The Human Akash

KRYON
Monika Muranyi

The Human Akash

A discovery of the blueprint within

www.ariane-books.com

The Human AKASH

Published by: Ariane Books

1217, av. Bernard O., suite 101, Outremont, Quebec, Canada H2V 1V7
Phone.: (1) 514-276-2949, Fax.: (1) 514-276-4121
info@editions-ariane.com
www.editions-ariane.com
© 2014 Ariane Éditions Inc

Cover design: Carl Lemyre

Interior design: Kesse Soumahoro

Cover Design by DeLisiArt:

Artist Deb DeLisi's description of her artwork:
When I meditated on seeing the energy of the Akash, I saw that it is
something within us and without us. It is in our DNA and in the unified
field that is accessible to all. When looking closer, I saw that it looked like
codes. These codes are in our DNA and in the Akash and they contain information that is accessed on a level that is outside of even meditating. It
is accessed through light! It is incredibly hard for me to even describe. The
codes are like a doorway or portal that one moves through to enter a high
vibrational state where the information flows. It is accessible to all. This is
the light-filled art that expresses what was seen and felt for the Akash. It
expresses a high vibrational state, full of potential, full of light and a joyful
and powerful connection.

ISBN: 978-2-89626-173-4

Distributed by: New Leaf
401 Thornton Rd. Lithia Springs, GA 30122-1557
Phone: 770.948.7845 — Fax: 770.944.2313
domestic@newleaf-dist.com — foreign@newleaf-dist.com.

Printed in USA
Ariane online store
www.ariane-books.com

Dedication

*This book
is dedicated to
you, dear reader,
as the New Human awakening on
the New Earth.
Together we are planting
the seeds of peace.*

Table of Contents

Acknowledgements

This book is the second in the Kryon trilogy series that features a compilation of subject-driven information from Kryon's channelled messages given by Lee Carroll. Many lives have been deeply enhanced and transformed as a result of Lee's partnership with Kryon. Thank you, Lee for saying yes to Kryon twenty-four years ago and for making it your life purpose to share these profound messages with the world.

Other beautiful souls have contributed to this book and enriched my life in numerous ways. Thank you, Kahuna Kalei'iliahi [Kalei]. Kalei carries with her the Hawaiian and Lemurian lineage. Her communication with the Ancients and her wisdom and knowledge as a Hawaiian High Priestess is a gift for us all. Previously this knowledge was sequestered and held by male Kahunas. In this new energy we have for the first time a female who is sharing these ancient ways with non-indigenous people. I hope you enjoy reading the channelled messages from Kalei.

Dr. Amber Wolf kindly shared her home, support and insightful comments as I compiled this book. Thank you for the wonderful times together and the opportunity to experience your guided mediation on "mining" the Akash. Thank you, Peggy Phoenix Dubro. Your energy work has transformed my life. Thank you, Laurie Reyon

Anderson. Your loving messages from the whales and dolphins continue to inspire all who read them.

At the eleventh hour synchronicity (via an email) introduced me to a brilliant editor who offered to edit my manuscript. Thank you, Lourana Howard for editing this book and for your continual support of the Kryon work.

I would also like to thank my publishers, Ariane Editions. I am blessed to be represented by a company with a high level of consciousness and a desire to help accelerate the great shift that is occurring on the planet.

Finally, dear reader, I'd like to thank you. As your eyes travel across this page I invite you to feel the energetic hug I have for you—a hug that also comes from the Kryon entourage and family!

Foreword

The wind carries the feeling of impending doom as it moans through the sails—a haunting voice that sailors know well. The salty spray of the ocean stings our faces as we stand in rank and steady ourselves on the swaying wooden deck, preparing to face our fate. The motion of our tall vessel is something we are used to, but it has increased in the last few moments as our captain continues to maneuver our warship to engage the enemy.

We are all afraid—cold and afraid. Many around me are silent and praying. I can see the movement of their lips as they say their final sweet words to their God. Some bring out small tokens of their wives and children, and hold them tight ... but we never let go of our weapons ... ever. Some are weeping, but no man is in judgment of this. Many of us are going to our deaths soon, and there are no "rules" among warriors in these last moments. These are personal moments, and each man has his own way of facing death.

The call to battle is imminent. In the semi-darkness of the morning dawn, the wind sweeps over the waves and is delivered to the sails of the ship as we continue to jockey for position with an unseen enemy who is very close, but hidden by the fog. The sails luff and fill as the captain jibs through the wind, trying to guess the position of the enemy. We are upwind, and the captain has given us battle advantage. The ocean speaks to us again, as a heavy northern swell pushes against our port side, tipping the deck in a way that foretells that we are maneuvering towards the battle line.

Books are filled with these moments, glorifying them and making them into some kind of adventure. But most will never know the absolute silence we are experiencing prior to battle between men on the sea. The ships must come together in a way that allows boarding, yet they must stay out of "profile range" of the big guns they both carry, to the last possible moment. No instructions are yelled or battle cries are heard. Instead, silence is maintained to allow the captain's steady non-emotional voice to be heard over the wind and waves, giving constant rudder adjustments, and instructions on final sail trims. The trimmers are on the yards, along with the archers and lookouts. We are over a hundred on deck with our armor and weapons, and there is not a sound except for these haunting surreal navigation voices and the creaking of the ship as it groans against the surge of the sea.

Out of the fog and mist appears the enemy, and they are enormous! Their ship is as we were told—much bigger than ours. A new cold wave of fear descends upon us as we see the reality of what is coming and we know the odds. No man says anything, as we simply stare at our fate. The enemy ship will meet us on our starboard side, and we on their port. Both of us will immediately lose headway to allow boarding, as the two ships slowly slide past each other at zero range. We watch as their sails are furiously collected to spill the wind. We are doing the same.

The explosions are deafening when the cannons of both ships erupt. The roar from both sides is almost simultaneous, and the deck immediately slants under our feet as our iron clad ship feels the brunt of the volley on the hull. Most cannons are aimed at the hull of the other, but some of the smaller guns are aimed at the rigging. The result of the damage is chaos on the decks of both ships, and we are in the middle of it all.

We must focus to stay alive and shield ourselves from our fear. Falling rigging is tearing into the deck where we are standing, and the wet, heavy lines and tackle are whipping us like attacking snakes, destined to entangle us and keep us from the fight. We are now out of rank, shields pointed up, dodging the flying debris and moving about furiously.

Next come the arrows. Our lookouts see this and the order to put shields forward is given. We see their archers strapped to the yards of their ship's foremast, allowing them to have a "first choice" aim as their ship comes alongside ours. Tying the men in this way helps to stabilize their aim, and many will die there, hanging in their harnesses like rag dolls, slowly staining the sails red. We watch as our archers try to take out theirs. We hear the exclamations of pain from both sides as arrows hit their mark. Then the death around me begins. Men are going down everywhere. Focus! Do as you are trained! Look for where the arrows are coming from and keep your shield pointed that way. Listen and watch!

The order comes quickly to move to starboard, where large sections of the railing have been removed in anticipation of battle. We must be quick! The wooden boarding ramps have been raised into the air, giving some shielding to the rain of arrows and spears that continues to assault us. More men fall, and we move forward to take their places. Focus! Don't help fallen mates. Don't look at them! You will be next if you do.

Less than a minute has passed since the first cannon fire, and a massive sustained battle yell comes out of our throats as we push forward en masse to the deck to the other ship. This is our protocol. Our commanders tell us that the noise frightens the enemy, but we know that our yelling is mostly meant to cover the cries of pain of those around us who are falling and stumbling from horrendous wounds that we are taught not to view. Don't look! Focus!

The cannons roar yet again, and my death is what my superiors call a "dumb death." It has no honor. In all the chaos, noise, and confusion, I realize that I was positioned on the very edge of the boarding gangway. The inertia of our own coordinated cannon volley pitched our deck and threw me down into the havoc and turmoil of the two ships grinding past each other. I must have been torn apart and drowned at the same time. I never engaged the enemy, and I never defended my country. I was a total failure. The ocean mocked me as it immediately closed over my dismembered parts and captured my soul. No one heard my screams.

I awaken in a pool of sweat. That dream again! Why do I have that dream so often? Was it a movie I saw or a book I read? It was so real! I could hear the sounds!

As I get ready for work, check my email, and text a friend on my smart phone, I ponder all this. Is it possible that this memory is something I actually experienced? Perhaps it explains my anxiety of the sea? All my life, my friends have made fun of me because I would not go into the ocean. Pools were fine; lakes were fine, but never the ocean. It wasn't reasonable, but fear isn't logical. I realized some time ago that I didn't just dislike the ocean, I hated it. I hated the feeling it gave me, as if it somehow knew me. I didn't care if I was swimming in it or not. I just didn't like it—and as far as boating or cruising went, forget it. Never! Some suggested therapy, but I had my own answer, and it worked. I just lived as far away from the sea as I could.

I still feel the residual fear and anxiety of my dream as I begin my commute to work. I start my car and move onto the road. I smile, and enjoy my daily peaceful drive to work within the vast plains of Texas, very safe from the sea.

From Lee Carroll

The above story isn't mine, but it could have been. Kryon tells us that these amazingly real dreams may very well be expressions of our past lives as they are carried over in that mysterious energy called the Akashic Record. Certain past lives, which are especially potent with drama, seem to be etched into our very cellular fabric. Can they affect us today? Do these residuals carry over and affect where we live or how we make decisions? The answer is yes, and the life-changing potentials are profound.

This book is about these amazing Akashic energies as discussed by Kryon in the last twenty-four years. However, it goes much further than simple information about past life experiences. In this new post-2012 energy, we are being told that we can actually work with our own Akashic energies in profound ways. We can even re-write the fear and anxiety of past experiences, and void the drama. How about mining our own past talents and body attributes? Is it possible to use them in our current life? After all, if it's inside us, then why not? Interested?

This is the second subject-driven book from author and Kryon archivist, Monika Muranyi. The first book, *The Gaia Effect*, was a carefully researched compilation of just about everything Kryon has channeled about Gaia. It was so well received, that she knew she had to compile and write about at least two more subjects. The book you are holding in your hands is number two in the series.

The Akash is complicated and often misunderstood. Again Monika pulls together what Kryon has channelled about this subject and surrounds it with explanations and commentary. In addition, she asks Kryon many questions to help further clarify certain attributes. These questions appear nowhere else, and are unique to this book.

Enjoy this journey into a subject that is a study of your own lineage on planet Earth!

Lee Carroll

Preface

My previous book, *The Gaia Effect*, was a compilation of the wisdom and teachings from Kryon relating to Gaia. It told the story of the profound relationship between humanity and the planet Earth, Gaia. This second book (in the Kryon trilogy series) is about the Human Akash. There is a circle of life and a grand system. Every Human Being has an Akash that can be accessed to enhance their current life and change the energies of their potential lives to come. *The Gaia Effect*, was an invitation for you to renew your relationship with Gaia. This book is an invitation to renew your relationship with yourself and awaken to your mastery.

Many humans on the planet have been here before. Numerous lifetimes filled with unimaginable events and experiences. Who are you really? What talents do you have? Why did you choose a particular job? What can't you live without in your life? What are your biggest fears? The answers to these questions are unique for each individual. Within each of us resides our elusive Akash, which holds the blueprint of who we are.

Think of your Akash as a spiritual jar. Within this jar is everything that relates to you. When you open it, out comes the wisdom of every life you have ever had. The spiritual jar is a metaphor for the spiritual learning contained within your Akash. It means that you don't have to learn everything again. You simply have to open it and reawaken your spiritual knowledge. So how do we open our spiritual jar? You have already started to open it just by reading this book. Spirit sees your intent! As you read the information that follows, particularly the Kryon channels, you may experience a feeling of remembrance. You are *remembering* your spiritual wisdom.

For the majority of my life, my passion was nature. It still is, but in a different way. This passion led me to university where I completed a Bachelor of Applied Science with Honors in Australia. Undertaking scientific research, especially the field trips in the great outdoors, was my ideal heaven. After university I started working as a Park Ranger for a national park agency in Canberra. Life was grand. I was getting paid to do something that I loved. It hardly felt like a job. For over 15 years I worked in numerous national parks across Australia and New Zealand. Without realizing it, my Akash had placed me where I felt the most comfortable ... in nature with Gaia. I was content and happy to be immersed in spectacular scenery and landscapes, away from the hustle and bustle of the city.

When my marriage ended in 2005 many issues came flooding to the surface. This event was directly linked with a major life lesson, although I didn't know it at the time. Over a slow process of spiritual awakening (slow because I'm stubborn) I gradually began to discover a whole new aspect of myself. My emotional breakdown was the catalyst to get out of survival mode. I had given intent to know more. In the process I had opened my spiritual jar. Slowly, out came knowledge and spiritual wisdom that led me to the energy work of Peggy Phoenix Dubro and the channelled messages of Kryon given by Lee Carroll.

My spiritual journey continues to unfold. Like many of you, I still have fears and challenges. Would you like to overcome your fears and challenges? Would you like to identify old energy patterns that no longer serve you and get rid of them? At the same time, why not pick up the talents and abilities of who you used to be?

If that is something you would like then this book is written for you. The purpose is to help you understand yourself better and enable you to access the wisdom and divinity within. It may also help you to understand others. The writing of this book has been driven by the Kryon channellings. Kryon can be described as a loving, angelic entity that gives messages of peace and empowerment for humanity. Lee Carroll is the original Kryon channel and has been giving the messages from Kryon for over twenty-four years. Lee is the author of thirteen Kryon books and the co-author of *The Indigo Children*, *An Indigo Celebration* and *The Indigo Children Ten Years Later*. These books have been translated into over twenty-four languages.

All over the world Lee Carroll has presented his lecture on the Human Akash. However, Lee regularly changes his lectures, in keeping with the dynamic new information from Kryon. If you would like to see Lee's lecture on the Human Akash you can view it online for a small fee at: www.kryon.com/lectures

The majority of information given in Lee's lecture is included within this book. This has been done with permission from Lee Carroll, so that others can discover the profound truths about the incredible Akashic system. This book provides a compilation of everything known about the Akash up until January 2014. In addition Kryon has provided profound answers to over thirty questions relating to the topics within this book, giving new insight and detailed explanations about how the Akashic system works. The Kryon channels used in this book are available as audio files from Lee Carroll's website: www.kryon.com/freeaudio

Are you new to the Kryon work? Perhaps you have never heard of Kryon but something drew you to this book. Be prepared to read about things that may seem unbelievable. Several subjects are covered within this book. The name of each chapter is a guide to the information presented. If some terms, such as Lemurian and Pleiadian, are new to you, detailed information can be found in my previous book, *The Gaia Effect*.

As we address the issues that are encoded in our Akash, such as karma and life lessons we change our own vibration, and hence the vibration of planet Earth. We are planting the seeds for peace and co-creating a life filled with enlightenment. Individually we open ourselves to a whole new level of freedom. Collectively we open the door to create an ascended planet. I deeply thank you for being here on the planet and honor your courage for taking the journey of self-discovery and enlightenment. It is not always an easy path, but the rewards are beyond measure.

Finally, it has not been possible to include everything about the Human Akash in this book. Additional chapters are on my website: www.monikamuranyi.com under the "Extra's" tab.

Love and blessings,

Monika Muranyi

Chapter One

The Human Akash

Have you ever heard the phrase *"the answers lie within"*? It used to drive me crazy! Now, I truly understand the answers ARE within. I just didn't know how to access them. Has this been a challenge for you as well? Perhaps learning about the Human Akash can assist you.

For over twenty-four years Kryon has given channelled messages about the Akash. The premise is, that you have an Akashic Record, and that the Earth also contains the Akash. What does that mean? Do you know what the Akash is? Do you know where it is? Learning about the Akash is the purpose of this book.

The actual word *Akash* is derived from a Sanskrit word *Akasha*. Akasha has different meanings in different philosophies. It has been described as sky, space and ether in an elemental and metaphysical sense. It represents mystical knowledge that is encoded in a non-physical plane of existence. None of that really tells us much. It simply highlights that the concept of Akashic Records and an Akashic system is not new. What is new is that we are re-discovering spiritual wisdom and knowledge about the Human Akash.

I assume you understand, or are willing to consider, the concept of reincarnation. Perhaps you even hold memories of a past life. The reason I mention this is that not everyone believes we have one soul that has incarnated many times on the planet. If you don't believe in past lives, there is not much point in reading further. Feel free to close the book and never open it again or pass it to someone else.

The earliest spiritual belief systems on the planet (such as Hinduism and Buddhism) believe in past lives. The belief in past lives remained that way for a long time. This indicates it was one of the first intuitive thoughts and concepts of the circle of life. At a certain point in history that idea was discarded. In the Middle Ages (in some parts of the Earth), if you talked about past lives, chances are you would be killed for heresy. It begs a question: If having a past life is a core spiritual truth, then why do many belief systems say there is no such thing? The short answer is for control.

Think about it this way: You only have one life. That means you only have one after-life. If you only have one after-life you better behave yourself and not screw up your only chance of eternity. The idea that you have an expression of life that keeps coming back makes it hard for those in charge of a "once only" belief system to compel others to conform to the established set of rules.

Kryon often says it doesn't matter what the Human Being believes as long as they are aware of the God inside. Many belief systems serve the Human Being in worship, even those that don't believe in past lives. The love of God is still there for every single life. Kryon says: "*Any system based in love is a good system. This is because compassion and love are the core issues...*"

Not everyone I know believes in past lives. That's okay. For many years I wasn't aware of it either. Remember:

You can't force spiritual awareness on to someone. You can only assist them on their journey if they choose to open the door. Besides you never know how things will unfold. One day they may come to you and ask for your wisdom and spiritual knowledge.

If you are still uncertain about past lives let me pose a few questions. Why are there thousands of people who can remember vivid details of a previous life? These include children who accurately describe things to their parents that a child of their age would not know. How can that be? Is it possible their experiences are real? The answer is yes. What a coincidence! (See Chapter Ten: Akashic Communication).

Why doesn't every one remember their past lives? The reason is that it is part of the Human set-up when we come into the planet. This is the duality that Kryon talks about. The multi-dimensional pieces and parts of you are hidden. When you give intent to find out who you really are, you start to become aware of the many "you's" Kryon has talked about.

The details of the many lives you have previously lived may not be conscious within your mind, but all of the experiences are with you right now. Your cellular structure remembers. Your Higher-Self was there for all of it. Understanding this reality starts to explain many things that remain a puzzle and mystery to those who "don't believe in past lives".

So if we have past lives, how does it work? What does the system of reincarnation and karma look like? The answer is complex but it exists within the Akashic System. Think of it as a type of energy accounting that keeps track of you—every expression of life you have had and will have on Earth.

Describing what the Human Akash is and where it is found is difficult. The difficulty is because the Human

Akash is multi-dimensional but it also exists in three dimensions (3D). The Akash is part of the circle of life—a circle of life that keeps coming back. Old souls keep returning for a purpose. We are given a chance to raise the vibration of the Earth and it is done by coming back many times—the expression of life. During the expression of life you have the opportunity to learn things. In the learning, you can raise the vibration of the planet or not. That is your choice. It is the free choice Kryon speaks of.

When you pass through the *"wind of birth"* and take your first breath, your unique life expression begins. The Akash is an energy that comes in with you. The term "Akashic Record" is a record of the Akash. The Akash can be defined as an energy that represents "all that is." Your Akashic Record is therefore a record of everything you have ever been and more. The concept of the Akash also represents the potentials of everything that can be, things that are potentially unrealized. Here is what Kryon says:

This is a story of an incredible thing, the amazing Human Being. This is not a story of a special Human Being. It's not a story of a Human Being that has super powers. It doesn't matter whether they're rich or poor or what happens on the Earth. I want to give you a story of the Human Being from my perspective—what happens when you leave my side of the veil, and what happens when you come back. This is you—every one of you. Listen, for this may upset what you've been told in the past.

You may say life starts simply, but it does not. There have been those who would love to trick Kryon. They ask ethical questions. The question, you see, is a trick. Because there's a lot of controversy for humans there, you see? So they wait for

4

Kryon's answer, and you're not going to like it, for it goes way beyond your seemingly ethical 3D mind.

There is a system in all this and it is beautiful. It's of birth and life and death. The potentials of who you will meet on this planet are known before you get here. The karmic attributes that you will enjoy when you land on this planet are all understood. The synchronicities of who you will meet are there! It's not fortune telling or predictions of the future. Instead, it's about pre-dispositions based on energy.

What are the possibilities that every potential that could exist is all mapped out? As complex as it might seem, before you ever step on this planet, you know of all the synchronicities that might occur. And in that, you pick your parents and they pick you. When does life begin? It actually begins eons before you're born. That's the love of God at work, and that should tell you something: There is no accident that you're here.

Oh, Human Being in 3D, you're not listening. For from the depths of your wisdom you chose parents who would make you an orphan. So you might say, It's because when you're on my side of the veil, you have the mind of God. Sometimes you will choose challenge so that you will help the planet with your potential solutions. Listen to me. No one came here to suffer. What you came here for was to unravel the puzzle of life, and the ones who are sitting in the chairs and listening or reading this are interested in doing exactly that.

Each one of you here is a piece of the Creator. Each one of you started on my side of the veil. However, my side is not a at all. You really cannot understand that, for in three dimensions there has to be a physical place where you come from. God is not in a place. God just . This is difficult for you to understand, for you are in 3D. But actually, you're a piece of that called God.

There is no physical attribute of God. Being a part of God is not explainable in 3D. I sit in front of you, but I am not singular. I am, like you, a piece of the soup of God. My name on the other side of the veil is not Kryon. That name has been created for you. I inhabit my partner's energy in this communication as a group. I see those reading this and I see those listening to this message. Can you even imagine that?

So you didn't start at birth at all. You always were! Before the Universe was created, you *were*. You belong to God and are of the family of God and you choose to come into the Earth for a purpose ... a purpose known to all (except you).

The reason for coming to this planet is something we have tried to explain many times. It's tough to do that, because it doesn't really have much to do with Earth. It has to do with the Universe. It has to do with future energies that you will establish from your experience here. It's tough to explain the outside world to a fish in a bowl, for the fish only knows of the bowl. If you tell the fish about your solar system and its surroundings, the fish has no understanding. It only knows of what it knows. So let us again say that what you do in this bowl affects something far greater on the outside.

You never believe it, but you wanted to come here. When you saw the potentials of your parents and where you would be born yet again, you said, *"Yes!"* You said, *"I can hardly wait to get back. Let me come in now."*

Each one of you knows what has happened in your own life. Now you're thinking, aren't you? *"Kryon, if I knew these potentials, I don't think I would have come."* This is the incredible Human Being, dear one. Yes, you knew. You knew the potentials of everything you've gone through so far. It was there as a potential and you walked right in and you lived it.

"Why is it that God loves humanity so much?" We've just answered that. You knew the potentials, and came anyway. It's because you love this planet as I do. Because there's something bigger going on. It's all about where the vibration will go on this planet. High? Low? For whatever happens there, it creates something far, far larger. And in order for this test to

be in integrity, Human Beings must be born on this planet and search for the hidden Creator within.

Listen to this: At that appointed moment of birth, and after the embryo is fully developed, I stand with you metaphorically in a place we have called *The Wind of Birth*. This is a portal between linearity and multi-dimensionality. It's not a place, but rather an energy that is divine. I look at your energy and you look at mine. What follows is what took place with each one of you, for I represent the group that says goodbye to you and hello to you. I'm Kryon, lover of humanity.

In that beautiful energy, I said to you, *"Are you ready? Are you sure?"* And every single one of you gave me a beautiful energy embrace. Then you disappeared, and an incredible process began.

[Pause]

Being born on the planet is not easy. The first thing you do is split apart. Not all of the piece of God you are gets transferred to the Human body. Some of it continues to reside on this side of the veil. But you knew that, didn't you? For you spend so much time looking for the piece that was separated ... the Higher-Self, wanting to connect to it. But with birth you become singular. It's lonely, you know? For you go from a multi-dimensional being to a singular, 3D one. The Higher-Self is the best portrayal of who you really are. It's the core soul energy, and it really is YOU. That's why it feels so good when you finally connect. It's a connection that you have asked for, and it becomes a remembrance.

So at birth you split apart. That's not all, and here's where it gets difficult for you to understand. Pieces and parts of your core Spirit stay on my side of the veil, which is not the Higher-Self. These energies, who are also "you," become your guides. I've just given you a secret: Your guides are you. That's why it feels so good when they're around you, and you feel so lost when they retreat.

7

"Kryon, I often feel so depressed and so alone." I've heard this so many times. There are those in this room and hearing and reading this who would say this to me. If you had a multi-dimensional picture of your life as I do, you'd see an entourage around you all the time. We've said this so many times: You're not alone. You can't be alone, but in 3D it appears that way, doesn't it? Some of you who are depressed have never really opened that door to Spirit, have you? If you had, you would have found that there is an energy ... the energy of the Higher-Self, which pushes back at you to let you know there is something actually there. Every one of you has this.

I often see the one crying in the corner, so depressed, so alone, in despair. I see the beautiful energy of the guides standing around him doing nothing ... because the Human never gave permission for them to do anything at all. Yet all of you have them!

So, into the Earth comes the Human Being, and in the DNA there is divinity. You have not split your divinity that much, only your dimensionality. Your DNA is filled with sacredness. It has to be, because if you're going to reunite with a Higher-Self, you're going to have to have divinity in your cellular structure ... and you do.

The first thing that happens at birth, is a multi-dimensional process that is timeless. The instant the child is born, there is a crystalline structure activated in the Cave of Creation. The Earth *knows you're back* or the Earth *knows you've just arrived for the first time.* For an old soul, the crystalline structure has been waiting for you, for really it's the essence of all of your lifetimes waiting for the next one. You realize, do you not, that you have had other lives here? It may seem foreign to you what those lives were, but you have a *friend* in each one of them. It's the friend called the Higher-Self. It's the same Higher-Self you have now. What that means, dear Human Being, is that those past lives were not a *foreign experience* at all. For *you* were there.

It's important you realize this, for it gives you permission to look, remember, even to pick up some of the talents that you had before. The crystalline structure of your own crystal is activated, and it's almost like rings of a tree. Each lifetime is represented and can be seen. Now here's something you should know: Everything you have done spiritually on this planet is imbued into that crystal. Everything you have learned the hard way is imbued into that crystal. It lays there in your DNA, transferred to your DNA at birth into two multi-dimensional energies, or layers, we've called the Akashic Record of DNA [Layers 7 and 8 as mentioned in Kryon Book Twelve, *The Twelve Layers of DNA*]. It's this way so that should you awaken or start asking spiritual questions, everything you've ever known or experienced through the ages will come back.

This is very good news to many who read this. It means that nothing is lost through your efforts here through the ages. When you come back, dear Human Being, everything you've learned in life is still there, and you don't have to learn it again. You don't have to go through anything again if you don't want to. Do you understand what I am telling you at this moment? For those of you who wish to push on the door, to find the God within, to actually reach out to the Creator, are literally opening the jar of spirituality of everything you've ever learned. Slowly, it pours upon you and you remember.

So many of you are asking the questions, *"What do I do? How do I do it? What is next? What are the processes, what are the procedures? How, how, how?"* And we have said for 20 years, that when you start opening that door, intuition starts to show you what you've already learned! You already know it. In order to make sense of it, new processes have been placed upon the Earth to help structure these things in ways that you can understand. These are processes that never existed before 1987.

The teacher, Peggy, is here [Peggy Phoenix Dubro]. Eons ago, she knew the potentials of what she might do here. She is a passionate steward of a new energy. But this information has been given to her slowly to help *you* make sense of God. Before 1989, the very energy she teaches would not have been possible to teach, and as the years passed since then and the energy of Gaia shifts, her work is enhanced. See how this works? Her "jar of knowledge" is being opened and realized by all.

Everything you do is registered on this planet as energy, and it stays in The Crystalline Grid after you are gone. Geologists know that most of the rock on this planet, especially in the crust, is crystalline. Crystals do something that most of you understand: they hold energy and have memory. Even scientists know about the energy of memory in a crystalline substance. So it shouldn't be much of a stretch of imagination or too esoteric for you to understand that everything you do is held in that memory bank.

This is what vibrates higher within the planet. It's what you have done collectively, all of your lives, which has stayed here and made this planet vibrate higher. This energy is currently amazing! For the incredible Human Being has changed even The Crystalline Grid in the last two weeks!

You live your life. Some of you find the *secrets of these things*, and some of you don't. The *secrets* are only things that are hidden from plain view. But they reveal themselves clearly when any Human begins to look for them.

As we said last night [at the channelling the night before], there is no judgment of any Human. However, in Human terms, in linearity, you want God to judge you, don't you? The thought that you might die and all of you get to go to the same glorious place does not make sense to you, does it? You say, *"Well, Kryon, what about the bad guy? I was good. He was bad. We're going to the same place?"* Yes, Human Being, you're both going home. Job well done. We gave you this information in the channelling, in your culture, within your scriptures. Did you see it? Did you understand it? It was called The Prodigal Son. This is *not* new information. Within this parable, the father represents God, and the two sons represent humans on Earth. One does everything right and one does everything wrong. Then they both come home to the same energy; they get the same party!

There will come a day when all of you breathe your last breath. It's not a sad day for you. It may be a sad day for those you leave behind, but not for you. You've all been there before. The ones listening [to the recording], the ones in this room, and the ones reading... listen to me: When you are finished with your natural life, you take a trip to the Cave of Creation. This is when you leave the essence of everything you've accomplished within the crystal. All the thoughts that you've had that were beautiful, all the thoughts that you've had that made you learn things, all your epiphanies, all imbued into that multi-dimensional object.

Then the part of you that was not Human (the multi-dimensional soul part) leaves this planet and recombines with the Higher-Self. All that which was split apart — the divinity of the cells, all of the guides, returns to the appropriate *piece of God* yet again. This, is what you should celebrate. I do! Because when I meet you on the other side, I meet a brother/sister. I'm doing it right now. I'm saying goodbye to those who are leaving me, being born. I'm saying hello again to those who have passed over and are coming home. *"Kryon, how can you be in so many places at once?"* You can't ask that and still understand. I'm not singular. I am a piece of the Creator, just like you.

Kryon live channelling "The Incredible Human Being"
given in Caracas, Venezuela — November 2, 2008

Is what you just read completely new information? Perhaps you were blessed and intuitively knew about the Creator inside since birth. Unfortunately, that was definitely not me. I didn't know anything about the Human Akash and the system that Kryon talks about until I was in my thirties. Many spiritual belief systems on the planet have a Human bias. The bias is that we are singular. What you just read from Kryon is that we are not. This is one of the most difficult concepts for us to understand.

Humans prefer the idea of being on a path of spiritual graduation. Many believe that we have some kind of debt to pay and that as you pay your debt you progress to the next level of learning and enlightenment. Once you have learned all your lessons you no longer reincarnate on Earth, but you learn lessons in higher realms. Kryon tells us it is time to get out of this old energy way of thinking. I can understand why the idea of 'spiritual graduation' would appeal for many. No one likes the idea that someone who commits a terrible act against you (or others) is not going to be punished! It offends our sense of justice. Rather, it offends our sense of Human justice based on a bias of singularity. This is not the mind of God.

When we are not on Earth we have the mind of God. We go from the limitations of a three-dimensional Human back into the *oneness* of all that is: the multi-dimensional soup of God. I realize this is difficult to conceive, but as you connect with your Higher-Self, you connect with the creative source.

There are many other channellers that mirror the same loving messages given to us by Kryon. Use your own intuition to guide you about the integrity of the information you read or hear. Some close friends, Allen Stacker and Debbie Morris in Australia, have a website that is dedicated to Lightworkers that are awakening in the new energy. Many awakened humans have gleaned valuable insights after connecting with the information on their site. In particular, Allen's post on Cancer in the New Energy provides a wealth of information for those dealing with this challenge. You can visit their website at: www.pointsofpower.com.au

Now that you understand there is more to you than you may have realized, let's look at your personal Akashic Record, where it is and what is its purpose.

Chapter Two

Your Personal Akashic Record

Your personal Akashic Record exists in three places (actually four but I will discuss the fourth one later). Kryon has said that our expression of life (many times) is to see if we can raise the vibration of Gaia and become an ascended planet. If this is the aim, doesn't it make sense that the Akashic Record is stored within Gaia as well as within us? The answer is yes. Within Gaia is the Cave of Creation and The Crystalline Grid. Within us is our DNA. Therefore the three places where our Akashic Record exists in the Cave of Creation, The Crystalline Grid and our DNA.

Gaia has a Magnetic Grid. Each piece of DNA is surrounded by a magnetic field. This means the transfer of energetic information between the several places that the Akash is stored is possible because of the attributes of magnetics, which is a multi-dimensional energy.

Have you ever wondered why Gaia records everything that humans do? The answer is because every single Human soul that comes to Earth makes a difference. The energy of each unique Human Being modifies the life force of Gaia so when that soul arrives, Gaia creates a record, stored as an energetic imprint. Gaia's intelligent consciousness therefore "knows" all about you. The life force of the planet is everything that is alive, including those things that most of us don't even think are alive. The concept of Gaia and the Akash is huge and very grand. It is part of a system that has been described in detail in my previous book, *The Gaia Effect*. If you haven't read this book, don't worry. In summary, the system is all about Gaia's co-operation in the Human spiritual experience. Everything revolves around the Human, even the planet's purpose.

So what is recorded within your Akash? There are many things within your Akash that start to explain the unexplainable. Within your Akashic Record there is:

- a multi-dimensional record of each life
- all the energies of accomplishment
- all the unfinished business (relating to your life lesson)
- karmic group attributes
- all talents and abilities grown over many lifetimes
- all spiritual growth
- a quantum record of what you have done and *all your potentials to come*

There are two things to note about the Akashic Record.

One: There appears to be a seemingly chaos of energy. This is because the Akash is constantly changing potentials, as it is always readjusting, based on what you are doing NOW. For example your friend contacts you and asks to have lunch with you tomorrow. You have changed your future potential by saying yes, or even when you say no! When tomorrow arrives, you have the choice to go to lunch or not. This is the free choice of humanity, to walk into what you planned or not. Depending on your decision to go or not, your potentials will change accordingly. The seeming chaos is because Spirit sees all of this at once, not as the linear progression of events that we experience.

Two: The term "past life" is not exactly accurate. This is because the past does not exist in a quantum state. There is no time in a quantum state. Time is in a circle, so you are always looking at the potentials of the NOW.

How does it all work? The answer is complex and best explained by Kryon:

There are two kinds of Akashic Record: One is global and one is personal. The global one is contained in that place we have spoken of so many times in this last year, the Cave of Creation. It is a physical place on this planet, filled with crystalline energy. You might say that every single Human Being who is hearing this or reading this has a crystal in that cave. That's not exactly multi-dimensionally accurate, but it's the best we can give you in 3D. This makes it simple for you to visualize. Each of you has a physical object in this sacred place that is sacred, is crystalline, and stays on this planet after you are gone.

The hard part about this explanation is that this crystal is timeless. That is to say, it carries with it the core energy of your Higher-Self when you are here on the planet. When you are not here, the energy of this object is placed upon The Crystalline Grid, which is global. All that you ever were on this planet is imbued, permeated, into the grid. Therefore, you might say that your Higher-Self still resides with Earth. At some level, you would be right. This also explains how a Human can "talk to the dead." For in a timeless state, everyone who ever lived is still here, within the crystalline.

An Overview of Coming and Going — The First Kind of Akashic Record

When you come into the planet, you activate this unique personal crystalline structure, and your Higher-Self is then responsible — the caretaker — for this crystal while you are here. The Higher-Self of each Human is always on my side of the veil, but it has tendrils, you might say, that allow parts and pieces of it to interface with you and the planet. These are the parts that you get in contact with when you meditate. Once you arrive on Earth, the energy of the Higher-Self is connected to Earth for as long as Earth exists.

The life that you live right now becomes etched upon this crystalline structure. The decisions you make, spiritual and otherwise, all of the things that you experience, what you go through as a Human Being, all are imbued into this crystal. The properties of crystalline structures are well known in your science. It is a mineral that has an atomic structure that has long-term atomic order. This creates a unique attribute discovered early, which is that of memory. In our case, it is way beyond anything your science will ever have... a crystalline structure that contains sacred life lessons, knowledge, memory and remembrance. What you don't realize, or understand in 3D, is that the crystalline [structure] also has the potential of the future imbedded within it. Difficult to explain, it is, but let's keep it simple for now.

You live your life on Earth. When you are complete and experience what you call death, which we call transition, you come back to the Cave of Creation for a moment. At that point, everything you experienced and learned gets sealed into this crystalline object, and then your earthly essence and the personal sacred portion of your Higher-Self leaves the planet.

You might say that this crystalline record is like the rings of a multi-dimensional tree. It places upon itself a lifetime at a time, everything you learned and all that your DNA has collected. This is far more profound than you expect, for the changes that have occurred in your awareness, if any, remain on this planet in the form of a vibratory shift. It remains here for the rest of the civilization, because it is placed onto The Crystalline Grid of the very earth itself. Therefore, you might say that the very earth resounds with your vibration ... past and present.

Nothing is wasted; nothing is lost, dear Human Being. What you do here stays here. All the things you did, all the decisions, all the epiphanies, the love, the joy, the drama and the sorrow ... they're not just for you, they're for the Earth. The vibration of the earth itself, therefore, is made up of the trillions of lifetimes of energy created by humanity for approximately 50,000 years.

It's not a time-capsule, for it's active all the time. A time capsule is passive. Multi-dimensional things are always in the "now." Therefore, there is no "time stamp" on any of this. It just "is," and is "seen" by the planet as always current. That means that whatever you experienced is still being experienced and is fresh.

After a period of Earth time, you may revisit the Earth. Most of you do, for a lifetime on the planet is like a day in the life of a grander scheme. The grander scheme is an overview of hundreds of your lifetimes, and Spirit sees you not as a Human in this life, but as a timeless, sacred entity that is part of the family of God, working for Earth, who has been here over and over in different incarnations or "expressions of karmic energy." This is very difficult for you to understand and accept, for you think life begins at birth and ends at death. That is no more true than a perception of life beginning at dawn and ending at dusk. It continues and continues and each life is like a day in a grander life. You continue to awaken and sleep ... over and over.

You have called this process reincarnation. An expression of your Higher-Self again comes into the Earth. It's the same

Higher-Self, by the way. Think about that for a moment... many lives, many faces, both genders... same Higher-Self. It comes in as it has before and places the new energy as a beginning addition into the crystal that is yours. You are then born on this planet and you continue the journey seemingly as someone else. Then you live that life. When you're finished, what you experienced and learned becomes another *ring on the crystal*. Over time, this sacred crystalline structure is imbued with hundreds of rings of lifetimes. One Higher-Self, many lifetimes, many names and faces... all YOU. That is the essence of the Cave of Creation and the process of The Crystalline Grid. It's how it works. Whatever you do stays here on this planet and contributes to the energy of all humanity that will follow.

That is the overview of the Akashic Record in the Cave of Creation. The difficult part to explain is how it also contains the future. For all the potentials of the lives you may live are also on The Crystalline Grid. It helps to posture who you'll be the next time around. I cannot explain this to you and I'm not going to try, except to say that there is purpose in all these things. Many have called it karma, a continuation of unfinished business, much like waking up tomorrow to the errands of the day that you didn't get to yet. The errands wait for you... they are the future. But in the case of a multi-dimensional energy, they have always been there, and will affect what you do when you wake up.

The Second Kind of Akashic Record

Now, let us move on to the teaching of today. There is another kind of Akashic Record, the second kind. There is a mini-Akashic Record that occurs in your DNA itself upon birth. It is shaped in the womb and given at birth. This is the Akashic Record of who you are and who you have been on Earth. It also contains the potentials of what you might do, carried within the layers of the DNA within you. This may sound like the same attributes of the crystalline record in the Cave of Creation, but it is not. The record in the cave is for all humanity. It is connected to The Crystalline Grid of the Earth. The purpose of the one in your DNA is personal discovery, awareness, karma, and life lessons.

It is esoteric. It is even odd to you, is it not? Some may even call it unbelievable that in your DNA is the record of who you ever were. Let us speak of that. We're going to talk about how it affects you. We're going to talk about what it means. All of these things we give you in a small amount of time, condensed into this message today.

Some of you are asking, *"Well, Kryon, right away there is a puzzle. I understand what you're saying. You're about to teach the fact that we come in with many energies from the past. But what about the first timer on Earth? They have a crystal that has no rings, you might say. It has no energy of past expression, no past experience on Earth. So what about that? What happens then?"*

This is a very logical question. There is a well-known energy of a newcomer that is unique to the planet. Most of you reading this have experienced it. Also, there are many newcomers! Know this: Kryon is very aware of geometric progression. That is to say, that the Human Beings on this planet grow exponentially in number. As the population grows, that means, dear Human Beings, that there are many, many first timers. For whatever the percentage of those who are old souls, there's even a higher percentage of those who have never been here. We know that. It's part of the plan and the energy of Earth. So this message does not apply to those who have never been here. At other times, we have discussed the attributes of the first timer.

Kryon live channelling "It's in the DNA!"
given in Kelowna, BC, Canada — June 28, 2008

Now that you understand what is in your personal Akashic Record, it is important for you to realize that one thing ties all the lifetimes together. It's your Higher-Self. Your Higher-Self is the same one in every life you have had and potential lives to come.

Understanding What a "Past Life" Really Means

Most of us have a Human bias that everything is linear. We find the concept of time being in a circle extremely difficult to understand. The evidence we see is that time only goes forward. That creates a distinct idea of a past, present and future. The idea of everything existing within a NOW reality is too removed from what we can see. Think back to when people thought the world was flat. Many believed, if you sailed too far in the ocean, you would fall off the edge. The idea that the world was round was too far removed from what they could see. Sound familiar?

If time is in a circle, which Kryon says it is, then there is no such thing as a "past life". All of the lives are with you now, because the energies of things you have collected are part of you. Instead of having "past lives," think of it as having current life attributes, some of which are realized and some of which are not. Sound confusing? Perhaps Kryon can help you better understand this concept.

There is no such thing as a "past life." When you leave this planet, you will be out of time [removed from the limitations of linear time]. There is no *time* on the other side of the veil. It's something that has been manufactured for your comfort and lifestyle in 4D [3D].

Let me tell you what this means. Listen carefully, for this is important. You think you've got past lives? You don't. You have multiple current lives all at the same time. When you get out of time, as you have known it, what are you going to call it? Think of it this way—it's a whole layer of lifetimes, but you're living them all once right now, so therefore they're all now lives... all of them.

But there's one on top of this layered stack who is in control, and that's the one that you are living now—the one you see in the mirror—the one that is currently occupying your body, who you think is the only one. This is the one who talks to all of the others in what you call the Akashic Record. This is a multi-dimensional concept and is also represented by one of the layers of your DNA... also invisible. This multi-dimensional layer of DNA reminds you that all of the other lives are still there being lived at the same time, but out of a linearity way. Why do I tell you this? Because there, my friends, is the storehouse of your power.

Isn't it odd how we must force multi-dimensional concepts into single-dimensional explanations for Humans? I wish to tell you about the infinite circle of lifetimes that are active within you, yet I must resort to an example of "stacking them up" in a simple linear fashion for you to understand it! Any way you can grasp this will be helpful for the next step.

How would you like to have the benefit of everything you've ever done as an angel, since you arrived on the planet? Lemurian, how about combing through 52,000 years' worth of experience for the best of it all? How would you like to have that, Lemurian? Well, I'll tell you, you connect to the Higher-Self and suddenly the quantum effect takes place and you're connected to all of these lives at the same time! Some of you know what I'm talking about and some of you don't. It hides from you... this wisdom of the ages. You can dig down into those lives that you are currently living all at once, and using the one who's in charge [who you are now], you can choose to pick the best parts of each, and bring many former attributes forward to use them.

Here's what I mean: We've broached this before in a different way, but I'm going to use my partner once again, even though he doesn't like it when I talk about him this way. [Pause while Lee considers what's coming]

About Lee

While in his early days, when considering being the channel that he is now, his exchange with Spirit went like this: *"I cannot write anything and I never have. I cannot speak in front of an audience and I never have. I'm basically an engineering hermit. I'm not social, either. I like to be quiet and unspoken, and I'm nervous in front of people. Therefore, how is it I'm supposed to proceed, since I don't have any of the obvious talents needed to do what I've been called to do?"*

Now, what we showed him, in a way he still doesn't understand, was that these talents were always there, but hidden as part of his personal Akashic Record. These are attributes that he carries hidden deep down into the past lives he thought were behind him in a linear spiritual history he thinks is over with. However, they are not gone at all, and are actually part of him, still active. In a process that is still mystical to him, he pulled out the one lifetime who was the writer. He pulled out the one who was the orator. He pulled out the attributes he needed, out of his storehouse, and you see the result. These were talents that always belonged to him, but that were not present when he was born, so he thought.

He reached down and pulled them out of the essence of the Akashic Record, which is alive and well and living within his DNA. The promise, therefore, from Spirit is that you can do it, too! But we use him as an example, since he sits in front of you, and you can see what we mean. So, which one of these things do you want, Shaman? Is this concept really that strange to you?

Rejuvenation

I'll give you something else to think about. If you don't believe in past lives, let me ask you something that only involves this current life. Do you remember when you were 10? The answer from most of you is "yes." Well, so does your DNA! How about that one? Think of it. Imprinted in your body is a memory that has a cellular stamp on it that remembers "10 years old." You see, it's still there. It's a cellular memory. How would you like to revisit it? And you might say, *"Well, why would I do that?"* When most of you were 10, your DNA was clean and pure and it was whole and young. Although that was long ago, your body has retained a memory of what it was like then.

So how would you like to instruct your body, in your next meditation, to *"Go to the 10-year-old DNA imprint, and replicate it?"* Why not? The body reproduces itself all the time, cell by cell. It rejuvenates. Let's go to the 10-year-old DNA—young, pure, fresh with the energy of the youngster—hard to even keep still [Kryon smile]. It's alive, you know? It's still there within the body's rejuvenation memory.

Concepts of the Future

Oh, and here's another one: This concept you have of the future. It's so limiting. Let me give you a snapshot idea about the reality of the future. *"Kryon,"* some have exclaimed, *"There's a dichotomy here. You say God can do anything, yet you also say that God doesn't know our futures. How can that be?"* It's easy. God knows all your futures, but does not know which one you will select!

Spirit knows the potentials of all of the things that you might do. It's extremely complex to you, but to us it is not. It's multi-dimensional and it loops around in a circle. We can see the potentials of every decision you might make throughout your life. Therefore, we know everything except one thing: In this free-choice situation on this planet, we don't know which future you're going to choose. That's up to you.

So I bring this to you so that you will think this through, and complete this circle of the "now." I've already discussed the past, so let's discuss the future in your mind. Do you agree that each lifetime is a graduate one from the one you had before? In other words, since you learn from each, and you re-incarnate with all of the knowledge from what you call the past one, the next life is going to wiser. Do you agree? You learn, learn, learn. If this is truth, and if what I'm saying is the way it works [it is], and if there really is no time on the other side of the veil, then why not go five lifetimes *up* the Akashic potential ladder and grab the wisdom that you are going to learn in your future? Pull it down and use it right now! How about that? That's called Ascension Status, dear Human Being! Learning to become multi-dimensional, therefore, is an invitation to "mine your Akash" and participate in the best of past and future. This process isn't for the faint of intellect... it challenges the very concept of what you have been taught are your 3D limitations.

Kryon live channelling "The Many You's"
given in Manhattan, New York — April 1, 2006

Do you see how we can change our current life by tapping into the energies of our past and future realities? Again, the one thing that ties them all together is our Higher-Self. It's the same Higher-Self every time. The Higher-Self is the portal to the other side. It's where we can go to get everything we have learned and what is yet to come.

Before we continue to explore your personal Akashic Record that resides within your DNA, let's examine the Akash within Gaia.

The Cave of Creation

It's important for you to understand some key things about where the Akashic Records are kept within Gaia. Kryon has given many channels about the Cave of Creation, and Lee Carroll has enhanced this information during his lectures. The attributes of this cave are that it:

- actually exists, but will never be found
- is crystalline in nature
- contains the Akash of all humanity
- has a record of every life lived and every potential life to come
- has a crystal for every Human
- has crystals that remain, even when you are gone

The Cave of Creation is quite complex. It is difficult for us to even imagine that such a thing exists and how it could possibly work. Kryon says there is a potential record of every life to come. Now this assumes that you are coming back. You may think that you are not, but you are! The reason you come back is that the consciousness on the planet is not the same as the consciousness on the other side of the veil. As soon as you pass over, you can't wait to come back, especially if you are an old soul.

Now, some of you are thinking, *"Wait a minute, isn't that predestination?"* Let's look at the word predestination. It carries the meaning of "determine beforehand" or "to decide upon ahead of time." The belief is that God has predetermined certain things ahead of time. Isn't it interesting that only *certain* things are predetermined. The truth is that there is no such thing as predestination. Instead, you need to view things in terms of predisposition. You are predisposed to do certain kinds of things. Just because you are predisposed to do certain things there is no absolute certainty that you will. Your current expression of life is not predetermined. You have free choice to change your karma. If you change your karma, it changes everything you do.

Every life to come, is based on the potentials of the NOW. Each time you shift your current life, the potentials of the lives to come also change. There is no time line, only a constantly updated potential of your next life, created by you as you walk the current life. KRYON 2008.

What if everything you are doing now, in your current life, is a set-up for the next? As you reflect on this question, what will you do differently? Do you want the same challenges you face today to be carried over into another expression of life? Actually, it is more than just creating potentials for next time. It is about the energetic footprint you place on and within the planet. Every accomplishment you achieve towards finding God and the divinity within you raises your vibration. In turn, you raise the vibration of the planet. As we raise the vibration of the planet, we change the planet's potentials. Look at all the things that have changed within the last twenty years. Can you see how the world is moving from war, conquering and separation to love, compassion and unity? This shift in consciousness is slow, but it has begun. There will still be those who prefer to cling to past potentials of doom and gloom. Kryon has said that old energy dies hard. However, against all odds, the planet is moving towards peace on Earth.

Another attribute of the Cave of Creation is that it remains static. The same number of crystals are always there. How can that be? How do we know how many souls are going to be on the planet? The linear thinker wants to know exactly how many crystals are there. They want to start adding them up. They look at the global population of seven billion people. They look at the estimates that predict there will be ten billion people by 2050. Are there ten billion crystals? Twenty billion? It doesn't work like that. The number of crystals (and therefore souls) are uncountable. Think of it this way. The seas and oceans of the planet are salty. How many individual pieces of salt are in the ocean? It is unknown. It is uncountable because the salt is dissolved in the ocean. It is part of the ocean and no longer a separate entity. The quantum state is difficult for humans to understand because we want to individualize everything and quantify them. We want certainties, not probabilities. A quantum state doesn't work that way. The number of souls that will come to the planet is a quantum potential. These quantum potentials are known by Spirit in a quantum state.

By the way, the expectation that our population will keep increasing is based on things remaining the same as they have been up until today. Do you think this estimate accurately reflects the future? What does the world look like today? There are developed countries and countries that are still developing. In developed countries the birth rates are low. This is because it is expensive to look after large families. More women prefer to concentrate on their careers. Increasing sexual equality has meant women have more control over their own fertility. Parents have a choice about how many children they have. Contraception is available and family planning facilities help with advice. Developing countries are the opposite. They have high birth rates because large families can help look after the farm. Parents have a lot of children in the expectation that some will die because of the high infant mortality rate. There is no old-age pension scheme, so parents that are old or sick rely on their children to look after them. There is often a shortage of family planning facilities and advice. What will happen as the developing countries become developed? Their birth rates will change!

Let's go back to the Cave of Creation and all the potentials. Against all odds the Armageddon that many predicted did not occur. Gregg Braden is an internationally known author and speaker. In his book, *Fractal Time*, Gregg Braden merges ancient wisdom with modern knowledge, to give a powerful new model of time. He combines the ancient concept of cycles with the modern laws of fractal patterns and demonstrates how historical moments of war and peace are the returning patterns of our past. These fractal patterns can be known, measured and predicted. The returning cycles carry a window of opportunity known as a choice point (decision point). It allows humanity to choose a new outcome for the cycle.

During our fifth decision point humanity faced a very-real threat of a nuclear world war. Moving beyond 2012 is passing the marker of our decision not to terminate. There was no nuclear war. What if we did terminate ourselves? What about the Cave of Creation? What about the potentials of every life to come? We have to abandon our linear thinking to understand what happens. The potentials of the life to come would be voided, but the crystals still remain because they were the potentials at one time.

What happens to the crystals after we are gone? To answer this question, you need to visualize the rings of a tree. The rings represent a record of the past in 3D time. Similar to the way tree rings record each year's growth pattern, the crystals record every lifetime, every accomplishment, every failure, every personality, every epiphany, every passion, all spiritual growth, every re-membrance and each gender over and over. All of this accumulates and is available for you to use.

How are the crystals organized? Kryon says they are organized by karmic group. This starts to explain what you may feel with other people. What does karmic group mean? Let's redefine karma. Karma is an energy that feels it has a purpose. Think about the people that are in your life. Do you think you have had past lives with them? Perhaps you're not sure but you feel a strong connection with some of them. As you journey through life you make many friends. Some become friends for life and others become friends for a while and you continue on your way. What happens when you change within yourself? Some of your friends become less prominent in your life. You end up making a new set of friends and it's almost like you get a new karmic family.

The concept of our crystals being arranged by karmic group (family) seems strange to us. How many times have you heard the expression *"You can choose your friends but you can't choose your family!"* Oh really? Sometimes this is very difficult for people to imagine. Why would anyone choose abusive parents? Why would anyone choose to be an orphan? Again, we need to re-member that the consciousness we have on the planet is not the consciousness we have on the other side of the veil. We come into our family knowing that we are presented with the potentials for change. The choice to void our karma is ours. The choice to view everything as though we are a victim is also ours. Each of us is pre-sented with an opportunity to move beyond our unique life lesson and move into ascension status.

What happens to the crystals in the Cave of Creation when we drop our karma? What do you think would happen? Is it possible that we leave this karmic group?

31

Not only is it possible but Kryon says when we drop our karma we move into the "no karma" group. What does this mean? It means that when you drop your karma, you remove yourself from your karmic group that is in the Cave of Creation. Your crystal is still there but it is no longer with its former karmic group. You create your own group on The Crystalline Grid while in your current life expression on the planet. Does this sound like your experience? Have you moved forward only to find that your family and friends are left behind, often still spinning their wheels in drama? If so, I would like to honor you for taking control of your life. You are no longer being pushed and pulled by your karma. You have literally taken up the metaphoric tiller to steer your own boat. For those who choose to keep their karma, understand there is no judgment as we are here in free choice.

Earlier I mentioned that the Cave of Creation also records every gender. What does this mean? Kryon has told us that part of the system of a Human Being who comes and goes on the planet is that we share both genders. Every single old soul on the planet has been both genders. It's carried in your Akash. You tend to be one gender for many lifetimes. It works better that way. When it's time for you to change genders and come back as the other gender, there is an unusual time, spanning at least three to four lifetimes where you get used to it. Society has a name for people that are going through this transition. They call it being homosexual.

There are always 10 percent of the population on the planet that are going through this transition. Now here is the truth of it. All of you have been through it and in the process there has been difficulty, discrimination and even death. It is time for humanity to start seeing homosexuality as part of a beautiful system. Attitudes change slowly, but it's important to take the first step.

You have the choice to plant seeds of enlightenment to create peace on the planet, or not.

Now that you understand about the Cave of Creation I would like you to read Kryon's description.

The Cave of Creation is a name that I gave that represents an attribute of storage for the Akashic Circle—the system of the Akash. It has been known in many forms and has been talked about using other names. There truly is no name for it, for it is a system and not a place, although there is a place involved. The place is filled with beauty, within the earth's crust, you might say, and yet lower than that. In a dimensional suspension that cannot ever be seen or found by a Human Being, there exists a sacredness that is the Akashic Circle. It is crystalline in nature, but it cannot be counted or notated. In a quantum state, there exists a crystalline structure for every single soul on the planet who will ever be here and who ever was. It's in the "now" representing no time, but potentials of time.

There is a plan. It's a plan of arrival and departure. Already existing there is a structure that expects souls to fill it and there are those coming from other places that come into existence on the planet for the first time. You cannot visualize this. Oh, you could put it in your three dimensions, but it won't be accurate. It doesn't need to be accurate. All you have to know is that it exists. You might call it Akashic accounting.

There is one soul per crystalline object and yet uncountable. You might say, *"Wait a minute. There's got to be billions of those crystals. Why can't they be counted?"* I say again that if it were soup, we ask you, how can you count the salt? How can you notate the flavor with a number? And this is the quantum state that is confusing to the Human Being, for you wish to individualize, separate, notate, quantify, and count—and you cannot do this with love. Yet I'm telling you there is crystalline for each of you.

One soul can have many lifetimes. Old soul, listen to this: On this planet, there is one identifying, energetic, crystalline, quantum source for you that allies you with Gaia. It's profound and represents the circle of life.

The Reasoning

Why do you think it was created as a cave? Why should it be under Gaia? Why should it be within Gaia if there was not a reason? You see, the system includes the Earth. It has to. Isn't it interesting that the Ancients knew all about this? The first thing an Ancient does, your most distant ancestors, is to understand the Earth. Look at the indigenous who walked in this area. The first thing they did was to offer the Earth a gift. To this day, the indigenous all over the planet understand the system. The Earth is alive, the mother. The Earth provides the food, just like the mother. And the first thing you do is honor it and supply a gift.

If the Earth is the mother, what about the life upon the Earth? The next thing you would do if you were an indigenous is to honor that life. Perhaps it exists in the forest in the form of the wolf, the bear, the beaver, the possum. They are all there as part of a life force of you and Gaia and they are the system that propels spirituality that you don't know about. The circle is the reason for your being.

The indigenous knew it. Do you think the indigenous wore the furs and the pelts of the animals for warmth? Yes and no. Many times, it was for honor. They would wear it on their heads to create their honor for the forest, the trees and the animals. It honored the planet and the Earth and the system. All of the lifetimes you've ever had are etched in a beautiful, multi-dimensional energy upon one quantum crystalline object. It's the piece of you that is the accounting object in the cave.

The Workings of the System

Now listen. It exists with all of the others, too — billions of them, if you singularize them. There is a confluence of interactive energy between the crystalline objects. This is to say that even though you want to stack them up and call them "souls" and put notches in them and call them "pieces of crystal," they're not. They're all together in one system and they morph with each other. We have never discussed this before due to its complexity.

As you accomplish lifetimes with others, sometimes you cross the energies of what we call this confluence and they become something else. One becomes two. Two becomes four. Families that work together in karmic interchange, especially in the old energy, actually change crystalline parts of this system, parts that don't even seem to be related. It is one of the most complex puzzles you've ever seen. Humans with humans. It explains synchronicity. It explains intuition, and it is alive with Gaia.

Gaia knows who's here and Gaia responds to the consciousness of you walking the planet, the personification, the embodiment of the expression of your soul in this life. It's the one with your face on it right now. It's the one who has active consciousness that can change what is going on with planet Earth. That's what Gaia sees. This is what you change. We have told you that you modify The Crystalline Grid of the planet, which is to say you are actually modifying and transmitting energy to the Cave of Creation with everything you do. Because there's a system — a complex one.

DNA

In your DNA you carry your *personal Akashic Record*. What have you done on this planet? How many times have you been here? What are the energies that you've experienced already?

Old souls have something that very few Human Beings have, and which none have when they arrive for the first time. You have a record. Every single energy of every single lifetime stays in the DNA. Yet they don't represent themselves as a stack to be read by an Akashic reader. Those who read what you would call *past lives* are reading energies, not past lives, for it all sits on the surface, intermixed, ready to be seen and read.

The most profound of all of the past lives you've ever had are at the top, since they are all together. There's no hierarchy. Humans want to see them in a row, organized by date. Humans see them as one after the other. Human Beings will report to a past life reader and say, *"Is it going to cost more to get a past life reading if the desired life is older?"* That's funny! That's linear. Many of you right now are awakening to one of the most profound lives you've ever had—the first one, the Lemurian one.

Lemuria existed for thousands of years as the oldest, most sustained civilization on the planet. It is one that has no historical acknowledgment, buried forever at the base of the mountain in the Pacific Ocean you now call Hawaii. That is by design. Humanity should not be digging up those things that are part of the creation story. It would bias you. It would give you a little too much information.

The puzzle is this: Can you find what is buried inside you? This new energy can be seen as a portion of the onion skin that is being removed, not only from the planet, but from you. Layers are being shed so that you can now start to see that which is the Akash in you. It explains why so many of you are starting to feel things in this shift.

Could it be that you really can do some of these things? The answer is yes. How many of you are now aware of the Shaman inside? How many of you are starting to acknowledge, personally and privately, the old soul that's there? Some of you are starting to actually receive talents that have been buried. Some of you are becoming that which is a writer, storyteller.

All the things that are creative — music, composition, art, color, design, are part of you. You know it's there.

Gender Switching

Old souls, let me tell you something. If you are old enough, and many of you are, you have been everything. Do you hear me? All of you. You have been both genders. All of you have been what I will call between genders, and that means that all of you have had gender switches. Do you know what happens when it's time for you to switch a gender? We have discussed it before. You'll have dozens of lifetimes as the same gender. You're used to it. It's comfortable. You cannot conceive of being anything else, yet now it's time to change. It takes approximately three lifetimes for you to get used to it, and in those three lifetimes, you will have what I call "gender confusion."

It isn't confusion at all. It's absolutely normal, yet society often will see it as abnormal. I'm sitting here telling you you've all been through it. All of you. That's what old souls do. It's part of the system.

Let me tell you about the circle given by the Cave of Creation, which is the Akashic Record of all things, all life, all souls. Interfacing with Gaia through The Crystalline Grid, you walk on top of the Earth with your Akashic Record and your DNA. You are using the information you have inside you and the circle is complete. When you affect The Crystalline Grid with your consciousness and actions, it then alters the Cave of Creation.

Everything is in a circle, dear one. It's beautiful. It's interactive. I can't explain anything more except that the higher you vibrate and the more you use that which you have known on the planet, the more it changes the planet. Inside the Cave of Creation is that confluence of quantum energy with billions of souls, millions that are not even here yet; it affects them, too. I will tell you why. Because you are changing the future as you work the past. You are changing the makeup of those who'll arrive and what they will do and what their consciousness will be.

What you do today plants the seeds of peace on Earth, so when they are born they will have what you have. It is more profound than you know and you sit in the chair and you wonder about gas money. Do you see what I'm saying? Maybe it's time to just suspend that for a moment and say, *"Thank you, God, that I know what I know."*

As you go from this place, I want you to know something: You are grand beyond any scope of imagination and you should hold your head high. You really don't know what you've done. Some call it sacrifice, which we call appropriateness. There are those in the room who have come to the planet on purpose for only three months. Then they die, and seemingly break a mother's heart. And you might say, *"Well, why would I ever do a thing like that?"* And I'll tell you: So your mother could find God, that's why. Because she wouldn't otherwise. She had to go to the darkest place, examine herself, and come out a Lightworker. That's written in the Akash! It's an energy that's in The Crystalline Grid! You don't think God knows that? That's part of the system.

Oh, I know who's here. Maybe you've been on the other side of that, mom. Now you know. Maybe you're sitting in the chair because of it. Do you think we don't know who's here? It is grand! You call it sacrifice, but it is not. You're here for three months, you go back home, then you come in again — often to the same mother. There's a system here! It's beautiful.

There are a lot fewer soul records than you think. This is because you keep coming back. How many people are on the Earth? How many people have been on the Earth? What does that add up to? A lot more than there is in the Cave of Creation, for you keep coming back. True, the Earth's population increases exponentially. That means there always has to be new humans, and there are. But Gaia knows who's coming.

The pieces of God around this Universe know who's coming. And the old souls at some level know who's coming. This, I would like to tell you in closing, is where the beauty is.

Now suspend belief for a moment. I would like to take you to a place. It's a beautiful planet. There isn't a lot of dissension there. Oh, there are differences of opinion, but not a lot of dissension. There are only a few continents on this place and it's surrounded by water. There hasn't been a war for 100 years. The ones on this planet don't always agree, but they don't kill each other anymore. Can you imagine such a place? Oh, there's unbalance because there's free choice. But they care for each other.

They don't kill each other anymore. It's not an option, since it's seen as barbaric. It doesn't occur to society to do it, like it doesn't occur to you to cut off your son's hand if he steals something. That's barbaric and isn't an option to an enlightened society.

I'd like to introduce you to this place. It's called planet Earth. It represents the result of the ones who are going to arrive in the cave. It will take as many generations as it takes, because the seeds are being planted today for it. It will occur slowly. You have the start of it now. Can't you see it? You're not going to have another world war. You just are not. You can't. There's too much benevolence in the system that you are starting to be part of.

Oh, it may not look like it. Look at the news! You are in transition from the old energy to the renaissance of Human consciousness. Could it be that you have come in, old soul, to accomplish something the ancestors have only dreamed of? Oh, how many generations will it take? It doesn't matter. It is slowly going in that direction.

Will there be wars? Sure. In the process of this completion, old energy will prevail and certain places will go backwards into the dark. That's what darkness does. But light will win. Slow it is, it must be generational, for the children must come in fresh. It is difficult for an adult to have a renaissance of consciousness in midlife.

And who are those children going to be, old soul? You! See the circle? What you are doing now is planting a seed so that when you return, you will be able to water it with the beauty of the love of God and nurture its growth. You are your own ancestors and you will be in the future. I would not tell you this if it were not so, if it were not in the plan of things, if it were not foreseen years ago.

Dear ones, there would be no Kryon speaking to you now if it were not for what you've done. I would not have been here if you were going to destroy yourself. I would not be here if the Earth was going to destroy you. Do you hear me?

You have free choice to do anything you want—all of you. But you've crossed a marker where the potentials are pushing into benevolence, where Human nature is starting to change, where what you want is starting to manifest itself—and it's about time.

Kryon live channelling "The Akashic Circle"
given in Totowa, New Jersey—July 17, 2011

I would like to share some additional information that Kryon has only given once before in Kryon Book Eleven, *Lifting the Veil*. Kryon refers to the three-day journey where we visit the Cave of Creation following death. This information gives us a glimpse of just how complex the system is.

There are, and always have been, other journeys that you might take besides reincarnating, and many humans choose this. They become part of the energy of the planet for a number of years in order to help certain situations. Some stop incarnating as Human for a while and become *guides*, but they're not guides with humans. Instead, they're actually a part of the energy of Gaia.

Some go into the mountains — actual Human reincarnated energy on the planet, but not in Human form. And when that's done, they'll come back very much like they came back before, then reincarnate as a Human Being again.

We haven't discussed this before, because again, humans, want a black-and-white scenario of what happens. They don't want to know about the energy part because many humans will worry and say, *"Which one will I be?"* as if you have the mind of God and could decide now — and you can't. It's all part of a grand plan. It's beautiful and part of a system that honors the "now" of what is next at the moment.

Let me give you a hint about something: Are you one who loves the Earth so much that you want to get down and roll on it? Do you hug trees? Are you one of those who the ground speaks to? Oh, there are many of you like this! I want to tell you that the *last time around* there is the potential that you were part of the dirt! Perhaps it didn't last long, but just long enough to put your energy in there so that when humans walk on the dirt they will feel your consciousness, love, and feel Gaia's energy.

Oh, this is complicated, but it's true. No one is ever "stuck." And if you hear that, it doesn't honor the grandness of the angel called the Human Being, or the system you've set up to help the planet. You have full choice when you're not here. The Human-Earth scenario is the only place where you receive a hidden persona where you don't know who you are and have to seemingly walk in the dark. When you're not here, you're a part of the whole of God. Death is a known transition, and not filled with uncertainty, error, mistakes or mystery. It's simply the closing of one door and the opening of another.

Kryon live channelling "Current Events"
given in Washington, DC — April 10, 2005

The Crystalline Grid

Kryon and Lee Carroll have said your Akash is found in three places: The Cave of Creation, The Crystalline Grid and your DNA. Earlier I mentioned it was actually in four places (as described by Lee) and after this section you will discover where. The Cave of Creation is like an Akashic library. The Crystalline Grid is therefore like a storehouse of energy and action. This means that The Crystalline Grid:

- remembers everything you do
- is immediately responsive to your present life (that means that the things you did in the past is there energetically so as you walk from place to place you not only feel energy of what happened there, such as war, you may feel what you did personally. It remembers actions and profound energies of what you did when you were here)
- carries the energy of all the crystals in the Cave of Creation (past lives)
- creates the vibration measurement of Earth (current vibration of life) which is its main function

Because The Crystalline Grid remembers every expression of life the energy recording remains permanently on the grid. Like a tape recorder the energy imprint can be played over and over again. This explains what we call hauntings. It also explains why a psychic/medium can tap into The Crystalline Grid and have a conversation with a Human that has passed to the other side of the veil. This was explained in my previous book, *The Gaia Effect.*

At our fifth decision point humanity decided to choose life instead of termination. This created a shift in

42

Human consciousness. The shift in Human consciousness resulted in a recalibration of everything. A recalibration of: humans, Gaia, the Universe and of course
The Crystalline Grid. This recalibration is discussed in
Kryon Book Thirteen: *The Recalibration of Humanity
2013 and Beyond* written by Lee Carroll.

The Crystalline Grid is being recalibrated towards
love and compassion. Previously everything has been
recorded in a linear fashion. There has been an equal
emphasis on war and love. That is starting to change. It
also means that the actions and changes made by the
old souls on the planet have a much higher significance
than those outside of this core soul group.

The Crystalline Grid always vibrates at the same level
as humanity. Because we have started to vibrate higher,
The Crystalline Grid also vibrates higher. This means
that future generations will come into the planet at a
much higher vibration than what you were born in. The
DNA of future generations will therefore receive a communication from the grid to vibrate at that higher level.
Can you see how this will change the consciousness of
the planet?

We are designed to have our DNA operate at 100 percent efficiency. What does that mean? What would that
look like? Think of the Masters that walked the planet:
Krisna, Sai Baba, Paramahansa Yogananda, Jesus and
many others. Their DNA was activated at one hundred
percent. That ought to tell you something. Kryon has
said that future generations have the potential to come
into the planet with The Crystalline Grid vibrating at
thirty-five to forty percent. Up until now we have been
vibrating at around thirty percent.

Do you understand how it all works? Do you know
that everything you do has a bigger impact than you
were told? If that is the case, what are the mechanics

behind it? How can something we do personally make a difference to anyone but us and those around us? That's the beauty of the system. The way it works was described by Lee Carroll and Kryon in Kryon Book Thirteen, *The Recalibration of Humanity 2013 and beyond*. However, the information is repeated here to reinforce your understanding.

The Crystalline Grid Explained

The Crystalline Grid is the mechanism of how humanity communicates with Gaia. It's not necessarily in real time, either, for it's cumulative. Let me explain: We have told you about a grid of the planet that is called crystalline. We have told you this is not something you can see, but it exists. It is a multi-dimensional, esoteric grid that covers the very dirt of the earth — all of it. It's under your feet now and it's wherever you walk. You might say it is a *shell of the planet that remembers Human energy*.

Crystalline attributes in geology are recognized scientifically as substances that can hold and store vibrational frequencies. So the metaphor of The Crystalline Grid is *a grid that holds memory and energy*. The energy that it holds best and that it was designed for is *everything Human*. The planet responds to you because of this grid. The consciousness of humanity is embedded into the grid through your actions every single day of your life, and everything you do has an energy of some kind.

For thousands of years, these energies that you have created as humans have all been similar. Human nature didn't change much, so it was a repeat of the same things. You can see this clearly in your past, for history repeats itself: war repeats itself, government repeats itself, greed repeats itself, and this is where the shift begins. You're starting to see the subtle changes in your daily lives: your children are changing, governments are changing, and regular Human Beings are awakening to the shift that is before them that will change the very essence of how they live...

...Everything that has happened etches itself onto The Crystalline Grid. For those of you who sense energy, let me ask you: When you stand in a battlefield that is only a few hundred years old, what do you feel? For those of you who sense this energy, you feel the emotion, don't you? Perhaps you feel the desperate sorrow or perhaps the release of death. Much goes on with humans during a battle and The Crystalline Grid at your feet on this battlefield knows it all. It stored it!

The Changing Crystalline

Up until now, the things that got recorded were always those things with the most dramatic emotion. If there was an emotional event on the planet, those who sense these things can go and stand where it happened and they will feel it. Quite often, it's the attribute of mass death and drama. These are also the things that Human nature remembers first and they are the most indelible—death and drama.

However, the attitudes on the planet are starting to change and the very attributes of what is important to humans is starting to change. Perhaps even Human nature is starting to change. The planet is starting to shift, and the idea that you are headed for a swift end is diminishing. This old attitude is a result of hundreds of years of prophecy that represented a very old idea that these times would bring an end, not a beginning.

There will still be those, including some old souls and Lightworkers, who will stand and say, *"This and that cannot change because..."* and then they will give a list of doom attributes, which is a list of all the things that you've experienced in the old energy that are issues and problems that had no solution. The assumption is that they can't be fixed or changed and tomorrow will be worse than today.

Why do I tell you this? If you have a more enlightened population, there will be more wisdom. You will receive solutions to the unsolvable. You don't know what you don't know. If you live with black and white sight, and all of a sudden the children start arriving with the ability to see in color, how do you think your actions are going to look to them? They will see things you never did. You will see these children as odd and strange, since they are talking about hues and colors and you are talking shades of black and white. That's what is happening. The very Earth will start to change how it works because *you are changing you.* This Crystalline Grid of yours has piled up all of these events of humanity and recorded them. This is the energy of the planet and it has been driven by feelings, emotions, death, love, joy and compassion. But within these, drama has been the king of energy for all these years.

Now I'm going to give you the attributes of how this is all changing. As you change yourselves, Gaia responds and starts to also become more multi-dimensional as Gaia is echoing your shift. The Crystalline Grid is going to change the manner in which it remembers things.

The Biggest Change — The Way The Grid Remembers

The primary change: The Crystalline Grid is no longer going to remember in a linear way. Here is what that means. When energy adds to itself as you pile things up, it seems to pile in layers. The things on the bottom were first and the things on the top were last, and whatever this all adds up to is a linear, unchangeable total. There is an assumption that those layers are forever and you can't go in and change them. But what if you changed the *importance* of certain energies within the existing layers? What if all the drama that happened in the past got reduced in importance? Imagine the grid responding to this, and all the horror and drama in the past got reduced in energy within all the historic layers. Do you understand that

46

this is impossible if time is linear? Linear time demands that it is static and unchangeable. What happened in the past is what happened — period. But quantum time is in a circle, so if the "rules" change, then as one thing in the layer changes, the energy of the whole circle changes.

If a quantum change were possible for the grid, then did you just change your past? The answer is no. The past is linear for you, but you can change your perception of how it gets remembered, and this is partially what The Crystalline Grid is doing — recalibrating itself for past, present and future. This, in itself, will change the planet.

Suddenly, The Crystalline Grid starts to clean itself of the old total (change the importance of the remembered layers) because now it is responding to light and dark differently. Up to now, it was driven mostly by things that were dark. That's Human nature. We have told you that less than one half of one percent of this planet has to awaken in order to have the entire planet change. Does that sound linear? No. But it's the same principle. Light is starting to trump darkness, and you are the ones who have this ability to impact The Crystalline Grid in a greater fashion than it has ever been impacted before. The old energy of the past, no matter how dark, will not have the effect it did before.

The Reaction of the Old Energy to a New Grid

The old energy on this planet creates a pattern and humans have gotten used to certain things, including the way The Crystalline Grid works. Old energy counts on The Crystalline Grid remembering things that are more dramatic than things that are not. That means negative things have more energy than positive things. That's what is changing, and the old balance of dark and light will react. You see, there is a *consciousness* of the dark and light balance that is perceived within the Human. There is an old balance of dark and light that has been here for centuries, but when it starts to shift, humans don't know how to react.

This is all metaphoric, describing the energies on this planet. But I will tell you that against all common sense, there will be those who take the old energy to their grave because they just can't help it. It's all they know. There will be those who will go yelling and screaming, not believing that what is around them is shifting and turning so greatly. You'll see it in government, you'll see it in politics, you'll see it in banking, you'll see it in insurance, and you'll see it in your drug companies. They are all counting on the old way and how things work used to work.

The Crystalline Grid is starting to awaken and be responsive to light and compassion instead of drama. If a battle occurs on the planet, the grid won't "see it" the way it did before. Gaia itself won't record the drama of it, and won't respond as it did before. Do you know what happens when a war doesn't get any attention? Pretty soon there's no reason for it, and that's what we're saying. Only the things that make a difference to light on the planet will go into The Crystalline Grid and be measured differently. It will not measure darkness and drama the way it did before, and it will not see the emotion of hatred and terror the same way. The things that had the most impact on Human nature in the past that you now remember more than anything else — death, sorrow, murder — will not matter nearly as much. Oh, it will still be there, but it's not something you're going to want to hear about, dear one. Stand by for that.

There's going to be a day when you're going to go to your news and you're going to expect the *good news channel*. When the old style reporting tells you something awful has happened and they "churn it", it will hurt your heart, and you're going to turn it off! You will turn it off because it doesn't suit the magnificence of the God inside you! Do you understand what I'm saying? When enough of you turn it off, those who produce the news will realize it and start to understand that Human nature is changing. Then they will change.

The Result

Human nature itself will shift, and drama will not hold the key that drives the Earth's grid anymore. That's the new news. This represents a difference, a recalibration in the way that you will communicate with the planet—a total and complete difference. That's what we want to tell you.

What are you going to make of this? What are you going to do next? Let me show you the profundity of this. There are those in this room with puzzles they don't know what to do with, and they are waiting for synchronicity and intuitive answers. In the process of the way you work with Spirit, dear ones, you become self-balancing. This means that no matter how unbalanced you become in 3D, there is a trigger that will create a self-balance energetically, and to which you will return automatically. You self-balance; that's what a mature, old soul does.

When you start to solve the problems that you came in with today, whether it's health or relationships or life's purpose, the solutions create light. This is a metaphor, dear ones, and the only way we can give you a visualization of what is happening. The solution to your problems, using the Creator source within, creates another energy, which is light. Solution and balance create light, and this light is immediately seen by The Crystalline Grid. It sees it as fast as it saw drama before. Light goes into the grid and it changes the planet incrementally in a way it never did before.

So as you leave this place, making decisions that are going to enhance your life, you are creating light and generating compassion that the planet knows about and records. That's what you're here for. That's your goal, no matter what you thought you were supposed to be here for. Everything you do is about the creation of peace inside.

We've said it before. Sometimes we give humans things to do to keep them busy! And you think you are working toward your goal? Your goal is to *exist and love God*. That's your goal, and in the process you have marriages and children and careers. There is sorrow and there is death during life. In the process, there are books that are written and friends who come and go. In the process, you self-balance and Gaia sees the light of your solutions through all of this.

When you are born, your spiritual instincts are driven by your Akashic Inheritance [instinctual remembrance of what you have learned]. You know God is inside; You know that help is there; You know intuitively of your seed biology and the love of those who seeded you. All of those things are inbred in you, and it creates a Human Being who can do what no other Human Being can do at this point in time — change this planet!

It's going to take a long time to steer this change to a full reality for Earth. But now you've created the ladder where there was none before. You have started to build the bridge where none existed before. Do not fear what comes next, for there are those energies that wish to pull you back. These energies are blind and have no idea of the amount of light behind you that will push you forward. They are blind to the light. They'll scream and yell and go into their own demise in total denial, but you're an old soul and you've seen that before. Perhaps this sounds cryptic to you? For now it needs to remain so.

So, dear ones, all is well. Can you look at your life now and say that? *All is well.* Can you believe that there is purpose behind your life? Young person and senior, it makes no difference, because you will swap positions soon. It's what you do. And you're not going to miss the ending of this Earth saga, I'll tell you that. All of you are coming back to participate in this renewing planet. This is what we see, dear family, because we've seen it before. This is a routine that you have felt many times but never on this planet called Earth. Now it's time.

Kryon live channelling "The Recalibration of The Crystalline Grid"
given in Portland, Maine — August 4, 2012

There are other attributes of The Crystalline Grid. There are places on the planet where The Crystalline Grid overlaps with Gaia. In certain attributes you get a build-up of energy that creates a node. There are three kinds of nodes: a portal, a vortex and a vortal. A portal is a node that overlaps and amplifies Gaia. A vortex is when energies collide and the energy is constantly moving. To some, being in a vortex may feel good for a while, but it's hard to live there. A vortal is half and half between a portal and a vortex.

In certain attributes, the overlaps will cancel each other in energy and you get a null. This means there are places on the planet that have an absence of The Crystalline Grid and the only energy you feel is pure Gaia. Nodes and nulls exist all over the planet. For more information look under the "Extra's" tab on my website: www.monikamuranyi.com

Whales and Dolphins

What do you feel when you see photographs or artwork of whales and dolphins? Is it joy and happiness? Do you find yourself smiling? Have you been fortunate to interact with living whales and dolphins? Did you feel a heart connection? These mammals are seen as special by our global population. The whales are protected by over 80 countries, including countries that are bordered by land, not sea. Why does humanity feel such an affinity for the whales and dolphins? The reason is that our cellular structure within our DNA knows that whales and dolphins represent a significant and special part of the Earth.

What do they represent? Your intuition already knows the answer. The whales and dolphins are the living portions of the grid system. They are the library containing the history of the Earth's evolution. All three Akashic systems are stored in the whales and dolphins. They coordinate and cooperate with The Crystalline Grid. The cetaceans of Earth are, therefore, the fourth place where your Akashic Record exists.

During April, 2013 I experienced a dolphin encounter in Cancun, Mexico. Previously, I have swum with wild dolphins in New Zealand and Hawaii but my Cancun experience was different. It was an interactive dolphin program located in the natural environment of the beautiful Isla Mujeres. This facility has around twenty-five dolphins, all born in captivity. Our small group included Lee Carroll and Lightworkers from Russia. We became acquainted with two female dolphins in a very personal and individual way.

One by one, we got to hug, kiss and play games with the dolphins. Working in tandem, the dolphins allowed me to be pulled across the water while I held on to their dorsal fins. They also gave me a foot push. All of us felt our hearts and consciousness expand. We were communicating with the dolphins both physically and quantumly. At the end of the day, Lee Carroll and Kryon gave us a profound message that I wish to share.

Greetings, dear ones, I am Kryon of Magnetic Service. Feel the wind and hear the ocean. It should fill your heart with sweetness, for this is the energy of Gaia that responds to Human consciousness and the part that is in love with Humanity. Gaia itself has a consciousness. It is difficult to conceive that the Earth can speak with one voice, but that's no more difficult a concept than God speaking with one voice. Here we are dealing with quantum language and something called *quantum intellect*. I'm going to tell you a little more about that in a moment.

The attributes of Gaia are complex. The very consciousness of Gaia was placed here as little as 200,000 years ago when the Pleiadians planted the seed within your DNA. It is necessary to say that before we discuss our subject, we need to pause. For today you touched the dolphins and so we wish to speak of these animals. We wish to give you a little more information. Perhaps it will continue to close the gap of awareness, because Humanity has already made the discoveries we speak about.

There is an axiom of truth — we'll call it "the rules of the way Spirit works." We do not give answers to any questions about science, or the way things work, unless there has been a Human who has already discovered it. This would be inappropriate for the concept of free choice.

Humanity must find its way to raising its own consciousness, and that is why Spirit is sometimes elusive. When you sit in channelled sessions and questions are asked about free energy, or about biology, or other items that have not yet been discovered, Kryon and Spirit may answer these questions poorly. This is because these things all belong to Humanity. But in the last year, there have been discoveries made, which allow me to speak as I do now.

What did you feel when you touched the skin of this animal? It's a cetacean, and in that family are what you call whales and dolphins. Indeed, they have something in common which I'd like to talk to you about. Today your experience was controlled, and these animals were born in captivity. But for our discussion, it doesn't make any difference. Were you able to look them in the eye? One eye turned toward you, as you might have noticed. Now, they didn't need to look at you, for they sense your presence with sound. But indeed, they looked at you with one of their eyes. Their vision is not binocular as yours is [eyes which coordinate to create one image], and these animals actually see rather poorly, with one eye on each side of their head. But what did you see today?

They checked you out and they looked at you carefully. Indeed they are trained, but you saw their interest when you came, did you not? Yes, they work for fish, but there is so much more. So let me back up and fill you in.

Is it interesting to you that there are so few cetaceans? In the scheme of animals on the planet, there are only a few shaped like fish, swim like fish, and live in the ocean. Yet they are like you. They breathe the air of Gaia as you do, and they are special, as you are. Human consciousness has always known they are special. But it has only been in the last 100 years that the countries of the earth have agreed to ban the catching and killing of these cetaceans. Even countries that have no oceans or seas have signed a contract to protect the cetaceans. In other words, there is an intuitive sense that they are special, and all of Humanity knows it and the governments of the countries know it. They have made arrangements to keep them alive and special. There is no other animal on the planet that has this attribute. So I ask you to look at this. Do you believe that this is a coincidence? It is not. It is, instead, mass intuitive action, and it should speak to you loudly about the connection between Humans, dolphins and whales, and Gaia.

Now I'm going to get back to the discussion of the Pleiadians, and their part in all this. There have been some discoveries made recently which have started to identify Human DNA as being unique and different on the planet — different from any other mammal. The discoveries show that you have two of your DNA chromosomes fused together, almost like they are welded together. The other mammals of earth have 24 chromosomes and you have 23. Something happened to your DNA. The DNA of the Human Being was altered, and I previously told you how and where. — It was by the Pleiadians, 200,000 years ago. It was designed, appropriate, and part of God's plan. It is your creation story.

When the Pleiadian home planets were in graduation, they had ascended energy to them. Your planet was now scheduled for the same test as theirs had gone through. They are your seed parents and now science is looking at their work — two fused chromosomes. What it means to science is that you did not evolve from anything here. This is the beginning of the proof that Human Beings did not directly evolve from any other species on the planet.

Two more discoveries followed: One was in September, 2012 and one shortly after that. They have finally identified the 90 percent of DNA that was previously labeled as "junk". They now understand what it is. Research shows that it is the instruction manual for the less than three percent of protein encoding parts of your DNA. It is data! So the 90 percent are the instructions, and less than three percent is the engine that makes the 26,000 genes of the Human body. Finally, science understands that the overwhelming majority of the chemistry are instructions — information. It's exciting news, for the discovery that followed had several parts to it.

Part one of the second discovery: linguists discovered that the information in the previous discovery was structured as in language. Let me explain this. You are listening to two languages (English followed by Russian translation). One language you understand, and one you may not. You are surrounded by other languages here as well (Spanish language spoken in Mexico). You may not understand these languages, but your DNA is wired to comprehend their structure, intuitively. You have quantum intuition that lets you *tune in* to the Human Being who is speaking. I'm speaking English through my partner, whose culture speaks English. But if you did not have your translator, some of you would still understand a great deal of the concept of what was being presented. Your DNA is built and structured in what we call engrams for language. Linguists now have seen the correlation of the 90 percent data of the DNA, to language engrams. This was not expected.

The second part of this language discovery is that the information in the DNA is not fixed. What this means is that it can be altered and changed. The data can be re-written! Some scientists are now working on how that can be done, and they're starting to correlate sound combinations and frequencies with the changes to the information in DNA. Is this starting to make sense to you? How long have you been told that sound can heal, or that sound can change your biology? Now science is starting to look at this same exact thing.

There is a connection with the animals you touched today. Through many years, and with a great deal of resources, science has researched Human DNA. I now encourage the scientists to put some funding toward the study of dolphin DNA, because what they're going to find is something similar to yours. *It is built for quantum intuitive language recognition.*

Human DNA is like a radio receiver for sound. Certain kinds of sounds, both audible and inaudible, can alter the instruction sets [the data] for DNA, and can send messages to Human consciousness. Certain kinds of sounds, audible and not, can send messages to the dolphins. You have this identical thing in common, and scientists will begin to see the correlation.

There'll come a day, dear ones, when you say, sing, or project the correct sounds to the cetaceans of Earth. They will see it as a structured language (even though it isn't to you), which they have been expecting. When this happens, there will be something they do which we will not tell you about yet. They are expecting you to do this. They "see" Humans as family.

Meanwhile, they feel you when you are there, through the energy of a quantum intellect. Some ask, *"Kryon, what would happen if you looked at a monkey's DNA, a creature much like the Human? Would there be similarities?"* Yes. You would see the expected genomic development, earth chemistry and similarities. But that's where it stops. Dear Human Being, there are only two kinds of DNA on the planet which are structured for quantum intellect. The Human Being and the cetacean. Finally, I give you this information: If you really looked at dolphin DNA closely, listen carefully ... you will also find that they are not from here. I will let that be what it is.

And so it is.

Kryon live channelling "Information about the Dolphins"
given in Cancun, Mexico — April 10, 2013

Kryon said that two discoveries have been made by scientists regarding DNA. A summary of what these scientists discovered is presented in Chapter Eight: DNA—It's More Than You Think. Kryon also mentioned that the whales and dolphins are expecting humanity to sing and project sounds to them. Does this sound too weird and spooky?

Every year, millions of dollars are spent by enthusiastic tourists undertaking activities with the whales and dolphins. Clearly, the whales and dolphins do more than just contain the Akashic Records of the planet. Many cultures from around the world have stories about their healing effects on Human health and spiritual well-being. There are also many cases of dolphins assisting seafarers during storms and saving individual lives.

In 1978, Dr. David Nathanson started working with children who were mentally handicapped or suffered brain damage. The unique approach to his therapy included the use of dolphins. The simple concept was to reward the children with a dolphin swim when they made a correct response. The startling results showed that the children retained more information and learned four times faster.

Since then, there are many organizations and institutions that offer dolphin-assisted therapy. There are also more individuals tapping into their gift as an interspecies communicator and helping others to heal physically and spiritually with the whales and dolphins. Many scientists claim there is no scientific evidence that whales and dolphins can heal humans. Try explaining that to those who have experienced a healing.

Dolphins use echolocation to investigate their surroundings, for exploring, finding food and communicating with one another. They create intense waves of sound above and below Human hearing that can be controlled to a fine degree. Many hospitals use a lithotripsy machine to break up kidney stones and gall stones in patients. The machine uses low frequency sound waves. These shock waves pass through the body of the patient until they hit the kidney stones or gall stones and break them up into tiny pieces, allowing them to pass out of the body. The physics of the machine are similar to a dolphin's sonar. However, dolphins can produce over four times the amount of acoustic power that lithotripsy machines produce. Dolphins can also shape the waves of sound that they send from their forehead from a wide fan to a narrow beam.

There is evidence that dolphins trigger the healing process in humans by boosting the production of T-cells and endorphins. Following a dolphin interaction, scientists have measured a greater coherence between the left and right hemisphere of the brain and an increase in brainwave activity. It is also thought to help increase attention span, and develop motor skills and coordination in children. Many therapists believe that a dolphin's sonar produces changes in a person's body tissue and cellular structure. The sounds emitted by dolphins can also help produce change, similar to the effect of music therapy.

Some researchers are finding some interesting similarities between autistic children and dolphins. Most humans vibrate between 13 and 30 cycles per second of brain wave energy in a conscious state. Dolphins vibrate between 250,000 and two trillion cycles per second of brain wave energy in their conscious state. A child with autism can process over 250,000 cycles per second of brain wave energy in their conscious state. This high level of brain wave processing is recognized by a term known as an *Intuitive Genius.*

When autistic children and dolphins are at this level of mental processing they can communicate through what is known as *thought transference.* They are able to read the energy from each other and respond within a split second. Children with this ability, therefore, operate at a higher level than what our language provides. Trying to linearize this into our language is difficult because they have to dumb down their ability to process at a genius level.

In Kryon Book Nine, *The New Beginning*, a mother of an autistic child asked Kryon a question related to autism.

Dear Kryon: I'm a mother of a seven-year-old son diagnosed with autism. I've worked with energy for what seems to be all my life. During the past five years, I've been getting concepts that I don't really understand. Your channelling has been helping. However, perhaps those of you who read this (I trust it will be read by whoever Spirit intends) may have encountered this as well.

Here goes ... my son's magnetics system does not feel the same as ours. Is there a possibility that his DNA may have different magnetic structures than non-autistics? I can almost see this in my mind as strands running through some sort of chrysalis-type prism. Okay, I know that sounds nuts. I also feel this same thing around dolphins. He is particularly drawn to the calls of hump-back-whale recordings. Is it possible that the cetacean connection to autism is in the magnetics? His communication (still nonverbal) has been progressing in leaps and bounds over the past year. Are the magnetic grid alignments becoming more compatible with autistics' systems?

Dear one, for you and the others who work with these children, I honor you! We told you earlier that they are mostly savants. These children are indeed born with DNA differences of the kind that are magnetically enhanced. The difference is that they are more geared to a multi-dimensional existence, rather than the 4D existence that you live in. So, yes, this is a magnetic cellular attribute. Some are even calling, autistics "rainbow children." Your intuition is correct. Here's more.

1) They wish to communicate and live out of linearity. They don't understand things in a row or in a line. They'll do far better with overall concepts that steer them to a pseudo-linear action, so that they can live in your world. If it were possible, they would love to communicate without "in-a-row," linear verbal speech. They would rather do it all at once using a "thought group." Their frustration is that everything around them is boxing in their expansiveness, and they have to stop and make sense of it.

Can you imagine what it would be like to be born in a world where you had 3D, and everyone else had 2D? Let's say there was no depth — only height and width. You wanted to "reach inside" things, and you could see how — only to have an invisible wall stop your hand each time you tried, or stop your mind each time. You couldn't even walk around! Others around you would call you retarded, as they watched the funny kid who couldn't navigate in a simple 2D world. You would spend most of your time looking at things, trying to decipher if what you were seeing was true or not for the reality you were in.

2) They tend to live partially in a reality that humans don't see or understand. Where are they mentally, you sometimes ask, as they stare off into space. The truth? They're actually seeing and participating in multi-dimensional attributes of life ... or trying to. They also can "see" the other life on Earth — the life that you don't even acknowledge yet. More on this some other time.

3) They're attuned to the energy of the dolphins and whales, but more specifically, the dolphin. There has actually been research on this from your scientists, so it's not as odd as it sounds. There's communication at a distance between autistic children and these sea mammals. If they ever actually establish a one-on-one relationship to a single animal, it lasts a lifetime.

4) Yes, the grid system of the planet is going to make them more comfortable ... and you less comfortable. We've been channelling over the last year about becoming multi-dimensional. Perhaps it's time that humans moved a bit in the direction of the autistics, instead of teaching them how to exist in yours.

Kryon Questions and Answers from Kryon Book Nine,
The New Beginning: Chapter Fourteen.

I'd like to introduce you to someone who has experienced the healing energy of whales and dolphins on many occasions: Laurie Reyon Anderson. Laurie Reyon is an internationally known Interspecies Communicator and Soul Healer. She has even been named "Standing Whale Mother" by the Native Americans. Many people have experienced the wisdom and healing energy of the whales and dolphins through Laurie Reyon.

Here is a message from the Dolphins as given by Laurie Reyon in February 2012:

The Dolphins have shared with me that they are the designated KEEPERS of the Human DNA template system. They receive infusions of DNA activations through the Earth's ocean systems from Creator. It is their given task to process this information internally and calibrate the actual DNA that is perfect and right for each person. They also hold the energy of LOVE and JOY for actual locations on the planet that are experiencing war and chaos. They work to create frequencies that are infused into these areas on the planet with templates of peace, harmony and healing. The DOLPHIN MATRIX supports DNA re-encodements for people and places through the energy code systems they use. THE DOLPHIN FAMILY OF LIGHT has created a TEMPLATE for the HUMAN DNA and uses it to monitor the overall template for the pure HOLOGRAPHIC POSSIBILITY equation for Humanity and Earth.

If you choose to connect with the planetary DOLPHIN family, you can receive these attunements directly from the dolphin group consciousness.

They are the masters of DNA recalibration and are able to shift old energies very quickly with their healing frequencies. Also, they work in a frequency of joy and playfulness that is perfectly suited to the energy of ascension and the "New Earth." Beloved humans, please listen to your hearts as the energies accelerate during 2012 and beyond. Call upon the dolphin energies, as they are the chosen emissaries of light. Their communications will be of valuable assistance in helping you to align with The Crystalline Grid system, your personal DNA upgrades and the dolphin matrix systems that are assisting in creating the "center" for the "New Earth."

Also know that the dolphin matrix of energy is assisting with the cleansing and balancing of the Earth's oceans.

"Currently, many scientific experts are saying that DNA plays a powerful role in newly discovered communications between dolphins and humans. An ongoing study at the Sirius Institute in Hawaii has revealed that dolphins and whales receive and transmit sound signals capable of affecting the genetic double helix. Using natural biotechnology dolphins can actually heal humans swimming near them "sono-genetically."

Fourteen years of multi-disciplinary study at the Sirius Institute has indicated that the expression of DNA traditionally considered the blueprint of life can be changed by the sound and electromagnetic fields generated by dolphins.

New research shows that our DNA is activated by waves and particles of energized sound and light that literally switch genes on or off.

Likewise, genetic inheritance is energetically transmitted bio-acoustically and electromagnetically through special water molecules that form the electro-genetic matrix of DNA. These hydroelectric structures are shaped like pyramids, hexagons and pentagons and they direct healing processes."

This amazing phenomenon explains how remarkable healings have been reported by people in our boats near the dolphins and by swimmers, following dolphin contact.

The cetaceans have had complex languages for millions of years and they have the largest brains on the planet. Visitations by dolphins and whales have demonstrated a history of friendship and cooperation and even partnership with humans.

The dolphins and whales have shown us that they are the ancient and wise super-sentient Beings on this planet. They are living examples for humans, showing us how to live in peace and in harmony with our planet. We encourage you to connect with the dolphins and the whales each and every day, energetically, telepathically and in the physical oceans whenever you can. They are the living ultimate expression of how we humans can begin to live in our hearts within the POD MIND, which is demonstrated by living for the good of the many, not the one.

Laurie Reyon & Master Cat Puddah and the Cetacean Councils of Light

The Sirius Institute quotes taken from the site: www.Dolphin-Spirit-of-Hawaii.com

Many of you have probably experienced a whale watching tour or even swam with dolphins. But have you experienced a dolphin or whale trip with an animal and interspecies communicator? You may want to consider participating in one with Laurie Reyon Anderson. At the time of writing this book, Laurie told me about a recent trip (July 2013). They saw approximately 2,400 dolphins and interacted with six blue whales! Take a look at one of her videos featuring the Blue Whales:

www.youtube.com/watch?v=ugLN8w5T2mA

For more information about Laurie Reyon Anderson and details about her whale/dolphin trips please visit her website: www.lauriereyon.com

Questions for Kryon:

Logic suggests that each planet of free choice has an energy accounting system. (On Earth it is the Cave of Creation and The Crystalline Grid). Is there an energy accounting system in the galaxy? What happens as each planet of free choice reaches ascension? Is this related to the expansion of the universe?

Answer:

In order to fully answer this, plus some of the other questions to come, I wish to display an attribute of the Akash that is really basic to this entire discussion. Prepare for me to disclose information that has been waiting for 2014. Much of what follows has never been presented in any Kryon channelling.

Did you ever look around and wonder about how evolution works? When a child is developing in a mother's womb, there are astonishing processes that go into creating a working, functioning Human Being. Each organ and system is "prepared" through a system of pre-knowledge, which we call templates. Ask a doctor how a lens is formed in an eye or how certain tissues start one way just to change to another way later in the womb. If you ever have studied this, then you would be awed by the complexity of a system that has stored the details of "what worked and what didn't". That's the nature of evolution. Things got better and better through millions of years, and the organism only *remembered* and kept what helped them survive, or helped them see better, or walk better, or find food better. Even the simplest of organisms on the planet have this feature, down to insects and even things you can't see.

Now, with all that in mind, I'm going to ask you this: *"What is the accounting system that is responsible for making all this work?"* There has to be one — an amazing one with benevolent consciousness and knowledge of physics. If you think your body came about by accident in a vacuum, then you are the one who would have no problem finding a specialized transmission for a Formula One racecar on another planet. You would say, *"The elements came together over many years and created it fully by accident, manufacturer's labels and all."*

The truth of life in the galaxy is far grander than this. Think about it. If the evolution of species was just to "create survival," then there would come a time when it was "good enough" and creatures would simply stop changing. What would propel them into having intellect? Why would they need more than food and the ability to defend and reproduce? There has to be something else that "pushes" the template to create something that is far more evolved than just survival.

Why are you reading this? Is there perhaps something in your template that "knows" there is something bigger than what you see? Humans are very interesting. They think they can "know" anything that is available to know. However, even as you sit there, there isn't even an awareness of the template! Humanity is like a fish in a bowl, thinking that food just somehow naturally drops in when they need it, and they never even question or see the hand that is attached to it — and they don't know there is a bowl!

So the template creates biology that eventually has intellect, against all odds. This would never follow the bell-shaped curve philosophy that you cling to regarding how "things work." When humanity was fully developed and ready, your *spiritual creation* was accomplished, and that came from the Pleiadians. Then spiritual evolution began, and that's a subject for another book. But the Akashic system came with your seed parents and all the systems involved with it.

So in answer to the first part of the question, we tell you that you inherited the same Akashic "accounting system" that your seed parents had. Their planet had the equivalent and still does. So you are looking at an *evolved model of spiritual conveyance* — a system that carries so many attributes that a book has been written about it! [Kryon smile; referring to this book].

Yes, you will find the same model all over the galaxy, just as you eventually will find the same kind of DNA structure in life, everywhere. Does this surprise you, that there is consistency of life? Biology is simply the extension and evolution of physics and shares structure with it.

The evolution scheme, as we have told you before, creates ascended planets [where the life is fully spiritually aware of itself], and this triggers the seed planting of another single planet. As each seeded planet grows or not, with free choice, it indeed changes the vibration of the galaxy.

Let's not get out of the galaxy. It's a big enough subject for now. The Universe is expanding for physics reasons that we have given you before.

The next answer will give you a better idea why a system has to exist at all. It's complex, and beautiful, and millions of years old.

As our global population increases, new souls come to the planet. At some time in the future our population growth will stop and possibly eventually recede. In this circumstance will old souls have precedence in coming back? Can you explain more about which souls are chosen to incarnate on the planet?

The growth of humanity is part of the "soul accounting" that you have asked about before. It's not accidental, and the incoming soul balances with old-soul returns in another beautiful system that has not been fully explained.

Logic and math will tell you this story if you think about it. The more souls on the planet, the larger the pool of return potential. Almost all souls return. This is an absolute, and it's very funny when Humans think they are not coming back. They have no idea what it is like to have the "mind of God" and think they will still have the mind of a Human when they are gone. Again, they are like fish in a bowl, so when they ascend, they get a bigger bowl and are eternal fish. Therefore, all their decisions will be just like the ones they make as fish now. The truth is that the very system of soul return you all "signed up for" lasts *until planet Earth is complete.*

So let's be clear. Since almost all souls who start on the planet return, there is no precedence or hierarchy of who is coming back. They all are! So the only variable here is how fast they come back, and that is measured by the vibration of

Gaia. Some are special (see next answer below), but there is a complete system, and we will review a bit of it.

In the beginning, after the seeding, virtually none came back. But at the end of each Human life, the souls went into the "pool of souls scheduled to return when ready." That pool grew and grew, but new souls were the only ones on the planet. We even have given you information about Lemuria [referring to Hawaii], in that there were no returning souls! We needed to build up the returning pool numbers — experienced souls who had been Human. We also told you that Lemurians were not necessarily Earth-savvy. This is one of the reasons a few of them had to live very, very long lives. It was the only way to keep the wisdom and knowledge pure, since there was no Akashic build-up yet. There simply were no returning ancestors! They even had dysfunctional leadership (imagine that). So it's time to demystify all the ideas that Lemuria was some "perfect civilization in the past." It was a society that is "home" to many of you, but you only were there one time — guaranteed. This was the plan.

Thousands of years went by like this, building up the pool of return souls, and finally after the core Lemuria [referring to the Lemurian civilization on the mountain Hawaii] started to disperse, the system of returns began. At that point, there were far more in the return pool than you needed. It meant that for a long period of time, the only Humans born on Earth had actually been here before. This was a needed attribute, kind of like they had some training in Humanism.

Today, ALL souls come back, and you always have a larger and larger pool of returning Humans. There is also a system of "family return," but this subject should be discussed separately. Today, there is a mixture of returns and new souls, due to your exponential growth rate. However, more souls coming and going creates more returns, since new souls automatically go into the "return pool" when they are finished with the first earth life. Slowly, the returns become wiser and wiser, and they influence the balance of consciousness. The percentage of souls who have been here before is far larger than you think. However, they are not all "old souls." That takes hundreds of lifetimes.

Throughout 30,000 years, there have been plagues, vast wars where millions have died all within a few years, and also an era of very short lifetimes. Add to that a mystery that we have not disclosed much about — four complete start-overs of humanity! But the pool of available return souls grew and grew, no matter what. So as we said, there was a time when there were far more candidates for an earth soul than the birth rate of Earth! The warehouse of souls was, therefore, created with time, lots of time.

So this may temper the very idea of *who* is actually arriving on the planet as a newly born baby. Again, think out of the box: Earth has birth and death, but souls are forever. Do you see how that might change the dynamic of who is here? ONE soul becomes Human many times, over and over, eventually moving into an old soul status. The dynamics are this: The larger the population of the planet, the more returning souls there are. Understand? Yet there is that funny idea that because your population is increasing at such a rapid rate, most newborns "arrive" from somewhere else and never were Human! That's not exactly true.

So the resource pool of souls who come to the planet has a quantity potential of hundreds of millions of lives lived over thousands and thousands of years. Exponential growth is only about current lives on the planet. So there are far more returning souls in the mix than you think. This is also the plan.

There will come a time, dear ones, when your growth slows down, and where all you are doing is recycling souls and there are no "new" ones. Guess what happens then? The proportion of old souls slowly begins to dominate.

So, where do the "new souls" come from? New souls come from a common-sense source. They are almost all from a pool of former Pleiadians, just like you. Think about it. You carry their spiritual DNA, so wouldn't it be obvious that you also carry their Akashic spiritual lineage? They have a pool, too!

When a child is born on Earth, do you ask what planet it is from? This is common sense, yet there are many esoteric thinkers who have remembrances of other planets and feel they are not from Earth. Well, they are right! Their spiritual Akash contains engrams of remembrance of their entire lineage of Pleiadians, and those who seeded them, and those who seeded the ones before them, on and on, all on other planets.

The earth has Human biology and you are a product of Earth. But after what many call "the creation story" (the seeding of spiritual awareness), you received what we call "spiritual inheritance." That inheritance could only come from one place—the Seven Sisters, which seeded you with their history. Therefore, you have the evolution of a Human with altered DNA from somewhere else. Both of these attributes play into who you are today.

There are planets with evolved biological life like yours who never were seeded. They have intellect without awareness, and all the things that go with it. Some have even visited you but never returned. That's a different story for another day.

The Crystalline Grid responds to Human consciousness. This sets the level of vibration for Earth. When souls arrive on the planet they inherit the level of Earth's vibration. The Masters on the planet are exceptions. Can you explain why some souls can come into the planet and have DNA that vibrates at a higher level? Is this related to their Akash or is it part of a system of balance on the planet?

Certain souls have a full and complete system that is their own. It is not "hooked" to Gaia in any way, as most souls are. These "mastery" souls come in many types, however, and some are not what you think. For instance, just to catch you off guard, I'll tell you that Nikola Tesla was one of these. So was Beethoven. These "specialist" mastery souls only come in when they are needed, and their DNA is tuned to what they need to do, and not to Gaia.

You think they are most likely spiritual masters, but that's not so. Although spiritual masters are part of this system, the majority of them are artists, inventors and Humans who will change the planet and create new paradigms. This is given to Earth when it needs to be in order to bypass Akashic timing and fast-track certain energies to the potentials that humanity has earned.

These souls then stay out of the Gaia Akashic system until needed again. You have one in your own backyard. His Lemurian name is Yawee [referring to Dr. Todd Ovokaitys]. Other recent ones were John Lennon and Steve Jobs.

These specialists don't always "vibrate higher," as you say. Many of them simply come in for their specialty. Only the spiritual masters who need it have advanced DNA. Some may actually seem very unenlightened. I know this does not follow your current teachings or ideas of how things work, but it should make more common sense to you in this accurate form. If the Earth needs flight, radio, alternating current or smart phones to move quickly into new paradigms, you don't send Gandhi.

Many humans have experienced a healing after interacting with whales and/or dolphins. Can you explain more about how and why this happens? Can you tell us more about the special interaction that occurs between dolphins and children with autism, and children who are mentally handicapped (or suffered brain damage)?

I'll do more than that. I wish to explain a bit more about the whole subject.

71

We have brought you information before about the cetaceans of the planet. They are part of the "Gaia group" and represent one of the nine attributes of the Human Being. They carry their own kind of time capsule or *template for future humanity,* and they have altered DNA that the Pleiadians gave them. Therefore, you might say that they are "tuned" differently from any other animal on the planet.

Part of what they carry is "increased dimensionality." Warning: This is not something that is going to be widely understood, since it is not recognized yet. There simply is no teaching at this point about relative dimensionality. We will make it understandable in a very basic way. Imagine what evolved Human DNA will someday be like. *"Kryon, how can we know that?"* Just imagine what you think it might be like. Since you carry the template already, you will be accurate. Evolution is simply the process of activating templates that are already there. So it's in your consciousness to imagine it. But you knew that, didn't you?

Imagine thought transference, singing to someone through love and having them *hear* it [the love], sending a pure template to a sick template and having spontaneous remission. Do you follow me? These things are already in the DNA of Humans, just waiting for the thousands of years it will take to bring them into reality.

Bringing them into reality must also be accompanied by a slight dimensional shift of consciousness across a barrier, a kind of elusive membrane between dimensions (something mentioned in earlier science channellings). The process for this coming shift is in data held in the cetacean time capsules, along with much more. In other words, these animals already have some of these very attributes, but they are whales and dolphins, not Humans. So they are just carrying them around for eventual release to you, like a living, traveling, Pleiadian grid.

Quantumness is odd to you, since it does not follow your reality construct. For instance, there is no "place" where anything resides within a quantum system. In fact, something with quantum attributes has the potential to be "everywhere" at the same time. Since these cetacean time capsules carry these futuristic attributes, they have a quantum residual, a spill-over of energy into certain Human Beings who also have a spill-over of the same kind. These are Humans born with DNA that is more ready to work into the *dimensional shift of the future*. All this is simply part of the biological evolutionary process. I have told you that some of the autistics are in this group — futurists, savants. However, for this discussion, suddenly the Human and the cetacean can "hear" each other!

Think of a music transmitter [radio station] that is slightly off of its frequency. Nobody can hear it because it moved off of the normal vibration place on the dial. Now think of a receiver that synchronistically is tuned slightly off center as well. Instead of a very clear music signal, now it has a very faint, hard to hear signal. But aha! Something else is being heard or sensed as well. It's the transmitter, which is also off, transmitting other music that is actually clearer and better. So both devices have to be slightly out of normal range to have this happen. You might say that both are moving into relative dimensionality. New information: A specific dimensionality [the description of a reality paradigm] is relative to the perception of the dimension it is moving to. See, I told you this would be hard.

Let me explain more. When you read the answer to a previous question about the autistic child, you saw something that has been hiding. Magnetics is multi-dimensional. It has a quantum attribute. The workings of magnetics are used daily, but the full scope of its definition and higher attributes are still a mystery. At the atomic level, it's far more than electrons being attracted to nodes and nulls of unequal pairs. It's a quantum dynamic that will eventually posture very high vibration on the planet, and it is the engine for eventual consciousness change.

So the autistic child relates to the magnetic grid, since he senses the new dimensionality paradigm that his DNA is looking for — *nonlinear higher thought*. New: The rules of dimensional action state that, "Dimensional differences always seek a more complete solution." Let me state that in other terms: The soup of dimensionality always seeks a higher purpose and never will marry to a lower one. This, my dear ones, is the reason for "intelligent design." It defies randomness and is "physics with an attitude."

Meanwhile, the autistic child and the dolphin are now on the same frequency! The child relates to magnetics because he senses quantum energy, and the cetacean swims the magnetic flux lines of the planet. Both are entangled just enough to relate to each other through what the magnetic grid brings them.

So rather than the magnetic grid of the planet being responsible for anything that is happening, it instead is the equalizing energy that allows the connection. It is the broth of the quantum soup that allows the frequencies to be heard and recognized.

The question asked by a mother of an autistic child earlier in the Whales and Dolphins section is related to all of this.

Did the Lemurians share a special relationship with the whales and dolphins? Can you tell us more about this?

Not really. These animals were seen as the perfect vehicle to store the time capsules of the future in a way that could never be plundered or eliminated. So they were there already. However, with changed DNA, these animals then became "part of the Pleiadian family," if you know what I mean. So it was after the seeding that they carried the data that would help enable the future of humanity.

When these animals became "complete" with this change, they also developed a connection with humanity that is to this day still palatable and mysterious. No other animal on the planet has this.

You feel it, don't you?

Chapter Three

Akashic Inheritance

Most of us are familiar with the term genetic inheritance. The genes, within our DNA, are the means by which we inherit physical characteristics from our parents. These include your gender, blood type, eye color and height. Many health conditions or diseases are genetic. The Human Genome Project (HGP) was undertaken in an attempt to identify all of the genes within Human DNA. This is further discussed in Chapter Eight: DNA—It's More Than You Think.

Current understanding of our DNA is limited and there are many things we still don't understand. However, this is beginning to change. Science is starting to validate the information given by Kryon about our DNA. Scientists are now recognizing that within DNA there exists information that provides instruction sets for our cells. Perhaps the reason it has taken so long to discover is that parts of it are quantum (multi-dimensional energy).

Kryon told us our DNA contains multi-dimensional information. Lee Carroll presented a detailed study of this in Kryon Book Twelve, *The Twelve Layers of DNA*. Our DNA contains the following energies:

- the tree of life (our biological layer)
- the divine blue-print (our life lesson and the duality of life)
- ascension and activation (our spiritual awakening)
- your angelic name
- your Higher-Self
- your extra-dimensional sense layer
- your personal Akashic Record of your core soul
- your healing layer
- divine belief
- wise divine feminine (pure compassion and mother energy)
- Almighty God (the life force of God within the Human)

As mentioned previously, your DNA contains your personal Akashic Record. Therefore, as each Human is born on the planet, they come in with their own Akashic Inheritance. But what does this mean? Is there any physical evidence of this? Kryon has given a detailed description to explain Akashic Inheritance:

The beauty and complexity of *Akashic Inheritance* takes two paths. Because you are linear thinkers and are in three dimensions, you have always assigned the idea of Akashic Inheritance to your genomic 3D chemistry. The man in the chair before you [Lee] is fourth generation Irish. His chemistry goes all the way back to his seed country. So there is the thought that his Akash (past life information) would also be carried in his 3D chemistry. But it does not work that way.

There are two complete separate paths for inheritance that seem to compete, but they are actually a meld. There is 3D body chemistry and there is Akashic. That is to say the man before you in the chair, although he is fourth generation Irish and has Irish blood, might have come from India the last time — and hate meat and potatoes! You might say, *"Wait a minute, how can that work?"* That's the point — it does. So it doesn't matter about the lineage of your parents when it comes to your past lives. That is totally chemistry dependent and the genes that are represented there are part of a three-dimensional genomic system. That system gives you eye color, some of the Ancestors' attributes, and even some of their talent propensities. You might also have their looks, but you might not have anything else that has to do with them if your last lifetime was in India.

So in all honesty, you have a non-linear puzzle before you that is almost not explainable to you. You can have the lineage of many generations of Irish blood, yet have Indian Akashic attributes that drive your eating habits and much more.

When it comes time for your re-entry into the planet as a reincarnated Human, dear one, you can make many choices for many reasons. Some of the choices are to continue within a 3D chemical pattern and have your Akashic Inheritance match your chemical lineage. But you can also step-into another race, and another continent. But as you step into that new body, it will have a 3D chemistry that reflects your parents in that other race.

Here is an example taken from my statement above, and it points all this out: Let's say you're going to come into this planet, to be born in America, perhaps of Irish descent, just like my partner. Let's also say, just as an example, that your immediate past life experience is from India. So you might not want to eat certain kinds of American food. You will become vegan, and it works well for your body. But those around you will wonder what happened to you, and why would you do this. After all, a good Irish person would not wish to eat that way.

Now, there is a propensity for many spiritual teachers to stand on their soapbox, so to speak, and say, *"Humans should eat a certain way for spiritual and health reasons."* Let me re-write this statement for you, personally: *"I will eat based upon my Akashic Inheritance. This is what my cellular structure wants and it will give me the healthiest and most spiritually appropriate balance for my chemistry."* Teachers can't give a generic food statement for all Humans, because all of you have a different Akashic Inheritance. That means that each of the body chemistry attributes of everyone reading this has a built-in template for their personal Akashic remembrance of health. Your cells are tuned in to your past lives in a far stronger way than you know. Some might be matched to the 3D chemistry of your parent's lineage, and some not.

Some people will be just fine with everything that's put into their food with no problem at all. Even places that don't feature healthy food may still be what the body chemistry wants, remembers, and can process. As an American, you might have over two hundred years of American experience, and the chemistry is recognizing and dealing with the preservatives. But others of you may come in to this life and immediately react, because you've never experienced this food. Now, again you may say, *"Wait a minute, that's chemistry!"* I told you it would be complex. Chemistry carries quantum information and 3D information.

Akashic Inheritance and chemistry inheritance meld together in a very odd way and create a scenario that is not explainable in linear terms. I've just given you something to think about, but it starts to perhaps explain some of the things that don't make sense to you. How you can have certain attributes of your parents, and yet other attributes are completely absent? Then the big question: How can you have strong attributes that your parents or your parent's parents never had? Well, a past life reader may help. [Kryon smile] Can you see the complexity? Now let me stir in the last complexity and this won't make any sense either.

Incarnation as Family

You tend to incarnate in Akashic family groups. This explains why suddenly you might shift from one race to another, or one continent to another. You are "following" a karmic family pattern of old souls who need to move around for spiritual purposes.

Right now in this room before me, family meets family. Maybe you haven't looked at everybody's eyes here, but there are those here in your Akashic family. Not your mother and father, sister and brother, but you knew that didn't you? Oh, there is chemistry and they [mother, brother, sister, brother] are aligned in certain ways also. However you feel the bond but that's not the spiritual bond. You incarnate as family and it doesn't necessarily mean that you find each other right away. There's no timing here. Your linear mind wants to think you all come in together, but you do not. Instead, you often find one another in odd synchronistic ways, and then group together over time. The Akashic families are starting to change, however, as you drop your karma. More on this later.

So in closing I will say this: Listener, reader, in this room you are meeting family and you are realizing you're aligned through the love of God. This includes all things living, which even includes the air you breathe and the rocks in the earth. It also includes those who you have not yet met, who are your ancestors on other planets and who know what you're doing.

Finally, we stand together in congratulations. Do not be discouraged, for you are in the infancy of enlightenment. A full planetary shift will not take place in your lifetime, or even the [lifetime of the] youngest ones here. But you are the seeds for this shift, and you know it's coming. You'll be here when it happens because you are coming back. All of you are coming back. You're going to want to, because when you awaken the next time, there will be an Earth that is couched for your enlightenment. You will not have difficulty with it, and you won't have to struggle like you did this time, or re-learn like you did this time.

The Crystalline Grid resounds with this and will co-operate with this. Gaia awaits what you're going to do next and will then morph to compliment the energy that you create. That, dear Human Being, is something to celebrate today.

Kryon live channelling "The Greater Akashic System" given in Laguna Hills, California — July 15, 2012

I would like to emphasize that the best choices you can make for your own cellular structure consider Akashic Inheritance. Kryon mentioned this in the previous channel and has covered this topic in various other channels. The information below provides us with a greater understanding:

Every single biology [Human] in the room is different, and now we bring up something that we have not brought up for some time, but you need to hear it again. What works for you in health is based almost completely and totally upon your Akashic Inheritance. Where did you spent the most lifetimes? Perhaps it was in Asia? Perhaps India or Tibet? Perhaps it was in the Southern Hemisphere? Each of those places and cultures will have had different food, which worked to keep you balanced and healthy. Yet, here you are in the Northern Hemisphere, in this lifetime. What I want you to know is that you are significantly influenced by the kind of diet that you used to have [in your past lives].

Perhaps you were vegan. Perhaps you ate only grains. Therefore, your cells will crave that diet to feel balanced. Do you understand? There are others who come mainly from North America, from Europe, and who never had those kinds of diets from Asia or the south. Therefore, they won't have any trouble at all with the food of the land. Listen: There is no one, generic answer to the question: *"What should I eat for Spiritual health?"* There are no "shoulds." Instead, there are good signals from "Innate" inside you, which gives insight as to the most healthy things for your own body. In other words, listen to your cells!

Now, why do I mention this? Because you're going to get advice from people on what to eat to correct what's wrong with you as you recalibrate. So I'm going to tell you right now, ignore them. Instead, go inside and let your own Akashic Record tell you what is going to work for you. Don't be surprised if some of you come up allergic to some things you've always eaten. I will tell you: Your biology is recalibrating. This attribute will be necessary for you to move forward, for you to shift to the place where you can be balanced with the most wisdom.

Many of you might not like some processed food, because you're not used to it in your Akash. Do you see what I'm saying? If you're going to pull the Shamanic energy up from the depths of the wisdom that you have learned and walked through over and over through past history, some things are going to come with it — like your balanced diet, for instance — and you're going to have to deal with it. Don't fight it.

Expect these things. They're there for you to see and feel. See them for what they are: recalibration. *"Dear Spirit,"* you might say, *"thank you for this recalibration, for caring enough about me to know that this is where I want to go and what I want to do."* Human Being, how you recalibrate now will determine how you will come back in the next life. You won't have to go through this again — ever. Akashic Inheritance is far more than the genealogy of those Human Beings you came from [parents]. You know this. An inherited Akash represents those things that you've experienced in all the lifetimes, regardless of your parents' genes. Sometimes, these are the most predominant and heaviest things that you have to deal with.

Kryon live channelling "The Recalibration of the Human Being" given in Red Deer, Alberta, Canada — January 7, 2012

In summary, your entire personal Akashic Record of every lifetime is in every piece of DNA. The energy of your entire existence on Earth is with you all the time. You have the ability to "mine" the Akash. This is simply pulling upon what you have already experienced and worked on. It's already yours. It's you with you and will be discussed in Chapter Five: "Mining" the Akash.

Heredity and Birth

What does a child come into the planet with during birth? The child will have its parents' contributions (genetic inheritance); Human nature imprint; Astrology overlay; and its Akashic attributes, such as past life lessons and Akashic Inheritance. Kryon has said that the life of a Human starts at their first breath from the moment of birth because that is when they have free choice. Before birth they still had a soul, but they were aligned with their mother's choice. The mother could choose life or death for the child, but once the child is born it has free choice to make decisions.

Before my spiritual awakening I only believed in what empirical science could prove. My understanding of the world was quite limited. I observed many things that had no explanations. I only saw pieces and parts of a system. I simply accepted possible reasons, theories or best guesses to explain the unexplainable. Often these explanations would be inconsistent.

A question many have asked is: *"Where does your personality come from?"* Science still doesn't know the answer. All we have are conjectures. For example, many say that our personality is derived from our genetics and the environment of our upbringing. Others say it is attributed to the complex wiring of our brain. What about our fears and phobias? Where do they come from? Again, science does not have a definitive answer. Many believe that our fears and phobias are attributed to genetic and environmental factors; a result of a trauma; a reaction to someone else's trauma; or a gradual development over time. Sometimes, that is the case but what about when people have seemingly totally irrational fears that they can't link to anything in their current life?

What about the difference between twins who are almost genetically identical? Why are children who come from the same parents and grow up in the same environment so different? Why do they have different personalities, fears and phobias?

Let's examine some attributes of two children from the same biological parents, growing up in the same environment. You may even recognize your children or children you know in the following description. Perhaps it represents the difference between you and your sister or brother. By the way, Lee Carroll presents this in his online Akash lecture in a wonderful graphic illustration.

First Child	Second Child
Moody and angry	Happy and balanced
No self-esteem	Self-assured
Anti-social	Leader
Few abilities	Talented
Slow learner	Advanced learner

What could possibly account for such a difference between these two children? Do you think it is due to genetics and the environment? Is it the order of birth? On a slightly different subject—what creates child prodigies? A child prodigy is defined as someone who, at an early age, develops one or more skills at a level far beyond the normal ability of children their age.

Some well-known child prodigies include:

Wolfgang Amadeus Mozart—learned to play the piano at the age of four, composed his first pieces of music at five and wrote his first symphony by the age of eight.

Kim Ung-Yong—by the age of twenty-four months was able to read in Japanese, Korean, German and English. Kim was a guest student of physics at Hanyang University from the age of three until he was six. At the age of eight he was invited to America by NASA. He completed a Ph.D. in physics before he was 15.

Akrit Jaswal—performed his first medical procedure at his family home when he was seven. His patient was a local girl who could not afford a doctor. Her hand had been burned in a fire and her fingers were closed in a tight fist that wouldn't open. Akrit had no formal medical training or experience in surgery, yet he managed to free the girls' fingers and she could use her hand again.

Cleopatra Stratan—is the youngest person to score commercial success as a singer recording her first album at the age of three. She holds the record for being the youngest artist to perform live for two hours in front of a large audience.

Michael Kearny—spoke his first words at four months and learned to read at the age of ten months. He finished high school at age six and received an Associate of Science in Geology and a Bachelor's degree in anthropology by age ten. In 2006 he became the first million dollar winner of an online reality game, Gold Rush, and in 2008 he won $25,000 on the television show, Who Wants to be a Millionaire?

Akiane Kramarik—began drawing at age four and was painting like a master by age six. At four years of age Akiane says she had a life-changing spiritual transformation, bringing her atheist family to God. Her art and literature are inspired by her visions, dreams, observations, nature and God. Her artwork has been exhibited in museums around the world since she was ten. Akiane is the only known binary genius in both painting and poetry.

Where did their talents and abilities come from? Scholars have been fascinated by child prodigies for centuries, but the puzzle remains a mystery. Could there be a viable explanation? Could this also explain why children from the same parents in the same environment are so unique? I believe the answer lies in our personal Akashic Record, our Akashic Inheritance.

When a child prodigy plays the piano like a master, is this something done by random chance? Is it possible they are simply continuing on from their last expression of life? Understanding what is in our Akash begins to explain the anomalies that we see, especially when it comes to children. But how does our Akashic Inheritance work with us? Kryon tells us how:

A child is born and the DNA carries energies of the Akash right into his personality. Immediately, these energies can be seen by all. The first thing that happens is karmic residue. Karma is real. Some of the most profound belief systems on this planet, which are esoteric, speak of this. Some of the oldest belief systems you have teach karma first. They know of this system of coming and going and what it means to have it.

We told you 19 years ago that karma was one of the first things that you could change in this new energy. We told you that the Lightworker will automatically drop it when they give pure intent to move to greater awareness. We told you it was the "implantation of permission to drop karma." [Back in Kryon Book One, *The End Times*, it was called "the implant."] Karma is the energy carried over from a former lifetime regarding unfinished lessons, which need not be learned this time around for any of you. That is one of the gifts of the great shift upon you. This is not new news. Within our example above, the child that is born receives it. Most Human Beings born today have karma, for not enough time has passed to create a karma-less Lightworker group that is being reincarnated. In our example, it is later that the child will decide to void his karma or not. [If voided in one lifetime, old core karmic issues do not carry over to the next.]

The set-up of life lessons and the energy of a child's personality is based upon the crystalline Akashic Record and is transferred to the child at birth. You might say, another day begins and the Human continues their overall "story" on Earth. The child begins to grow, and I've spoken of this before. I again say that mothers will agree, because they see that it doesn't matter where a child came from, or who the parents were... the child assumes the Akashic Record and the energy from their own past lives. Mothers know this, for they experience children coming from the same set of parents who are vastly different from each other. One will have talent, one will not. One will have fears, one will not. It only can be explained, dear

Human Being, by what I am telling you that is in the DNA. They are resonating to the Akashic Record of their own past. They are coming right from the Cave of Creation where they have their past life's attributes imbued into their DNA, and they start their journeys. Genealogy considered, they may look like the mother and father, and even have some of the personality attributes of their parents, but the core issues of their lives [life lessons] come from their own past lives. Let us discuss what they get when they come in [arrive on Earth].

Fear or non-fear: A Human's "fear quotient" will depend upon what they've learned and what they've gone through in the past. Indeed, if they're old souls, they're fearless about life, for they've walked through the major fears over and over. Some are warriors and very strong. They walk into situations as if they own reality. If they've only been here a few times, less than 30 or 40, they are still afraid. Some come from a fearful lifetime where all they did was fear. There was fear in their death and fear in their life and you can see it in their eyes. They're afraid of life itself. Mothers all over the planet spend much of their time trying to take their children out of fear! They love their children and can't understand why they are so tentative about everything. But the mothers know that they didn't create it. It came from somewhere else.

Desires: Watch the children develop their own personal desires. What do they like regarding food? What do they like regarding music? What do they like to entertain them? What soothes them, or irritates them, or makes them angry? They're all very different and don't necessarily relate to the biological parents. Interesting, is it not, why this would be? Let me tell you a secret: Watch what kind of food they like, for it will tell you where they used to be. Look at this, for it gives away a lot about what the DNA got used to, and again desires.

What music do they like? What soothes their soul? What do they look at? What attracts them? They're all different, but it's shaped by the DNA of the Akash ... who they used to be, what they learned, and what the crystalline past gives them. Children love the fads of today. First timers will simply go with the flow and enjoy all the new things, since it's their first trip. Others will start that way, but will soon tire of them and go to the things that are "calling to them from their DNA." This will include their past talents and interests. Many go "retro" immediately, much to the surprise of their elders. In their DNA is the record of all of the past lives that shapes who they are now.

Talent: They either have it or they don't. They can carry a tune or they cannot. Some of them come in filled with talent! Some are artists at birth, only carrying over what the Akash has given them in the immediate past life. In the DNA are life-times of drawing, colors, shapes and beautiful music. Some come in as maestros, and by the time they're three or four, it's only a matter of them finding the dexterity in their fingers again to play the keyboard or pluck the strings of a guitar. Some of them are drawn immediately to the instruments that they used to play, and their talent is way beyond what has been taught to them this time around. How do you explain this, Human Being? The Akash shapes it all.

Personality: As the child grows, their personality is shaped seemingly by their environment, but sometimes it's pleasing and sometimes it's not. As a parent, sometimes it seems completely out of your hands, yet you did everything right! You might wonder, *"How did my child turn out this way? Why not the way I did? Why do I have to fight in order to get them to understand something like common sense? They really are not like me or my family."*

Later, as adults, they may go in ways that you didn't expect ... ways you didn't teach them. You will wonder how your child could do something horrible like that. Others will say, *"Isn't it beautiful that my child has a perfect consciousness. They think like I do. I was good at what I taught them."* Let me tell you the truth, dear Human Being. Your children are often your parents [from long ago]! They come into the karmic group to keep teaching you, and you them. Families incarnate with families in groups of training, especially enlightened training. That is to say, there is a system of enlightenment. Did you expect this? That is to say this, dear Human Being, the reward of your work on this planet — listen to me — the reward of your work on this planet will be etched in the crystalline as the potentials of who is born from the loins of *you*. Quite often the enlightened child is only picking up what they taught you originally ... remembering their own past experiences and their own life lessons. It's easy for you to take credit for it, but it wasn't really you who gave it to them. It's a circle of training — child to parent, parent to child.

This means that you, sitting here, will probably populate Lightworkers in this planet, even if they don't believe what you believe. They will be children of light. That is to say, their hearts will resound with the information that you had in your cellular structure. That's what you passed to them. That's part of the system. It's complicated. It's a combination of who they came from, their decisions in the karmic way of who their parents were, who they were and what energies they wish to continue. But I will tell you that the desire and the permission is there in the DNA of both of you. When you get to the other side of the veil, you choose your family for the next expression, and you can come back and you can say, *"I want to be in the same family,"* and continue in the lineage of light. Profound, it is. Difficult, it is. Beautiful, it is.

All grown up... the adult: The growing is over and there stands the adult. Fears, desires, talents or not, personality traits and phobias are all intact. This is common to man. And here's where it gets good: Up to this point, this is what you accept, dear Human Being, as who you are. Automatically, this is who you are and you begin to work with these attributes. You feel they are the "way of it," normal, and that it is like nature... something that just "is" and can't be changed. And the only thing that we say to you is, "How 3D of you!" For that is the only way you think: *This is the deal that has been given to me this time around. It's the hand that has been dealt and I am this.* And you begin to walk through life working with whatever "this" is.

The Next Great Ability of the Human Being

For years, the psychologists have been telling you that you could actually change yourself by what you think. Even out of a spiritual context, they say, *"The power of positive thinking can actually change your life."* They know this. It's about energy, and they are correct. It's also a hint of what's wrong with your thinking. New energy came in 1987. The grid shifted and the crystalline moved. The Earth itself vibrates differently today than it did back then. We told you when we arrived, "You have changed your future." We told you about new gifts and now we will describe one of the best ones. It was always there, only now it is enhanced.

Why did you decide that the cells in your body could control you? Why did you decide that the genes that you have biologically were forever? Who told you this? Let me give you an old energy paradigm: *"Whoever I am, I am. God created me this way for a reason and so I'll make the best of it. I will do the best I can with what I have been given."* Doesn't sound too bad, does it? To some of you, it sounds fine. Now I'm going to say it again: Welcome to a multi-dimensional shift, for the entire thinking of the Human can be revised to include the new gifts!

"Whatever I was born with doesn't matter. I am in control of my biology, my immune system and my awareness. God created me as a

divine creature able to claim the past energies within my Akash ... and to totally shift my biology and my countenance and strengths into whatever I desire."

Does this sound impossible? There are profound teachers right now instructing humans how to "think above the gene."* Medical science is telling you that your DNA is not your destiny!** In other words, this whole idea is occurring to all of humanity, since it is time.

* Dr. Bruce H. Lipton — *The Biology of Belief*
** Discover Magazine — September 2008 — *DNA is Not Your Destiny.*

> *Kryon live channelling "It's in the DNA!"*
> *given in Kelowna, BC, Canada — June 28, 2008*

It is worth your time to view three videos on YouTube. The first one is of a four year old boy playing the piano like a master. Notice his hands as he plays: his left hand crosses over the right. This is NOT intuitive. It is a trained technique. The second video is of a seven year old girl playing the violin like a virtuoso. The third video is of a ten year old girl singing on America's Got Talent. When you listen to her it doesn't seem possible that the exquisite opera she is singing is coming from her small body. These videos are examples of what Kryon says about artists being born as maestros, picking up from their last life expression.

Four Year Old Boy Plays Piano Better Than Any Master
http://www.youtube.com/watch?v=omuYi2Vhgjo

Incredible 7-Year Old Child Violinist Brianna Kahane Performs "Csardas" on a ¼ Size Violin
http://www.youtube.com/watch?v=GEOZ31HeZT4

Jackie Evancho first audition America's Got Talent full with result and comments
http://www.youtube.com/watch?v=3d_XTvLalJk

Our Akashic Inheritance carries our desires, fears, talents, personality, our past life lessons and karma. All of these things contribute in making us who we are. Nearly everyone I know has heard of the idea or concept of karma, but not everyone understands that we have life lessons that are separate from karma. Often, there are conflicting descriptions about what karma and life lessons are. I have even heard the term "karma lessons" used. How do we determine the truth? Is there a difference and does it even matter?

Yes, there is a distinct difference between karma and life lessons. I don't think it is critical that every Human Being understands this completely, but to help you understand the channelled messages from Kryon, it is important that you understand exactly why the two terms represent different attributes of your Akash.

Karma and Life Lessons

Even before I awakened spiritually I had heard about karma. When someone did a negative thing I would think that karma would catch up with them one day! When I did a good deed towards someone else, I would think about the good karma I just created. Where did I get this notion of karma from? To be honest I can't remember. It probably came from my peers and the culture around me. I'm sure a lot of people continue to have misguided ideas about what karma and life lessons are.

While everything is related to everything else the role of karma and the role of life lessons have distinct purposes. Kryon has given many channellings to explain the differences between these two energies. The main difference is:

Karma is about situations with other humans, unfinished business, feelings to be completed and a system in interaction.

Life lessons are totally and completely personal and only about you with you.

Kryon has said that karma is ancient and slow. It is about the group around you, your place in it and the emotional energies that are developed from that. It is the unfulfilled energetic puzzles that often drive us to do things. You might say that karma is the default guide of direction for all humans on the planet. It creates four and five generations of firemen, policemen, doctors or military officers. You "fall into the groove" of what you think you are supposed to do, or what your parents tell you to do and you do it.

Karma is an old driving system and not needed in the new energy. In the old energy, karma pushed you to places to do things and meet people. In the new energy, you don't need karma to push you anywhere, because you are able to put yourself exactly where you are meant to be. These new understandings bring a level of responsibility—a total responsibility for all that is around you. No more playing the role of a victim and no more accidents. The choice is yours whether you wish to void your karma or not. Perhaps reading the following channel from Kryon may help you in dropping your karma.

If spiritual awareness is never upon you, the energy of karma remains. It is part of the system of the Akash. You must be aware that you have lived many lives and have had other lives. These lives build upon each other energetically and the past life experience shapes the potentials for your current life experience. The name of this ancient system is karma.

Those of you who are parents in this room, let me ask you about your children. Were they born like blank sheets of paper for you to teach them everything? You know they were not. Who taught them to be jealous? Who taught them to be angry and go into a rage? Who taught them to be afraid of things like water or certain animals? It wasn't you, was it? Then where did all that come from? Why would one child be so prolific in one talent and another have no talent at all? Why is one such a lover and the other one is so wise? Ah, you know what I'm talking about, don't you? [Kryon smile] Why is one a warrior and the other is not? And the answer is karma. They come in with an energy of predisposition. This is upon them all their lives and will push and pull on their consciousness with the energy of unfulfilled resolution.

All humanity has this attribute unless they individually choose to void it, and this ability has only been available for 20 years. Now it's available to everyone who sits in the chair before me or is reading this. I will tell you something, dear ones: Of those who sit in these chairs right now, some of these things are still in you. They're responsible for some of the challenges you have since you never gave permission for them to go away.

Here is a review of the process: You void this incomplete energy called karma, get off of the road of predisposition, and you start creating a new energy for yourself as though you arrived on the planet with no karma at all. Some of the very attributes of your life will change. Your fears will drop away since they're part of karma. My partner did it. He can point to the place he did it. For the man in the chair is a left-brain engineer [speaking of Lee]. He had the passion for naval military service in front of him and had the attributes of a hermit. However, when he gave permission to open the door to voiding his karma, those things dropped away. Now, his right brain has developed as much as his left. Seemingly, many of the things he was born with are now gone... replaced with the things that he wishes to be. Blessed is the Human Being who makes this choice, for it is uncomfortable at first, then rewarding when they realize that they are actually in charge of their own futures.

We'll close with this: When the Human Being stands without the karmic energy they came in with, it is truly like they are exposed before God. For they don't know where they're going. They don't know what synchronicity is going to come along to help them. They have no idea what to expect or where they stand. It is as though they are fresh and new, ready to create a path they have never seen. This is uncomfortable for a Human. However, here is the promise we gave you with shift number two. I dare you to celebrate that state—a status of uncertainty. I dare you to celebrate it. *"Well, here I am God. I have no idea what I'm doing. Isn't that great?"* And your relatives and your friends will look at you and they'll say, *"You really are crazy."* And how can you tell them that you stand there with a legion of angels holding your hand?

You've got a grand support group and this fourth shift is when the support group really starts to show itself. This shift is the one that allows you to walk into the darkness, whistling a tune, unafraid of the pitfalls of a three-dimensional system. You see, this shift allows for understanding of your own participation of your own creation. How can you be afraid of what's going to happen when you're creating it? How can you be afraid of the disease in you when you're creating your own healing? Don't you think I know who's here?

Kryon live channelling "The Eight Shifts of Enlightenment Part One"
given in Mexico City — October 20, 2007

There are two other attributes about karma that I would like to share. The first one relates to time cycles, as mentioned in Kryon Book Two, *Don't Think Like a Human* while the second one relates to a very unique and specific karmic group, as mentioned in Kryon Book Three, *Alchemy of The Human Spirit.*

There is a Human attribute that also is a soul attribute. Some of you previously have determined that a Human has a time cycle while on Earth that is either fast or slow or somewhere in between. You measure it in years. You use this to help explain why a person takes a very long time to make changes, or does so quickly. This is not the variable you might expect. Although you are mostly correct in the method of determining the cycle for an individual, what you do not know is that the time cycle will also be the same for that soul. It will be the same for that soul each time it comes into expression. It was the same in the last expression, and it will be the same in the next. This is a soul attribute and relates to universal pattern of vibration as well as your time cycle on Earth. It is one of the several attributes that are carried into expression that belong to the soul, and are permanent. This attribute is not biological, but is universal in its origin. I cannot explain this pattern variable that belongs to entities such as myself, and yourself, for it deals with terminology and concepts that are not comprehensible for you in lesson.

The new information is that there is also a cyclical lifetime pattern that matches the time cycle. If you know a person is a 3 time cycle, then you should also look for significant lifetimes of karmic importance in groups of three as measured backward from the current one. Not every lifetime is one of tremendous karmic importance. In fact, most are not. That is why many humans live uneventful lives without apparent upheaval, distress, learning, clearing, or enlightenment. Many lifetimes are lived as rest periods between the ones that are meaningful. Remember that time is not important to us. It is only an Earth concept, and therefore, what seems like a very long and arduous process to you is all in the "now" for us. Your soul needs periods of light karmic involvement between the heavy ones, just as you need balance in Earthly things for health...

...This is also a secret to the kind of karmic lessons that are involved. Those with long time cycles (such as a 9) would tend to have heavier karmic attributes fall on every ninth lifetime, and they are more prone to need help with clearing them. A person with a 2 time cycle will have more attributes spread over every second lifetime, and will be more able to clear them with everyday living. Look for tragedy and physical specter with the longer time cycles, and more Human interrelated karma with the faster cycles. These are generalities and as with all karma, there are exceptions based on the groups...

...Generally, it works like this: there are three basic groups for karmic consideration — the 1 to 3 group, the 4 to 6 group, and the 7 to 9 group. There is no cycle higher than the nine. If you find a Human who does not fit into a repeating cycle, then you could be dealing with a special few souls who have multiple attributes, and can vary the cycles if desired.

Those with cycles from 1 to 3 are sent in with an appropriate karmic imprint to allow for fast turnaround of many small but potent lessons. These more frequent lessons deal with interrelations with others in lesson. You know these, dear ones, for they are all around you. These are the ones who need to clear the attributes of what has happened with those who have abused them, and those they have abused. They have serious on-going current lifetime problems with parents or children, or other relatives or friends. They seem to be perpetual victims, or feel the need to strike out and get even, or constantly defend themselves. This is the kind of karma in the 1 to 3 group. As you might expect, the 1 gets a slightly different dose than the 3. Those in this group who are able to clear the karmic imprint will most likely be involved in helping others on a spiritual basis. All of these need to learn the important lesson of tolerance, a difficult one for all humans.

The 4 to 6 group is more evenly spread in all types of karma. These not only get to have some of the Human situations to work through, like the 1 to 3 group, but they also get to have some heavier events to consider with it. These are the ones who must also work through lessons that deal with more violence, usually Human against Human. Perhaps they burned someone to death in the name of God, or worse yet, learned to use negativity for control of others. They are the ones who often meet terrible death at the hands of other humans. There are many leaders here, and many humanitarians. Their main lesson is one of forgiveness ... of others and of themselves. There are more of these than of the others.

The 7 to 9 group gets the heavy Earth karma. They also figure highly in leadership positions of all kinds, but often die violently, due to accidents such as falling, burning, or drowning. Their lessons are mostly to overcome the big fear they carry over from these past events. The fear is so great it often makes them appear unbalanced in their current lifetime. These are the ones most likely to become mentally sick — or totally balanced. The reason for this is that they carry such heavy attributes that action of some kind is usually demanded to exist even at the most basic level of normalcy. The reason they are often leaders is that they seek power as a method to gain control over their fear.

Kryon answer in Kryon Book Two,
Don't Think Like a Human; Chapter Six

Now that you know about the cycles of your personal karma, here is what Kryon has said regarding group karma:

As we study group karma, we have to tell you there is another attribute that has to do with "energy accounting," for there is one group on this planet that must always remain in the same group; they may never change. It is like a staple of group karma, an anchor or starting base for the system of groups to work. We call these, therefore, the "astrally pure-bred" of the planet. In other words, the group always incarnates into the same group over and over. (Those who step into the group remain within the group until they wish to leave it, never to enter again.) The group is large enough so that this can take place all over the planet, and the newcomers that come into this group will always remain in this group as long as they wish, and they know this in advance. Now, some of you already have guessed what this group is. For it is so often that Kryon takes you back to the lineage of the Jews. This group has an attribute on the Earth which is like no other. My partner continues to be filled with awe at their lineage, and now he knows that this is the reason. For they are the ones who are astrally pure-bred. They are also the ones who have played such an important part in all Human history. Being astrally pure-bred carries with it the attributes of a double-edged sword. Being in the same group over and over strengthens knowledge of how things work. As you work through your lessons, you come in again with cellular knowledge of your past accomplishments. This creates cohesiveness, wisdom, and seemingly an unfair edge over those who change groups often. To compensate for this, the astrally pure-bred have agreed to take on the heaviest karma of the planet.

Now, Spirit does not create a hierarchy of favorites. The astrally pure-bred are loved just as much as any other, and they are not set aside as being God's chosen, except that they are different from other humans, in that their karma is pure. We invite you to notice an interesting biological attribute: The Jews are not recognized biologically by your Human science as a separate race, yet they act like it, since karmically they are.

This indeed is their great lineage, for they helped to found the planet, were here from the very beginning. There is much to be said around this. Your history has shown the reaction of the other groups to this pure karmic group, and the events that helped create many heavy lessons, all planned by those who decided they wanted to be the astrally pure-bred on planet Earth.

Kryon live channelling "Karma"
given in Kryon Book Three, Alchemy of The Human Spirit. Chapter Seven.

I hope you have a greater understanding about the role of karma.

What about life lessons? Life lessons, unlike karma, are far more personal. Life lessons may be related to karmic energy, but they stay with you even when you void your karma. So it's more profound than karma and belongs to your individual core soul, instead of a group. It is carried from every expression of life, just like karma, but in a different way. Each Human has more than one life lesson and each Human comes in with this as an overlay. When you solve your life lesson, the solution is carried over to your next life and never has to be learned again. Here is a list of typical life lessons to be learned. They only belong to you if you feel they do. There are many things not on this list that may apply to you. Remember, everyone is different and has their own list.

Learn to love
Learn to listen
Learn to receive
Learn to love yourself
Learn to speak your truth
Learn how not to be a victim
Learn not to let anyone define you

Learn how to feel your own mastery
Learn how to live with others humans
Learn how to get out of blaming others
Learn to move out of duality [drop your karma]
Learn to take care of yourself more than others

Each life lesson is profoundly personal. Life lessons don't involve family, a karmic groove or group energy. They are yours personally and you work on them for lifetimes, just as you do karma. However, in the new energy, they are all on the table to be solved. Isn't that great news? I can already hear some of you asking. "How will I work out what my life lessons are?" Kryon has given information that may help you identify what your life lessons are.

What is your Achilles' heel? What do you react to most? What is your purpose? Some of you have come here with profound reactions to authority. Some with a spiritual overlay. Life lesson is not karma. It's the big issue that is often developed from what has happened with your energy before. Some of you have come in with a life lesson that has to do with abundance issues. Some of you have come in with a life lesson that is only about love. What have you created for yourselves around love: the love for one another, the love of your children, the love for your parents? What have you created for yourselves? What is the life lesson? Who are you (really)?

This is all imprinted on your DNA—your choice, your pattern, your permission. Contract is only a beginning setup. There has to be a framework of reality for you to live within—a framework that you can change—a beginning posturing. Here is an unspoken thing we have never said: As you change your reality, all of you change your contract. The most profound part of co-creation, the missing piece that you have never truly understood, is that you do it with you! It is not procedural.

103

It does not require anything more than your claiming the "intent" of the reality that you have—then requiring it to move. It is an opening structure only. Therefore, it is changeable!

Those of you who said, *"I signed a contract and I've got to do this and that,"* misunderstand what this and that is. How many signatures are on a contract? Two! Whom is it with? It's with you! Therefore, when you give intent to change the contract, both signatures change simultaneously. We give you this metaphor so that you might understand the power you have to take the path you think you designed and to move off of it, designing another one.

Kryon live channelling "The Grid and DNA"
given in Breckenridge, Colorado—July 14, 2001

What will you do with this information? Hopefully it will help you gain a different perspective on some of the challenges you are currently facing in your life. This is where free choice plays a part. You can choose to void your karma. You can choose to move through your challenges and gain the wisdom of learning your life lessons. You do not have to do anything if you don't want to. However, most people that have chosen to void their karma and work on their life lessons move into a new vibration that creates peace in their life. It often opens you up to a whole new level of freedom.

Questions for Kryon:

Lemuria was the core population center for divinity. Jews carry the pure karmic attributes of humanity and the core seed of humanity. This would mean that many Jews could also have been Lemurians, but not all Lemurians would have experienced being a Jew. Can you explain a bit more about the relationship between Lemurians and Jews, and clarify the different role each group has?

Answer:

You have already answered your own question regarding the timing. Yes, Israelites were Lemurian, but not all Lemurians became Jews.

You have to start appreciating the time. Lemuria was 20,000 to 30,000 years ago, but the complete history of the Jews is fairly recent. There is also a dynamic that is totally hidden to all of you, but is barely being discovered. The civilizations on your planet have gone through four complete cycles and restarts. For various reasons and typical ones for a developing planet, you almost terminated and started again several times.

The fourth start was like the others, a fresh one where you set up a history that was filled with culture and attributes very different than the one before. So there was no strong "remembrance" of anything before. This fourth era is the history you study on the planet right now, and the only acknowledged one by your historians.

It was during this history that the karmic set-up of the Jews was established. As old as they claim to be, they are the new and most current history of the planet. As we have told you before, many of the original spiritual masters of this new start were Jewish masters, and they had a kind of "purity" that others sensed. Each era had a group like this, and it has to do with the DNA template—who starts it and keeps it.

Along the way, you got to see how they were persecuted, eliminated, and hated for what they carried. In the guise of a cry of "Eliminate the Jews!" is a hidden message that says, "...and let us have the template they carry." The Ark of the Covenant carried the template information for humanity. Are you starting to see the issues? From the Egyptian slavery, the wars with other cultures, right up to Hitler, the Jews carry something that others saw and often resented or wanted. We gave you the names of [the layers of] DNA in Hebrew. Do you now understand why?

What happens to our DNA at birth?

This would seem like a wonderful question, with a potential of revealing new information. But the truth is that the Human body is a beautiful instrument of quantum potential. Even the newborn comes in with a complete Merkabah (his quantum field of DNA). So biology is biology and the DNA is reproduced according to the scenario that pre-existed before the child was born.

By the time birth happens, the templates are set, and the Akash is already activated and planned. So a better question would be, "What happens before birth?" as was already discussed in the very first question.

If karma has been the mechanism for raising the planet's vibration, what happens when all souls on the planet have dropped their karma? Is that when a planet reaches ascension status?

No. It only means that everyone on the planet realizes that they don't have to draw on past energies to move forward. So it's really a sign of spiritual awareness and maturity. It's like taking the training wheels off of a bicycle. It's a form of enabling, but it only lets a Human move to a more empowered state of free choice.

Karma is an old energy template that pulls on past life experience to help set energies for a new life. When you drop it, it's a sign that you are ready to "steer your own boat", and you no longer need to fulfill any past contracts or walk through things that are "residuals" from the past.

You might say that dropping your karma would be the first step in spiritual evolution. But from then on, you must learn to live without it. Some find this difficult, and the real challenge begins.

So karma is only a portion of what raises the Earth's vibration, which worked in an older time frame. Now you have

106

progressed and graduated to a much clearer and sophisticated system of free choice. Old souls are the first to see it and clear their karma.

When humans drop their karma, what happens to the others from their karmic group who choose to continue to carry their own karma? How are they affected?

Human interaction is the catalyst for the planet's ascension and maturity. Nothing happens without the Human Being working with another Human Being. Let's make this clear. If everyone who dropped their karma went into a spiritual box and never came out, the Earth would not change at all. The whole "engine" of Earth change is the change of Human consciousness. That means that the few affect the many, and the many then have free choice to also change.

Dropping karma creates balance, and if you are a more balanced and joyful Human, then you create synchronicity in your life, as well as a safe haven for friends and others who wish to be around a "balanced being". Balance is attractive! Regardless of your dramatic TV shows, you would not actively choose dysfunction around you. Dysfunction will shorten your life and make it miserable while you live it. Those who live in dysfunction live in chaos, and it actually creates mental distress. Balance is what humanity seeks, and also common sense solutions to everyday issues.

There is an axiom of spirituality and benevolent universal design that says that *consciousness will always seek a more balanced and complete state*. I already told you that physics is the same. You might say that consciousness is "benevolently predisposed". Earth history has not shown this much, since Humans have free choice to find this balance and the benevolent predisposition, or not. Up to this point, you have been in survival mode, and like children on a playground, your civilization did not share much. It simply took what it wanted. This is what is changing, since Human nature is "growing up".

So in answer to your question, you have to know more about a "karmic group". Like karma, your karmic group is only a set-up to push you around when you get to Earth — [Kryon smile]. When you drop your karma, you also give a signal to those around you in your karmic group that you are "disconnecting" from all the spinning energies around them as well, for their karmic attributes are always linked to yours, hence "group karma."

So the direct answer to, "How are they affected?" is this: Their karma is not affected at all. However, your change gets their attention since you are dropping out. It often creates a change in their behavior, since they often have to deal with your situation! If, they see a balanced and more productive and joyful "you," it might be attractive to them, or not. Many times, they just want to distance themselves from you.

But other times, they might be interested enough to ask you more about what you did. Then you can share your beautiful *connection with the divine inside*. This is the "share your light" principle. They see your light and are attracted to it, or not. But if you have noticed, they can't just ignore it, especially if they are family members. Many will walk away, but some will not.

So my question to *you* is this: What kind of Human have you become if you have elected to drop your karma? Are you easier to be with or have you simply walked away from them and climbed into the "people with no karma box." If they have pushed you away, then this is their issue and you are correct to stay away. But if they sit there stymied and continue to try to "engage," then it's up to you to show them balance, patience and unconditional benevolence toward their "God inside." Get out of your box and let them see your balance.

When new souls come onto the planet, they are only just be-
ginning and therefore do not have an Akashic Record or even
karma, so what drives them and what opportunities do they have
to raise their vibration?

The new soul is "innocent in the ways of the planet."
Without a karmic imprint, they drift quite a bit, being unde-
cided about everything. They don't have the maturity of "how
things work" to even have common sense, since there is nothing "common" yet in their experience.

But each Human is driven by the original template from the
seed biology. This template tries to find beauty in all things
and solutions to unbalance. However, this is often their puz-
zlement and anxiety engine, since what they see around them
doesn't really help! They expect "A" and a more mature (and
cynical) humanity will give them "B."

They don't understand "the rules of the road of life," and
often stumble and then wonder what happened. They are
sensitive and very easily wounded. They are not "Earth street-
smart" yet. Some call them "newbies" and they stick out in society as often being "clueless". Sometimes, however, they also
go to creative endeavors, being fed up with trying to relate to
others. They often are artists and musicians—not the best,
but going for beauty at any cost. They are also very attracted
to organized religion, since it's simple, beautiful, and they can
feel the love of God with all the structure around it, already
set up for them—a nice, comfortable box in the strange wil-
derness of logic and life.

So they have to live a few of these lives before their Akash
becomes "Earth smart," and that's the time they begin to
balance.

By the way, did you notice who seems to be very, very good
at being "Earth smart?" It's the Jews of the planet. Their pure
karmic group means they are the only ones who continue to
incarnate with the same group over and over. Other humanity

moves around, but the Jewish lineage is karmically pure. Once a Jew, always a Jew, until the Human wishes to step out. Then they never can "step back in." The result of all this is that the Jews know "how things work." Did you notice this expertise from them, all over the world? They run things! It just shows you what I'm talking about. Of course, I just did something politically inappropriate. I pointed out a truth that shows that not all of you are created the same.

Human bias results in many people thinking there is a hierarchy of learning levels. How are life lessons chosen? Do we progress through life lessons? Do we ever reach a point where we no longer have a life lesson?

You are correct about Human bias. Because your brains learn this way, you fully expect all spiritual things are also this way. That is the "bias" we have spoken about. It's normal and worldwide.

Life lessons are complex and are part of the planning that you do with other souls when you are NOT on the planet. Here are two things you should realize: 1) Karma is a group attribute, and 2) Life lessons are an individual attribute. So nobody comes in with a shared life lesson with a group. They may have group karma, but a life lesson is singular.

You choose life lessons before you get here that will enhance your life if you work on them. There is full free choice to never work on it! Do you know people who are absolutely "stuck" with the same issue over and over? You can see the dysfunction clearly, and you might even tell them about it. They nod and agree, then they do the same dysfunctional thing again. They are often miserable and always telling others that they just can't get it together. Things "spin" around them and drama is king. They solve one thing and then another hits them. The life lesson of this person is to step out of drama. Simple. But it is a comfort zone of sorts, and they will not take the risk of stepping away. The fear is that then they will have to look at themselves without the crutch of the spinning.

Next time around, they will probably have the same lesson. It tends to repeat and repeat until it gets solved. This is, indeed, allied with karma, for they attract people in a group to help them with their life's lesson. It's interactive with karma, but it's an individual issue.

When you are aware of your life's lesson, then you can work on it. It's often revolutionary to see it and work on it. Things immediately begin to change, since awareness of issues is the key to solving or changing them. You end up thinking differently, choosing different friends, and beginning to create the balance you desire.

There is no stair step for this. Conscious awareness has no ladder, and it's not linear. Each Human brings his focus to his individual lesson in his own way. This is also why it's very difficult to teach this. But when the Human is "fully aware" of the life lesson, he has really solved part one, the largest part—"Identification of what it is". Part two is then to implement solutions of his own design.

Once a life lesson is identified, the hard part is over. Working with a life lesson will take, well, a lifetime! (After all, it is a "life" lesson.)

The process: Life lessons are derived from past experience and things that you need to work on for more balance and joy. Once you identify and work on them, they can either come in again for further work or [you] move on to another one. You never move backwards in this chain of benevolent self-help. The system is always about completion and balance with benevolent purpose.

You have mentioned that there are always Masters on the planet and this relates to a balance of energy. You also mentioned that all of the Masters, avatars and prophets have now returned to the planet Earth within The Crystalline Grid as a direct result of the shift in Human consciousness. Can you tell us more about how this works? Also, if a Human has once been a Master, will all their subsequent incarnations be at the same high level of DNA efficiency?

This answer might be difficult since it requires a nonlinear attitude in your logic. Thinking out of singularity is not what Humans do. Everything is singular around you in your life — one body, one soul, one life, one brain. You are isolated in your consciousness, and don't share it. When you look in the mirror, you see one body that contains your entire life's chemistry and life-force. You are not aware of anything outside of your skin that also might be "you". In fact, if you did see it, you would then go get mental help! *"Doctor, I'm hearing voices from beyond!"* So, it's a "singular bias" to everything. By the way, that's why channelling is immediately suspect. It's out of your box of bias.

All souls are part of the "soup of God." When you are not here, your most cherished core, the one you think is "you," is part of a nonlinear, multi-dimensional energy that you call God. It is part of the creative source of the Universe and is separate, but together. We use the term *soup*, since it's something common for you to compare it to. The soup has separate ingredients that stood alone before they went into the soup. But once they are blended, they are then part of the whole. Are there still separate ingredients in the soup? Yes. Are they altered? Not really, but they are now *blended* with all.

So you are no different than the masters of Earth. Your soul and their souls are part of the soup. Add to this the super difficult issue for a Human — part of your Higher-Self, and your very core, is not with you. It's with the God soup on the other side of the veil. So in effect, you are not all here! (I think there are some on the planet who might agree.)

Now, here is the thing that will make you want to skip to the next question. *"Too hard, Kryon!"* The soup of God allows soul parts to be split when in 3D. Did you ever wonder how so many Humans claim to be someone from the past, the same one? How could George over there be Beethoven when Mary is, too? (So she says.) The odd thing is that they both have amazing attributes of this past musical master! So who is correct? The answer is that both of them are. (I told you this was hard.)

Humanity has no problem with a God that can be everywhere at the same time, listening to millions of prayers all at once, and also be in every Human heart. We call it the "Santa" syndrome. It's OK for God and Santa, but when it comes to you or past Humans, you draw the line. Well, you can't. It's the same for you, too, since you are part of the multi-dimensional "soup of God" as well.

The Human soul is infused with the benevolent system of "completion." It cannot go backwards and return into a lower vibrational state. But up until recently, it could return without awareness of that state, and with free choice, never see it. But that is changing, and now many old souls will be far more aware when they are born. This is the new energy at work.

Parts of the past masters of the planet are in ALL three grids. They are in Magnetic, Crystalline and Gaia. This was always the prophecy, dear ones, wasn't it — that someday they would return and help the Earth? Well, it's happening! Again, Humans took a metaphor and linearized it to the max. They expected the skin and bones to return with a face, a singular body and a voice. They did not see the enhanced truth that once you passed the marker of 2012, all the masters would come back, and they have. I ask all of you reading this: Can't you feel it? Can't you tell? Energy worker, use your intuition and sensitivity out of 3D. Can't you tell this?

Can you explain the difference between the following two humans:

The first Human (A) awakens spiritually. He finds the divinity within and understands the circle of life. He practices mastery in his daily life, and he expresses love and compassion to others.

The second Human (B) does not awaken spiritually. He proclaims to be a non-believer. He lives by his own moral codes and his daily life is filled with expressing love and compassion to others.

Both humans show love and compassion to others, but one is aware of the Creator within and the other is not. Is there a difference between how much they raise the vibration of the planet? What is the difference between these two individuals regarding their next expression of life?

Delightful! What a wonderful question, for it will show a principal that is "hiding" and seldom asked.

Both Humans are practicing "compassionate action" in their lives. But did you ever think, *"Where did Human (B) get the idea to express love and balance in his life? Where did that come from?"* The answer is that it is, indeed, in his Akash, and he had awakened to the principal of balance before. Note: Maturity and balance do not occur in a vacuum. They are experienced and learned. But typically, his Akash also carried the "seed fear" of spirituality. Here is a Human who never has to go any further than being "nice" to accomplish his sense of balance on the planet. He does NOT wish to read this book, and he may not need to! But, a past shaman could still be in his Akash!

But Human (A) has something more than just compassionate action. Human (A) is actively pursuing the connection with his Higher-Self through the portal in his pineal. The result is that Human (A) is in touch with the "soup!" That "soup of God" is the creative source and is working with the grids, the time capsules, and everything that is part of what you are studying here.

Human (A), therefore, can be updated through the connection. Human (A) can raise his own vibration. Human (B) cannot. Human (B) is running on battery power from a stored source and is static. Human (A) is connected to the main source and is dynamic.

However, they both raise the vibration of the planet in their own way.

Can you explain the difference between an old soul and a soul who is awakening? You mentioned before that an old soul will often skip a generation and that this explains why old soul parents will not have old soul children but the grandchildren will be old souls. Can you tell us more about this and how it works, for I have frequently seen very enlightened parents with their children together at Kryon meetings?

The generation skip is complex, and it contains much that doesn't seem to follow this rule. But in its simplest form, it is because parents have a very difficult time being "friends" to their children. But grandparents have no problem at all.

So the system works with this normal issue to enhance the ability of spiritual teaching. Grandparents far more easily can show balance and compassion than a parent. A parent is always in the way of this, trying to keep the child alive! Survival training creates a barrier to life's more gentle issues. The soldier won't turn to his drill sergeant for love advice, but he might ask his platoon commander.

So different levels of awakening are assigned to help with this generation skipping. There is no OLD SOUL quantified definition, however, so really you are dealing with different levels of awakening over many lifetimes, and with two kinds of teaching (the parents and grandparents). So it's a very general kind of "rule" with families.

Sometimes the children will be "older souls" than the parents, but they are both "old souls." Do you see the complexity of trying to define this system or the players? [Kryon smile]

Chapter Four

Ancient Akashic Wisdom

What exactly does Ancient Akashic wisdom mean? To what is it referring? In many places across the world, ancestor worship is an integral part of social and religious life. Nearly every indigenous culture honors their ancestors. Their ancestral spirits are a part of everything that they do. They also esteem their elders. They give great honor to their deceased forebears, the same as the grandmothers and grandfathers did before them.

If we look at the oldest spiritual systems on the planet, such as Buddhism and Hinduism, the departed forebears are venerated by each passing generation. If Buddhists or Hindus perform acts, such as service to others, meditation and pilgrimages during their lifetime, they believe that they share these merits with family members who have already died. They believe these acts help their departed loved ones move closer to enlightenment and bless the living in return. There is also a belief that this allows the present generation to rid themselves and their predecessors of negative karma (although we know from Kryon that karma is not positive or negative, it is simply Akashic energy—see Chapter Three: Akashic Inheritance).

Several Asian cultures revere their departed loved ones. The extended family is central to society. In China the single most significant religious activity is ancestor worship. The Chinese honor and memorialize the actions of the deceased and place great importance on paying respect to parents and elders.

In Japan, ancestor worship is an important mechanism in which the living feel they are spiritually connected to the deceased family members. This ensures the continuity of family lineage.

In Korea, there are several different types of ancestral rites to honor and worship their departed loved ones. Tea rites are held four times a year on major holidays. Household rites are held the night before the anniversary of an ancestor's death. Seasonal rites are held for ancestors who are five or more generations removed.

In Vietnam, the anniversary of the date when a loved one died is an important occasion. Family members often gather for a banquet in memory of the deceased. Incense sticks are burned and offerings are given on the ancestor altar. Many Vietnamese have an ancestor altar in their home and business. Offerings are also given during important traditional or religious celebrations. Family members may also give an offering when they are in need of guidance or counsel.

In India, ancestor worship is predominant. When a person dies, many specific rituals take place, during which the family offers tributes to the deceased. Each year, the family members repeat the ritual on the anniversary of their death. They also have separate rituals, during which families remember and make offerings to all ancestors.

The worshipping of the ancestors was prevalent in the Philippines until the 1900s, when the American missionaries arrived. The rich cultural heritage of the tribes in northern Philippines has been preserved in museums and includes examples of the carved wooden images of ancestors that were honored as a memorial to the ancestors.

In Thailand, several religious ceremonies take place to honor ancestral spirits. Respecting the ancestors is an essential part of spiritual practice and there is a strong sense of social hierarchy. Those who are elders govern family decisions and ceremonies.

Ancestor worship is also prevalent throughout Africa. Many African societies believe that the ancestors, spirits and Gods live in another world and they can affect the lives of the living. Ancestors are called upon for important events and ceremonies in life. The presence of ancestors will also bring protection and good luck. The spirits of the ancestors are believed to reside in places such as a tree, rock or a spring of fresh water. Sometime shrines are built for the ancestors.

In most western cultures (including Europe), the concept of honoring the ancestors is foreign. If you mention the word "ancestors," there tends to be a narrow view of the immediate family lineage. There may even be thoughts towards the "skeletons in the closet," referring to disreputable departed family members. Growing up in Australia, I never participated in any ceremony to honor the ancestors. I never called on them for spiritual guidance or support. If anyone told me they had contacted their ancestors, I would think of them seeing a psychic/medium or doing a séance. Communicating with the ancestors was not a part of my reality. What about you? What do you think of when someone talks about honoring the ancestors?

During my formal education at school, I learned about Aboriginal culture. As a young woman I dated an Aboriginal man for several years. During that time, I was immersed in his culture and become a member of his extended family. It gave me an insight into the rich tapestry of family kinship that exists within Aboriginal families. This experience greatly assisted me later on.

I started my career as a Ranger in the mid-1990s. While it was always important to incorporate Aboriginal culture within national park management, I didn't work with any indigenous employees. Since then, several changes have occurred. It is now common for national park agencies to have indigenous employees. There is also a recognition of the indigenous being the Traditional Owners of the land. There is a greater emphasis on consulting the elders about park management. There is still more work to be done, but at least the process has started.

Nearly every indigenous group has a profound connection with nature. They have a deep understanding of their environment, way beyond what I learned at university or working in the environmental field. Their connection with nature is something I also feel. To the indigenous, nature is more than just knowing about plants and animals. Nature is life itself, as represented and personified by Mother Earth—Pachamama—Gaia.

I often pondered why the wisdom and knowledge held by the indigenous didn't have a place in our fast-paced modern world. Many of our indigenous brothers and sisters around the world have grown up in a society that places little value on their wisdom and knowledge handed down from generation to generation. Many indigenous suffer from low self-esteem. Statistics show that they often have the shortest life expectancy, the highest rate of heart disease, stroke, cancer and diabetes, the highest infant mortality and the lowest family income.

Slowly, Human consciousness is changing and recognizing the indigenous peoples as the wisdom keepers of Earth. The indigenous across the planet all honor Gaia. All of them honor the ancestors. They intuitively know that they are their own ancestors. They understand the circle of life. When they honor the ancestors they are getting in touch with their own Akashic remembrance. Every indigenous ceremony that I have participated in across the world has always begun with an honoring of the ancestors.

I have experienced several sacred ceremonies with a Hawaiian Priestess, Kahuna Ali'i Wahine Kalei'iliahi is a Kanaka Maoli of Hawai'i. She was born and raised in the lush Kalihi Valley on the island of O'ahu. Her ancestral roots trace all the way back to the stars, to the Makali'i (the Pleiades), to Papa (Earth Mother) and Wakea (Sky Father) and down a long line of Kahuna Ali'i Wahine and Kahuna Ali'i Kane (Royal High Chief Priests and Royal High Chiefess Priestesses). Kahuna Kalei'iliahi's family God is Lono, God of Peace (also of Fertility, Abundance and Agriculture). Lono is uncle to Goddess Pele of whom she is a descendent.

When Kahuna Kalei'iliahi chants and invites the ancestors, I feel the most amazing love wash that pours all over me. Sometimes the feeling is so strong and powerful that I weep with emotion. When I see others in the ceremony openly weeping I know that I'm not the only one being affected by the portal created by Kahuna Kalei'iliahi. She told me once that when we weep, we honor the ancestors. Kryon has said the following about Kahuna Kalei'iliahi:

Spirit has placed upon Kahuna Kalei'iliahi a high energy of re-sponsibility, one that she has earned through her Akash. She carries the Royal Blood of a pure Lemurian and has awakened to the core seed. — KRYON

If you would like to connect with Kahuna Kalei'iliahi you may wish to visit her website: www.kaleiiliahi.com

I asked Kahuna Kalei'iliahi why the ancestors are so important to her. I invite you to read her response.

The Importance of the Ancestors

For the Kanaka Maoli, the aboriginals of Hawai'i, ancestral worship is central to our Spiritual thinking, being and the core of our connection to the divine. This divinity is within us all and our ancestors live within us. We carry their memories and their wisdom in our DNA. They are an inherent and insepa-rable part of who we are. All that they held sacred, we hold sacred within us as their Ambassadors. It is our kuleana, our responsibility, therefore, to honor their many gifts to us by keeping them alive in our daily lives ... in all that we do, for we represent them. We want to make them proud...

Ancestral communication is an innate part of my being. Without their guidance and their love and their wisdom, I would wander aimlessly in the dark, trying to find my way. They are my Light. They are the Source from which all the se-crets of the cosmos come, they are sacred and revered, for they represent all that is holy within me. They guard and pro-tect me ... there is no security system in the world more pow-erful than that of their Love. It is grand and mighty, yet gentle and safe.

As an indigenous of these islands I am so very blessed to be born of such a lineage. Each time they guide me into right thinking and right action, I increase my sacred mana. Sacred mana is the Spiritual Energy I carry from them and it is my kuleana to spread it wherever I go. When I touch others with my love, I am touching them with the love of the Ancients who walked before me. Today they walk behind me as my entourage and they are mighty, because of their Aloha. This is probably the single most precious thing we Hawaiians have received from them ... their Aloha. It is our nature to love, for that is what we are.

We worship our ancestors, because we know that when they leave their corporeal selves and give it back to the Earth in gratitude, they return to the Spirit World, where they enter into their full godliness. They know we are all part of the Creator, that the Creator lives inside us, but the body cannot contain its full power. In the Spirit World they become One with God in the truest sense. It is because my ancestors understood the divinity within man, that they honored each other, both in this world and in the Spirit Worlds. They knew this divinity was expressed as love, as Aloha. This word is sacred and means far more than hello and goodbye ... far more.

The word "Aloha" is two words: Alo and Ha. Alo is the face and Ha is the sacred breath of life, a gift of our divinity from the Creator. In ancient times, to greet someone with "Aloha" was an invitation to share the sacred breath of life by bringing your faces together, noses touching and inhaling and exhaling at the same time. It is an ancient ritual called "honi" that honors the divinity in the other and in yourself. It is about Love. Through me, that love increases as it is shared with humanity. It is why I am here. Now I bring a powerful aspect of love to others as well, and it is their compassion that flows through me like a river and never stops. It is boundless and limitless. It is the highest expression of their love I can give. It heals all things. Compassion, a grand gift from the ancestors.

Many people come to me and ask me how I communicate with my ancestors; they want to know because they have forgotten how. I tell them that their ancestors never leave them. As a seer they [the ancestors] are visible to me, I can see the entourage that stands behind them, just as mine do. They long to communicate with you, but they cannot without permission. They cannot interfere. They can and do touch you with their love in many profound ways through the planet itself, through nature. This is why we Hawaiians are so deeply in tune with nature ... at least those that have not forgotten the ancestors. Yet you must call upon them to open the mutual communication and then enter into the silence where you will hear them. First you will feel them; that is necessary, for they speak to us through emotions. You have to have an open and pure heart and trust that they are there. When you have the feeling, then you will have your own Higher-Self translate it into a language that you can understand. Often when you do this, your ancestors are weeping with joy ... they miss you more than you know...

The question was asked: Why are the ancestors important to me? I have given you some reasons, but there is only really one needed ... it is because of their Aloha, their Love.

Now that we are more aware of the importance of the ancestors, I invite you to open your heart and connect with a special message from the ancestors, given by Kahuna Kalei'iliahi.

Even as I get ready to channel this message I am crying... so profound is the love energy that is present from the Ancestors. Here is their message, offered to you in Divine Love...

"We are weeping with you, beloved Children of our Hearts, for we have been waiting thousands and thousands of years for the potential of this moment to occur ... and now it is here. The joy we feel at this communication cannot be described. The longing within us to speak to so many who have both remembered how to speak to us, and especially to those who forgot, is profound. We weep and sit at your feet in honor of you, for you have made it through the storms, through the fire, through the darkest of nights and the bleakest of times for humanity on this planet. And you have triumphed over it. We weep with pride and love and joy for what you have done!!!

It is no easy task to become of flesh and bone and walk the Earth Walk. We know because we, too, have shared that same tortuous walk, filled with challenges. We have also seen the miracle of sunrise and of sunset and all the beauty of this sweet and precious planet. We know what you have been through, for we have stood beside and behind you every step of the way. We have never left your side, ever. We live inside you. Even if some of you do not remember us, we never forget or abandon you. It is impossible, for we are eternally connected.

We have a message of great love and hope for you today, precious Family: You will walk this Earth Walk in these new times with a greater ease and with greater confidence than you have [before]. You have earned this right. Your thousands of years of work and sacrifice and giving of yourselves have earned you the right to have this portion of your journey made easier. It is how the Elders have always been treated and even if some of you do not think of yourselves as Elders, we assure you that you are indeed an Elder, worthy of respect and honor on this portion of your walk. It is time for the Elders, such as yourselves, to be the ones served. Oh, you will still serve others, but you will be also served, you will be esteemed and revered as an Elder has always been by the Indigenous. These things do not change. Even in the Spirit World there are those who wear the badges and the colors of the Grand Elders and they are the ones whose feet we wash ... you are among them. Even if you don't think you are an Elder or have done very much or could do more, we assure you that we see all you have accomplished over the thousands of years and we honor you!

Some of you have felt frustrated and others afraid to shine your light because within your cells are memories of having suffered so much in the past. You are surrounded by a Light that is brighter than you can fathom and it protects you now and will all of your life. It is a light you carry inside you ... and we put it there. Take our love and light and fear not. Accept the honor bestowed upon you in these times and celebrate what you have done and are about to do. All living things on the Earth know you by name...all living things know you by name! Including the rocks! There is a light inside you that took thousands of years to create, and we did it together, for we are One.

Today is a holy day, anointed and remembered and recorded in the stars. It is the day when humans opened themselves to ancestral communication and allowed us to pour our love and honor into your hearts and minds and souls. Today is a day recorded in the stars and in the Earth itself. 10,000 years from today this message of love and hope will still be echoing throughout the Universe. And so it is."

Kahuna Kalei'iliahi

What do you feel when you read the words of love from the ancestors? What do you feel when you read the words of love from Kryon? Many call this the new age, but really, it is the age of remembering. We are remembering the wisdom and knowledge of our ancestors. We are getting in touch with the core Lemurian energy. The Lemurians, who were given the seeds of enlightenment by the Pleiadians, are our ancestors. We are therefore studying what the Ancients knew and what many indigenous still hold within their culture. We are accessing Ancient Akashic wisdom.

I have a question for you. Who are your ancestors? Do you come from a family where ancestor worship is an integral part of life, or are you like me, in that the concept doesn't exist in your family? We often spend a great deal of time tracing our family tree and looking at the lineage of our biological ancestors. What about your Akashic lineage? Your Akash is a soup of energy, so there is no list of whom to pay tribute. Instead, the energy of your Akash communicates with you. It draws people to certain places. It means, for instance, that someone who grew up in China with a Chinese family can go to North America and instantly feel a strong connection with anything that relates to the Native Indians who lived there. What if you have never been a part of a family or an indigenous group that honors their ancestors? How do you then honor them?

I would like to share how I personally honor the ancestors. I am a first generation Australian. My parents are both Hungarian and immigrated to Australia in 1969. My family tree reveals many generations living in Hungary. I was, therefore, exposed to both Hungarian and Australian cultures. I have also lived in New Zealand and South America. Everywhere I go, I like to give thanks to Gaia for being here and for loving us. When I feel my connection to Gaia, I feel the connection with the ancestors who walked the land there. When I participate in indigenous ceremonies, I feel the love of their ancestors greeting me. I don't think it matters if they are within my lineage or not. Perhaps you feel this as well? I also feel the connection to our spiritual parents, the Pleiadians. So when I think about honoring the ancestors, I not only feel my immediate biological ancestors, but I feel the pieces and parts of divinity that is within my Akash, which connect me to the Creator source. The Lemurians and Pleiadians are my ancestors as well as yours. We are family. As we honor our ancestors, we therefore honor God and ourselves.

Kryon has told us that many of the Lemurians and Pleiadians have remained in a quantum state within the dirt of the earth. When I look upon breath-taking views of majestic mountains or the sweeping desert terrain, I feel the energy of the Lemurians and Pleiadians. The global awakening of old souls means that we are connecting with our core Lemurian and Pleiadian ancestors. The invitation is there for you to honor them, as they honor you.

What about our spiritual grandparents and great grandparents? Let's not forget them, for they have different attributes than the Pleiadians. Kryon explains:

The Pleiadians are your parents. When their planet went into ascension and they had the full God within their DNA, they finally realized what they had gone through. They finally knew what they were there for, and they received a full pineal connection — 100% efficient DNA, but still in the physical [They remained in physical bodies]. Do you know what that's like? Don't look for their 3D ships. These beautiful beings are entangled with you and they come and go as they wish. However, they do it by just "thinking" about it.

You [on Earth] were the next ones, and the only planet after them to be seeded. But did you know they had spiritual parents of their own, just like they are your spiritual parents? The names of their parents and the parents of their parents are Arcturian, those from Orion and from Sirius. All of these also had spiritual parents of their own, and they then had parents of their own. Listen: Every single one of these groups is part of your "creative source group." Some are your spiritual grandparents, and some are your great-grandparents. Some are even more than that. There are also Ancients on your planet from other parts of the galaxy who are "just here to help".

Let me ask you this: What do you know about the attributes of biological grandparents, that your parents don't have? How do you feel about your grandparents, living or dead? You look at them differently from your parents, don't you? Your parents are hands-on, but your grandparents are not. Your grandparents are the ones who want to entertain you and help you and take you places. Mom and dad? They're a little different. They are here to make certain you survive, and give you the rules of life.

The Pleiadians seeded you and they're the ones who are responsible for the information as you open the time capsules. They're the ones who are putting you through all the tests of The Crystalline Grid and other systems they have created to interface with you for your spiritual awakening and survival. They're the ones who are saying, "Come on, let's go!" Ah, but the grandparents, they're the ones giving the most gentle help, since they are more available and do not have the same kind of responsibilities that the parents do. They also are a far more mature and ancient group than the parents.

Do you understand where this is going? The Arcturians and those from Orion and Sirius are in your DNA, because you have "galactic Akashic Inheritance." You know them, and they know you. They're probably the most helpful groups on the planet. Don't separate them out from the others, and don't worship them. See the system, dear ones, for what it is. Absorb all of them, and know that right now they are with us in this room, in this communication. They love the fact that we are now helping to de-mystify who they are. Those who channel them may say they're from here or there, but I want you to look for the metaphors within their information, for these metaphors will point to the truth. The reason these groups are here helping is that they are your spiritual grandparents and great-grandparents. That is why they feel so good to you, and that is why some of the channelling coming from them is so pure and so excellent. If the channeller is pure, you will see who they are. They love you and they know who you are.

It's important that the old souls who sit in front of me are understanding what I'm saying, and know that I'm not talking in code or in metaphors. Right now, I am talking about reality and spiritual common sense that is beautiful. This information is right from the creative source, which you call God. God is bigger than anything that you've been told, dear ones, and as you start to perceive this, I want you to remember one thing before we say goodbye: As you start to perceive the wonder of the Creator, I want you to remember where it came from, for your *Akashic lineage* is God. Ponder it. It's about time you picked yourself up, stood tall, and claimed this lineage. Say, "hello" to your grandparents.

Perhaps they've been waiting a long time for this? Is this too spooky? For some it is. For others the truth rings like a bell of purity and answers the questions that they've been asking a long time. Dear ones, you've got help. Acknowledge it, work with it. Use it!

Kryon live channelling "De-mystifying the New Age Part One"
given in Tucson, Arizona — January 18, 2014

So what does all this honoring of our ancestors have to do with creating peace on earth? Actually, our ancestors have everything to do with creating peace on earth.

I wish to speak of the history of the Ancients. Let us start with a phrase that you might have heard that says, "History will drive the future." If you speak to a modern sociologist or a modern anthropologist, they will agree with this. However, this is a cynical statement, for what they see is history tending to repeat itself, as though humanity never learns from mistakes made in the past. It may even seem that they are correct, for in the last few thousand years, there has not been much evidence of any progress.

As I mentioned before, the sticks that you hit each other with have just gotten bigger over the years. That's the only change. Survival is still survival, so it would appear that the history statement is correct. Many believe that the history of the planet will repeat itself and drive you into the future without a great deal of evolution of consciousness. You are doomed to repeat all the issues of the past.

Now let us go back even further in time and look at how the indigenous looked at it. Every single indigenous culture on this planet starts their ceremonies [by] honoring the Ancients. For there is a recognition that the template of wisdom lies somehow within the very bones of their own ancestors. So they ask the past to help with their future, but it is not a cynical request. Instead it is a beautiful hope that the future might be influenced by the wisdom of the original grandfathers and the Ancients, as far back as they can look.

Acknowledging the Wisdom of the Past

Now let us turn another page and look at this in a quantum, non-linear way. Outside of three dimensions, and climbing into the esoteric box that you have chosen for today, answer this: What is your past, Human Being? What is your quantum past? So I'm asking you to look at the template that has been placed here by the Pleiadians—the one that is in your DNA. The Pleiadians are the Ancients for you, so indeed, history may drive the future. The history of the Pleiades!

Could it be, that a graduate planet, featuring the wisdom of the real Ancients, (the ones you carry right now in your DNA), is possible? Perhaps the indigenous had it correct all along, except now when you apply the quantum aspect to it all, you go further back than this planet's history. Now you're looking at the history of a graduate, divine, aware culture, and that is the door that you are opening in this new age.

Kryon live channelling "The Compassion Choir"
given in Cancun, Mexico — December 8, 2013

As we get in touch with our ancestors, as we connect with the templates placed within us and Gaia, we open the door to the portal that holds the wisdom and knowledge of what humanity can do to become a graduate, divine, aware culture. The Ancients and the Ancestors are here with you right now, celebrating as you read this and, of course, some of them are you!

Question for Kryon:

Our spiritual parents and grandparents are the Pleiadians, Sirians, those from Orion and the Arcturians. Will we eventually have remembrance or awareness of the wisdom and knowledge of our galactic ancestors? How can we enhance our communication with them?

Answer:

Tens of thousands of Lightworkers all over the planet are already tuned into the wisdom, love and help from these groups. Sirians, Arcturians and those from Orion are favorites, as well as many, many others. So you might say that old souls already have full awareness of the groups, but they simply don't know how they are all related. They just feel the love and caring.

The interesting thing about this question is that it is right after the one about grandparents! These groups are your seed-grandparents! The Pleiadians, being your seed biology (spiritual parents), are far more involved in their teaching from the time capsules, the grids and the other profound systems they have put into place on your planet. This removes them from the "gentle, mature, easy-going" type of help that the others have. If you look at the information, as correctly channelled from many, you see how helpful they are with everyday life. The Pleiadians are far more interested in your "growing up" than holding your hand.

I am slowly giving you at least these four generations of your creation, but there are many more. The time, as measured in your Earth years, is awesome — for each planet has taken up to half a million years to go through its process and be able to ascend. (You are only in the first 100,000.) Some took almost a million. It also means that you are the "new kids on the block," as you say. The galaxy is far, far older than Human life on Earth. But Human life has been around for about two billion years in other parts of the galaxy. You do understand, don't you, that these ancestors are Human? Again, DNA is a staple in the galaxy. It develops with the same kind of system everywhere. Humans are everywhere.

Communication can be enhanced through the same process as the connection with the Higher-Self. As you increase your intuition through working on the connection through the pineal, it enhances your Innate body intelligence as well. This opens communication that is far more multi-dimensional everywhere. These groups communicate through the same portal as your connection with Spirit. You seldom find anyone who is channelling these groups without also having full awareness of their "God self." If you do find anyone claiming to do this who is obviously out of integrity, what does your intuition tell you? Perhaps they are not channelling at all...

Chapter Five

"Mining" the Akash

In my opinion, the phrase "*mining the Akash*" was first introduced to the planet by Lee Carroll and Kryon. Prior to this, I never heard anyone else talk about it, particularly in the way that it is expressed and described by Kryon and Lee. At the time of writing this book, I discovered that many other authors have written about the Akashic Records. However, the main focus of these books relates to accessing your past records and reviewing them like you would in a library. What Kryon says is that, because our past lives are actually part of our current life, we can pull upon our Akashic attributes and rewrite the scripts. Kryon has also said the Akash contains the potentials of all our lives to come. In addition, there are time capsules filled with spiritual wisdom waiting for release (see Chapter Six: The Time Capsules of the Akash).

Why do we need to know about our Akash? How can *mining* the Akash change anything? Perhaps the following channel from Kryon may help:

What is it you wish you could do? What are your blocks? What are the things that you think are you that can't be

135

changed? In the Akash, there is also you, many of them. Why don't you go there and replace the current *you* with the former *you*? That is *mining the Akash*. That's a quantum Human Being, and it goes way beyond what you were told past life energies were for. You were told they were for karmic exchange. It's the old idea that past life experience builds up in your DNA so that you will be disturbed by it, so that it will become the *sand in your oyster* and then you have to accomplish something to get around it. It is very old information, and now you can go way beyond that.

What if the whole reason for the Akash is just the opposite? What if it is a gold mine with your name on it? You lived all those lives. Think about that. It's life experience; it's wisdom, shaman. Now, go mine it. That's what the quantum Human Being does. It creates mastery. Think about that.

Kryon live channelling "Becoming Quantum"
given in Sedona, Arizona — June 13, 2009

Kryon often talks about mining the Akash. How exactly do we mine the Akash? The answer is difficult, because of our bias in linear thinking. We want a step-by-step process. We want an instruction guide on how to do it. The linear thinker wants a list of who they were in every past life. They want a list that shows their talents and abilities, fears and phobias. The next thing they want is to find out how they can be the skinny person without weight issues, or the wealthy and successful person that doesn't have any financial problems. We can't help thinking this way. The difficulty is that it doesn't work that way. It just doesn't work that way!

Our Akash is in a quantum state. That means your talents, abilities, fears and phobias are in your Akash as a soup of multi-dimensional energy. Trying to mine your Akash for the skinny person is like trying to extract salt from a bowl of soup. So the first step, if you like, is to get out of linear thinking. How? How do we get into a quantum state? The answer is complicated. Instead, let me ask you something. How do you fall in love? When you fall in love, you experience being in a quantum state. You lose track of time and just want to sit in the energy of the other person. When you are in love, when does logic enter your thoughts? Are you acting rationally? The energy of love is the closest example I can give that demonstrates being in a quantum state. It is like this when you get in touch with your core and hold the hand of your Higher-Self.

So being in touch with your core is a good way to begin accessing your Akash, which is quantum. Kryon explains, in the following two channels, the process of how we can mine the Akash:

In your Akashic Record are attributes that you need, dear Human Being. This time, right now, in this new age, you need these tools. You need this mastery. You need this quantum patience. Why don't you go into the Akash and ask your Higher-Self to activate it? Your Higher-Self is going to go get it and make you a patient person. Do you believe that?

"Kryon, I can change my attributes of my personality?" That's what this is about, and that's the new tool. Oh, it goes beyond that. How would you like to be slow to anger? How would you like to have a personality that never goes into drama or fear? How many lifetimes have you had to choose from? You could go get it. It's there. It lives in your DNA. That's why it was stored there, Lemurian. Now go get it!

Mining the Akash is what we have called this. It's the new tool. Go get the pieces and parts that are you, which you lived and you deserve. What have you learned in this life? If I gave you time, if I gave you all evening, would you then start to enumerate what you've learned in this lifetime? As a woman, as a man, as a Human? And you'd say, *"Well, I'd need a lot more than one evening to write that down."* Yes you would! Now, multiply it by several hundred lives and you've got a library of experience and knowledge. You've got a large storehouse. You've got an immense amount of experience, but instead of being in the past, it's all *now*. It's all you...

...Now, some of you have done this in other ways, because what you've gone through in a past life was fearful. Perhaps you've come in with the same fear you had last time around? There are some who even say you're cursed with an energy of some sort, and you can never get above it. I will tell you that this energy is in your Akash and you brought it in ... a fear that's so strong it affects your life lesson, your Higher-Self and all of your Akash.

Isn't it time to get rid of it? You can! You can reach right there into those energized layers of all of those lifetimes and pick out the one that had the hero, self-assured, courageous, loving, peaceful, and healthy...

...Can you feel the love of God here? If you can, it's a good beginning. I'll tell you this: If you can *feel* this message, you can accomplish what it teaches. Each one of you is unique on the planet. Each one has a life lesson that is unique. Each one has a unique pattern of lives lived in the past. That means your Akashic Record is like no one else's, and your Higher-Self is also unique. This limits my ability to give you some kind of 3D generic list or way to heal yourself, since you are dealing with the specifics of "you." So instead, why not sit down in a quiet moment, with purity, and say to Spirit, *"I would like these things. I give permission to activate the energies that needed to be activated in my life, to accomplish the purposes I came for. I want to have joy in my life and to find the joy in my full Akash, for I deserve it and I've earned it. I've had positive, joyful lives, so I want to pull on that energy."*

Let's say you want self-esteem. You call it out. *"Spirit ... body, I want self-esteem, because I don't have much."* What happens next is the Higher-Self will go into the Akash and bring back the warrior on the battlefield ... you in another life. This individual stands tall among Human Beings, and is courageous in battle. You are not asking for ego, but rather "an assurance of personality." Remember, you are asking only to dip into what you have already created!

For the one who wants to write the book, or go find the orator and the author in their DNA, do it! They're there. How do I know? Because the very people who will ask are listening and reading. They are the old souls of the planet and have the fullest Akashic Records ... the most experience of any humans.

For the one who wants spiritual knowledge, go find the *spiritual jar!* In there is the Shaman you were, or the teacher of spiritual things within your village. It's all there. I know this because I know you!

Kryon live channelling "Beginning the Activation of DNA"
given in Riga, Latvia — March 15, 2009

Everything you have is changeable, right down to the diseases that you currently carry in your blood. It's only the Akash, you know? It's part of *your* DNA, so it belongs to you. Listen to me: If the storehouse of who you used to be, which is contained in your own DNA, included a beautiful, young, healthy Human Being, it is, therefore, still there! Perhaps it included the ability to do certain kinds of things, being an artist, being the orator, the writer, the warrior, the self-confident one, the one who could stand tall and walk straight? Do you understand that this is all "you?" It's all still there. But, you say, *"That's a nice thought, Kryon, but it's in the past. You can't touch the past."* I say, how linear of you! For the new gifts are you, in a nonlinear attitude towards cellular structure. Delinearize your life and you will find that not only can you touch these things, you can mine them (extract them from the source). You can glean them easily! *"I like the idea, Kryon. How do I do it? I'm ready."*

Mining the Akash

I'll give you the first step. *You've got to believe it.* Don't believe it because I said it's there. You've got to believe it so strongly that it's as real, biologically, as your arm. When you look at your arm, you say, *"I have an arm and it is there and I can see it."* There's no question, and your brain knows it, too. The matter around you knows it, and to prove it, you can pick up things with it. No question about it. It's your arm.

Now, how do you feel when you say, *"I have an Akashic Record in my DNA. I have a record inside me of all that I ever was, which I can access."* Tell me what parts of your body object to that statement. I'll answer — *all of the linear ones!* Logic will yell at you, *"You can't do it. You cannot change who you are."* And it will be wrong about that.

You can all do this. It is part of being in this new energy and I want to tell you that many already have who are in this room. It can be done slowly and in small increments. It can be done quietly with nobody noticing, and it can be so obvious that your best friends no longer recognize you. The energy for this comes from the storehouse that is you. It's in your DNA, every single piece, trillions of them that all are synchronized to your will.

There are three levels of difficulty: Simple, medium and hard. I will tell you what happens in each one. Do you understand the premise? Do you understand, Human Being, that you're not asking God for anything? What you're doing is changing yourself to the degree where you can go in and get what you have already learned ... what you already worked for. The key? You have to understand and believe that the one Higher-Self was with you each time. That means that your central consciousness was involved in all of them. You are *not* a different entity this time around. You are simply another expression of the same Higher-Self. Therefore, you were there for all of these things we are speaking of. You have to believe it. Does the Higher-Self know what's going on? Do I have to really answer that? The Higher-Self has been waiting for you to bring in the belief.

Easy: Fears. Phobias and blocks. They're easy to clear. Yet these are the ones everyone wants to change and have trouble with. How would you like to not be afraid of the things you're afraid of? We'll talk simply here. Are you afraid of stepping forward, afraid of change, afraid of what's happening around you? Some of you have phobias. That is to say, these are hold-overs, hangovers from past life experience. Are you afraid of heights, afraid of insects, water, afraid of this and that? You may say, *"Well yes, but it doesn't really affect my life, since I've learned to live with it."* Yes, it does! I'll tell you why, because it includes darkness in a study of light. It doesn't belong there. You don't need it. It interrupts your belief, your efficiency, your prog-ress, and you are constantly aware of it. It's not you this time around, since it reflects another lifetime ... from somewhere else. You don't need it anymore. It's like trying to be quick to change, but having to carry around a bunch of old baggage that you claim you never need to open and use. Make sense?

So begin. Start to work with what you now believe, in the same way you *believe in* your arm. Soon you find that the pho-bias and fears start to retreat and change. As they do, you start to claim that part of the Akashic Record that you used to be, but are rekindling. It feels just like you. It really *is* you. It doesn't feel like anybody else, for you are just claiming what you already own. The fears start to go away, too. You can feel it, and you can continue to challenge them and work on them so that your cellular structure feels it, too. Afraid of heights? Occasionally go to a high place to check yourself. You'll see how the fear starts to become less. You are no longer para-lyzed to look over the edge. These things start to go away to the point you will wonder why they were ever there! These are small challenges. The blockages from you moving from one energy to another are real, but they will subside, as you claim the power of what belongs to you ... lack of fear. It's growth, and it takes practice. But you will absolutely see the progress.

Humans don't like to change. Many of you have these blocks. They are blocks of awareness. What is it that triggers your anger? It's a block of peace, isn't it? Can you eventually be patient while a fool speaks to you about his foolishness? Can you be understanding about his process instead of angry? Yes. These are the simple things. You can pass these tests, change your life, and then start to work on the more complex issues. The beauty of it, dear Human Being, is that if all of you did the simple things, you'd have a group of peaceful warriors ... warriors of the light. You all would be unencumbered by fear, phobias and blocks. You would all send the light with purity, and there would be no judgment from Spirit if you did nothing else. But if you wish to, they get harder.

Medium: How would you like to get rid of your allergies and change your immune system? It's a little harder. You might ask, *"Well, how do you do such a thing? Do you just think it away? I either have allergies or I don't. My cells are allergic."* Oh, really? I'll tell you, dear ones, there are those in this room who have dropped their allergies because they realized they were holdovers for something they didn't need anymore. They went into the Akashic Record and they got the pristine DNA from the one lifetime that was never allergic to anything! That blueprint is still there! It represented an immune system that was hardy and whole and never had disease. They were strong and never allergic to anything. How would you like to not have sickness? How would you like to have strength and energy beyond your years? This is harder, you know? But it is so. Whatever you think *you are* can be re-written at the cellular level.

How would you like to have peace over everything in your life, no matter what? I didn't say the problems would go away. I just asked, how it would be to be peaceful about them? How would you like to get rid of the drama and the worry? It's an interesting thing about drama issues: When the Lightworker does not *work karmic energy*, drama disappears! When you drop your karma, there is no reason to continue the drama about something you don't need anymore. *"Kryon, I dropped my karma years ago when I decided to change my path. This sounds like it's still there."* It's not that simple. Giving intent to drop your karma is like clearing the path before you. But now you have to get up and walk that path. The karmic attributes shout at you: "Pick me up ... I'm yours!" But then you remember as you walk that your intent has created a situation where you never have to pick them up. But they will always be around, talking to you.

This is difficult. Let me tell you, old soul, anyone who sits in this room, or any Lightworker reading this, has been through a spiritual revelation. You have been priests, you've been nuns, you've been shamans. You've gone through these things or you wouldn't sit in the chair or be reading this esoteric information. In these medium Akashic attributes, you might say, you can develop a personality that is so peaceful that everybody wants to be with you. That is the answer, is it not? This is the peace that the masters had. This is only the medium part, so I've just given you the starting point. I've given you the simple. I've given you the medium. Now I tell you the hard one.

Hard: This is the unbelievable part. This is for the one who really wants to dig into the Akash and change the future. In each of you is all that you ever were ... eons of experience. In addition, if you're going to mine the Akash, that is to say, if you're going to go in and get these things, you will be voiding the things that you don't like about this life. That is the result. It's not that you're going into the DNA and getting something different to paste upon you. Actually, it's an exchange — one for another. That's the way it works. For the DNA claims everything you are. What you are doing is exchanging attributes ...

putting into the record what doesn't suit your energy, and claiming the things that do. You own them all.

There is something else: Each of you has what we would call a spiritual jar. That jar is filled with everything you have ever learned as a Human Being on this Earth about God, about guides, about angels, about interactions, about sacred communication. And the jar is *yours*. It does not have to be refilled every lifetime. It lays there ready for you to unscrew the lid and pour out everything you ever knew. It is part of the system of the spiritual Akash. It is the spiritual gilding of all that is, allowing a seeming novice on this planet to become a master overnight. This "novice" paid his dues and lived through it. Perhaps he even died for his belief.

Many of you are afraid of certain things because you died as a result. Some of you don't want to touch the esoteric because it carries a fear of enlightenment and death. Your fear is such that you don't want to open the jar. So many will reject this entire premise, not believing. Well, not really. You believe, but you just don't want to touch it again. I know who's here. So the first attribute in the hard category is opening the spiritual jar and placing upon you all that ever was learned by you. Are you afraid of this? For some of you were important in the history of spiritual things. That's the truth.

Not only do you carry spiritual knowledge, you carry the persona of who you used to be ... in the jar. This is difficult to explain to you. Overnight, seemingly, one who is not interested at all in metaphysical things may become a giant teacher. Out pours the jar and all they have to do is learn and listen to use the information in a linear fashion. Non-teachers become teachers. Those who had no knowledge at all, now have great knowledge. Those who were clueless have great wisdom. The spiritual jar—that's the hard one. It's there; all of you have it. Everyone in this room and reading this are included.

You can assume a personality that is completely and totally different than the one you were born with. Are you ready for that? Are you too attached to the fears, phobias and blocks? Would you like to have a more peaceful personality? That is a fear in itself, is it not? You might feel you are losing yourself, only to find yourself! It's available in this "hard" category. These are the things that can be given with clarity through connection with the Higher-Self. Growth in these things requires a greater communicative ability from the Human Being to the Higher-Self. Each step gets you more connected.

"Wait a minute, Kryon. You said we were connecting to our DNA, not the Higher-Self." Yes, I did. Where do you think the Higher-Self is? It's in the multi-dimensional DNA. We even gave you the information of which DNA layer contains it, and the Hebrew name for it. We even told you its number was six: the sixth energy of DNA. That core information, that Higher-Self, lurks in trillions of pieces of the DNA all working together to create who you are. Oh, you want to think your Higher-Self is some angel in the sky? It is not. It's inside you, imbedded in your cellular structure. That's where it is. There's so much here to know.

"Kryon, I'm confused. Where is God in all of this?" Right where you would never look, for God is the concept of a loving family of spiritual help that is somewhere beyond the veil. God is love, yet you can't really find that fullness outside of you. It is a constant search and humanity has been looking for God since creation. Now I again reveal to you that the system of God is inside you, and that the very essence of your divinity lies in the multi-dimensional DNA that is within your own body. Be still, and know that you are God. Let the search stop and celebrate victory in finding the truth in the most unlikely place ... inside.

We're almost done. How would you like to have talents that you do not have now? *"Kryon, how can that be? I'm either talented or I'm not. I either play the piano or I don't."* How 3D of you! There you go, deciding that it's finished. You feel like you are some kind of cake, and when you come out of the oven, you're finished! You don't understand that you are just the

145

beginning recipe, and that recipe shouts to be altered. In your Akash, that is to say, in your DNA, is the remembrance of talent that you don't think you have, but which you did have. This is again called *mining the Akash*. We've spoken of it before. It takes years. It's doable. It can happen, and it can be awakened. What are you afraid of? Why not begin?

You say, *"Well, I cannot speak in front of people. I'm not good at that."* What about the orator in the third century? Are you going to throw him away? After all, he was you! Would you like to go in and get those attributes? The orator will speak with authority and people will listen. That's a talent. Many of you have this within you, yet didn't when you were born. Therefore, you can't imagine such a thing. You can't live that many lives without having this talent. I'll say it again: There's such a variety of what you have in your own history that you can pull upon it, dear Human Being. It's yours to develop. Too strange? Ask my partner some day about it. He did it.

The hardest one: How would you like to change your DNA to such a degree that the disease that surges through it now won't even remember it was ever there? Go in and get the clean DNA that you had *before* the disease ever arrived! The DNA remembers what it was like. It was participating, remember? Begin to change your own DNA in a multi-dimensional fashion so that the disease will retreat, go away, and never come back. *"Sounds like a miracle, Kryon!"* Indeed, it is ... the miracle of shift into mastery.

Miracles are only things that are outside of your normal belief. Change your belief and they become ordinary. Sometimes when these miraculous things occur, humans lift their hands to God and say, *"Thank you, God!"* There is no understanding that they have activated their own DNA to such a power that they received what only the masters could give in the past. They simply exchanged what was theirs to exchange, in a non-linear way. They healed their own life. What was only thought of as available from the masters is now available to all. This is the enablement of the Human race. Less than one-half of one percent will ever do it. But you are part of that group, and you know it.

Kryon live channelling "It's in the DNA!"
given in Kelowna, BC, Canada — June 28, 2008

Are you beginning to understand how you can mine your Akash? You are the miracle you have been waiting for. What if you don't know where to begin? How can you mine your Akash if you don't know what you are looking for? Perhaps instead of creating a list of things you'd like, why not ask Innate to bring you the synchronicity you need. Coincidentally, as I was writing this section, I was fortunate to be spending the summer with a dear friend who did just that. She has created a meditative guide that helps others mine their Akash.

Dr. Amber Wolf has been practicing holistic healthcare for over thirty years. She is an internationally known teacher, author, healer and recording artist. Dr. Wolf is a regular Kryon team member and is the co-designer and facilitator of the very popular and profound KRYON DISCOVERY SERIES that has been held in many locations in the USA and overseas. Dr. Wolf is also the original creator of the Lemurian Sisterhood sacred circle. This was developed from her Akashic remembrance of Lemuria. During a Kryon channel given in January 2014, Kryon revealed her Lemurian name, Mele'ha. Kryon has said the following about the Lemurian Sisterhood:

The original *Lemurian Sisterhood* was practiced within all parts of Lemuria, both the mother mountain, and the descendant islands and mainland settlements. It lasted far past the "Akashic growth centuries," and continued to spread around the Earth until it was all but forgotten, due to survival attributes and the beginning of the conquering eras of your history. It outlasted the "exclusive expression" attributes of the original Lemuria and made it into some of the most secret societies all over the Earth. It was renamed and even denied by those women who kept it dear, but eventually the Priestesses, themselves, perished, due to the unbalance that was rolling over Humanity. But it never left the Akash of the old soul. Like the whispers of a past love, it was always ready to re-emerge and rekindle itself with the fire of compassion for all of Humanity.

KRYON 2013

For over two years Dr. Wolf was communicating with Lee Carroll and Kryon about mining the Akash, with the aim of creating a meditative guide. However, each time she tried to create it, the words did not come. Finally surrendering, she said, *"Okay Spirit, if you want this done then you need to help me!"* The next morning she woke up with a very clear instruction from Spirit to write her meditation immediately. Within (two years) and 45 minutes the script was done! Her meditative guide, *Mining Your Akashic Records*, allows you to relax and reconnect with your divine essence. In addition, Dr. Wolf uses binaural beats in her guided meditations. Binaural beats is a recognized technology for brainwave entrainment. This teaches the two hemispheres of the brain to synchronize and puts the mind into a deep state of meditation within minutes of listening.

I realize that many people find it difficult to follow a guided meditation and visualize what is being described. Does this sound like you? If so, I have a suggestion that may help. Allow yourself to merge with the intent of the divine Human that is guiding you into the experience. Don't worry about whether or not you are doing it correctly. There is no right or wrong. Simply relax and trust that your Higher-Self and Innate will bring you what you need.

During the *Mining Your Akashic Records* meditation, I experienced a sensation of being within a crystalline structure. I connected very briefly with my guides and Gaia. After the meditation, my body was buzzing. I honestly can't even tell you what attributes I activated in that meditation. All I know is that Innate pulled upon what I needed from my Akash and I feel a deeper sense of peace. I also know that with the passage of time this experience will become fully realized.

If you would like to know more about the Lemurian Sisterhood, Dr. Amber Wolf, or order one of her divinely created meditation CDs visit the following websites: www.lemuriansisterhood.com and www.sacredenergyalchemy.com

While writing this book, I became aware of an issue that kept pressing my "fear, panic and worry" button. I asked for help from my Australian girlfriend, Wendy Chadwick, who I met at a Kryon seminar in Hawaii. Wendy is highly intuitive and channels loving messages from beyond the veil. If you are interested in a reading from Wendy, please email her at: wendi@clarityclear.com.au

I asked Wendy for a channelled message to help me with my dilemma. One paragraph in particular got my attention:

Our dear precious one, we are with you always during these times of frustration, understanding that a practice of patience is required for all events that unfold in your world at this point in time. We acknowledge that this has been the way of things for quite a while in your linear world. This is a pattern that has come through from other lifetimes, a sense of feeling of waiting, waiting, waiting,

waiting, waiting,.........For you know clearly this pattern that sits with you and has for many incarnations. This is why it feels even more frustrating as you now clearly see this pattern; it has come to the fore so it can be cleared within the consciousness instead of remaining and wreaking havoc in the sub-consciousness.

This message felt so accurate that I immediately organized to receive an EMF (Electro Magnetic Field) Balancing session from a wonderful EMF practitioner and highly evolved soul, Debbie Morris. The particular session I wanted was Phase II which focuses on gracefully releasing the energy restraints of the past and promotes awareness of Self Direction and Self Support. I wanted to release this old energy pattern that no longer served me. I received a "distance" session from Debbie in Sydney, Australia, while I was in Santiago, Chile. We never arranged a time for the session, only the day; however, I knew when the session started, as I felt a gigantic blanket of energy that was followed by a strong energetic movement throughout my spine. I knew immediately something had shifted from deep within my Akash.

The next day, when I was communicating with Debbie, she shared some insights of what she received during the session. She had sensed that the patterns I had given intent to release were very old and very deep energy restrictions that were entangled or hooked in my spine. During the EMF session there is a specific movement that clears the spine. As Debbie was clearing the spine, she could see these old "hooks" as shadows in my spine. When she cleared my heart center, the words "broken heart from unrequited love" came through.

Without a doubt this EMF session (combined with my intent) was a powerful catalyst that helped shift and clear an old energy pattern from my Akash that I had carried with me through many incarnations. It also explained my traumatic reaction to when my marriage ended, as it had triggered my "broken heart" experience. This event propelled me into spiritual awakening. The synchronicity of having a major breakthrough in a deep Akashic memory while writing about the Akash is no coincidence. As always, it makes me smile the way Spirit works with us. Spirit sees our intent. As your Akash awakens, that's when you get the instructions.

Kryon has often talked about "The Teacher, Peggy" (Peggy Phoenix Dubro) and on December 21, 2012, Kryon revealed her Lemurian name as Alani'ee. Peggy sees humanity with quantum sight. No matter how far away someone is, she is able to reflect back their quantum energy. Since developing the EMF Balancing Technique, Peggy has gone on to develop two other bodies of work: Reflections and The Waves. Peggy is also a channel, who brings in the Wisdom of the Feminine Divine from within the Kryon Entourage. During the Kryon Summer Light Conference in 2002, Kryon revealed that:

My group is feminine, but my essence is masculine. I am a balanced group, just like you. Although genderless, the balance between what is absolute to you is variable with me. I am both, and I change to accommodate the circumstances. It's an honoring, and you can watch me do it.

Peggy has often channelled alongside of Lee Carroll—and now you know why!

Kryon has described The Lattice (taught by Peggy) in the following way:

The Lattice represents the personal Akashic attributes of a Human Being, a quantum energy that surrounds him or her that can be used and pulled upon. It includes healing, a balance of life, and even mastery. The DNA is only the physical vehicle of a quantum state. A quantum state is everywhere. This is going to be tough for you to understand, Human Being, but there are really no pieces and parts of your DNA right now. They are all over the Universe! God knows who you are, oh, Quantum One. If you start activating these pieces and parts, your Lattice will change color, did you know that? Oh, but we'll leave it to the teacher, Peggy Phoenix Dubro, to tell you about that. [Kryon wink]

Kryon live channelling "Beginning Activation of DNA"
given in Riga, Latvia — March 15, 2009

More information about The Lattice can be found on my website: www.monikamuranyi.com under the "Extra's" tab. For more information about the EMF Balancing Technique or to experience an energy session from Peggy Phoenix Dubro, please visit: www.thebalancingwork.com

Communicating with Innate with pure intent is another way that we can mine the Akash. The following Kryon channel explains the process:

Pure intent is that which is so pure you cannot go backwards once you've given it. It's absolute. You're going to co-create something with intent because the intent is *all of you* moving into an area where you've never been before.

"Come on, Kryon. This is information that we really can't use. Pure intent for what? How? Give us more."

Here is a metaphor that you'll never forget: When a Human Being stands on the edge of a lake and they desire to jump in, all of the muscles of their body work together with pure intent. They give permission to jump, and the attributes come together for jumping into the air. They've committed when they leap, and they can't go back. But there's more.

Right at that moment, there's a process that humans don't understand at all, but they trust it and work with it, and it's called gravity. Science does not understand gravity. Oh, they think they do. They think it's a function of mass. Well, it is related, but mass is only one of the attributes of gravity. Mass does not determine the strength of gravity. What you see in 3-D is a correlation that you have come to understand, however. Survival mode has taught you all about it. There'll come a day when you can control gravity, when you can make massless objects. Tesla did it. The science is out there ready to be discovered yet again, but meanwhile, you don't understand it. But, oddly enough, you all use it.

So here is an extremely complex process that has no understanding at all, a multi-dimensional attribute of the Universe, and you use it every day. You don't even think about it. You don't understand it, but you count on it always being there and always being the same. Now you've jumped off the bank and gravity is taking you into the lake.

Now, how many of you, after you're wet, get out of the lake and sit down with a pad and a piece of paper and want a list of how gravity did that? [Laughter]

Are you understanding what's going on here? Listen: There is a profound, divine rule and an axiom about pure intent. Let me give that to you another way. Your Higher-Self is a piece of the Creator. You're all born with it. It's the same soul you've had for every single lifetime. Are you aware of that? Every lifetime, the same soul. There's a friend in there who has been with you through every journey, along with Innate. Some of you have been able to reach out and touch that friend and that is when you're the most peaceful on the planet. Can you feel that? Do you remember that? How would you like to have that feeling all the time? It's like having all your parents back, wrapped up in one inside you, looking at you. You can touch them, they can touch you. You can touch their hands anytime you want. In pure love, it's the parents you always wished you had if you didn't have them from the other side of the veil. That's what it is...

... Now, here's the promise, dear Human Being: When you begin that pure intent, this process takes over and will work. It will work because this is what Spirit has been waiting for. Jump into the lake. You can't stop it. There is no delete key in the Human brain. You can't unknow what I just told you. Oh, you can try. But it won't work, because I'm speaking to that which is inside you right now.

Right now, some of you are starting to feel it. There are old souls here whose Higher-Selves are yelling at you: *"Listen, listen, listen, listen, listen, listen, listen, listen, listen, listen!"* It's because they've been with you all your life and all they've ever wanted was for you to touch the hand that's outstretched—that's all they wanted. It starts *the process.*

So the invitation this day is without steps, without training and without knowledge of what you are doing. Like it so far? However, you can trust the process just like you do gravity. Can it be that hard? It's there. It works, but you've got to take the leap. And when you do, you can't go backwards. It will take you into the lake.

Kryon live channelling "The Process"
given in Laguna Hills, California — December 4, 2011

Did you understand the metaphor that Kryon gave? There was a description of a Human wanting to jump into the lake. Now, there are humans who can want to jump in the lake but never do. Then there are humans who truly commit to jumping in the lake and they are the ones that will leap off the edge. The Human with commitment to jump into the lake represents the Human with pure intent to mine their Akash.

154

What happens to the Human with commitment as they leap off the edge? Another type of energy comes into play. It's called gravity. When the Human jumps off the edge, gravity takes over and pulls them into the lake. Even if they change their mind, gravity pulls them into the lake. In this metaphor gravity represents Innate. The Human who gives pure intent to mine the Akash will actually trigger Innate. Innate will then start a process that you cannot even begin to understand to bring you what you need from your Akash. This beautiful system means that you don't even need to tell Innate what to get. Innate will bring you what you need that is appropriate for your evolution.

The key thing to recognize is that mining the Akash is related to spiritual evolution, not acquiring three dimensional wishes. However, during this process don't be surprised if you notice three dimensional attributes changing. This is why Kryon has said we can get rid of our fears and re-engage the abilities and talents we have that are carried within our Akash.

Here is a clarification: Kryon will sometimes talk about asking our Higher-Self and other times to ask Innate. Which is correct? The answer is both. The Higher-Self and Innate work together as a multi-dimensional soup.

There are several ways to mine the Akash and I have mentioned a few. Other healing modalities and energy psychology techniques can help. Dear reader, if this is something you desire, trust that it will happen. Be alert and pay attention to synchronicity. You may be interested in *Quantum EFT and Mining the Akash*. This technique, developed by renowned Australian therapist and EFT practitioner Jenny Johnston, helps you clear past fears and mine your Akash. Visit the following websites for more information: www.jennyjohnston.com.au and www.quantumeft.com.au

Finally, Kryon has given us an example of a wonder-ful new vow to replace old energy vows you may have carried from previous lifetimes (you may wish to say this aloud):

"Dear Spirit. I am alive in the years that will save the Earth, and I am here to make a change on the planet. I hereby drop all the vows that would get in the way of that, for they belong to another consciousness and another energy. Instead, I renew my vows with the same Akashic energy that took them originally. All of the lifetimes that are now under me are my support. And like a rod of energy that I will put down this line through my own history, I take control of them all now. I will need the help of all the consciousness of these many souls who I was, from the time I first came to this planet. Together we will create a white light like the planet has never seen. The light of the many me's, focused through the current me. That's why I came this time, and that's why I have ex-isted through the ages — to be here now."

Kryon live channelling *"Human Lighthouse Filters"*
given in Newport Beach, California — December 3, 2006

Questions for Kryon:

How can we remember what attributes we have within our Akash, which are available to us?

Answer:

You never have to. Our teaching has been clear on this. Let the Human ask, *"Dear Spirit, tell me what it is that I should know."* This is always the system for a Human who can't be expected to dig into esoteric and nonlinear spiritual systems that are outside of his own 3D logic and consciousness.

Your Innate knows what you need to enhance your heath, stability and mental comfort. Your Innate is the "smart body" that we have channelled about many times. (See more in Chapter Seven: The Three Parts of a Human.)

So if it's "in there," your Innate will know it and help you to bring out whatever portions of your past life experience needed to enhance your health and life span this time around.

Often there are old energetic patterns that are deep within our Akash, which we are not consciously aware of. Sometimes this can interfere with our co-creation process. For example, in the Akash is a memory of poverty and lack. Then in this life, we would like to co-create abundance. How do we address these deep issues that we are unaware of during the co-creation process?

This falls directly into the area of "rewriting" the DNA engrams that are part of old past life templates. That is to say, much of your DNA (and, therefore, your Akash) is just data ready to be changed if you would like to.

So "mining the Akash" can also simply be *changing your reaction to the past*. In this process, you are finding a past life *without* the trauma and bringing the attributes of peace to this life. The past is the past, and the subtle, deep memories will always be there. But you can rewrite your *reaction* to it, and this is the part where Innate can help, as well as your connection to Spirit.

Imagine someone rewriting abuse or a horrific past event. It's so beautiful and powerful, dear ones, that you may even do it within your existing life, too. But most of the rewriting is done because of many lifetimes of poverty, persecution or bad health. Poverty tends to be a residual that is difficult to shake, even in a current abundant life. It explains why a person has money, yet constantly worries about having none, so they "penny pinch." The hypochondriac is a person who has the residual of bad health and then projects that template onto his current life. These are individuals who will catch many of the diseases they worry about, since the body tries to "please" what consciousness always talks about or focuses on.

Addressing these issues is the "teaching of the day" for Kryon, and it is all part of a process that requires a new paradigm of thinking, letting your intuition help guide you into something that is almost like a journey into the unknown. Start with belief that it is there, then on to communication with Innate. The body starts to "listen" and slowly you are actually creating what you are thinking about.

One of the challenges of being Human is having patience and learning to wait for synchronicity. Many times the metaphor has been given that our "train is coming," representing the situation or event we are waiting for, and that we should relax because we "have a ticket for the train." This represents our intent or request for what we would like. Waiting for synchronicity is recognizing that the train will arrive on Spirit's schedule, and not ours. Are there things we can do in order to speed up the timing of when our train arrives? How do we recognize when Spirit has a better plan?

By default, it is *"this or something better."* The more you look at your watch or try to figure out what the outcome is going to be, or the alternate might be, the worse you make it.

Never try to speed it up or slow it down. Never second guess why the train is so slow arriving. When the train arrives, don't be disappointed that it's not going where you thought it was going! These are the rules of mature synchronicity. Synchronicity is not something where you get an answer to *what you want.* Synchronicity is you agreeing to work on *"this or something better,"* and getting out of the way so it can happen. Spirit has a bigger picture, and you do not.

The Human was thirsty; no water in sight. He sat in the forest and it was hot and dry. *"Please God, make it rain. Please God, make it rain. I will wait for the synchronicity."* Slowly the days turned into months and still no water. The Human sat and was tired, frightened, and more thirsty all the time. No end was in sight, and he was ready to give up.

Autumn came and slowly the trees began to lose their leaves. Now the Human was panicking. *"The trees are dying! The leaves are falling, and I'm next to die."* Here is where the Human could just stop and call it quits. Many do.

As the leaves fell, the absence of the foliage cleared the way for the Human to see something that had always been out of sight. There! Look! Through the trees, he could see a lake! It was a beautiful, fresh-water lake filled with precious water. It had been there all along. But he had to wait for the time and the season to reveal it. This is a metaphor for synchronicity. Did he get rain? No.

Chapter Six

The Time Capsules of the Akash

For most people, the term "time capsule" refers to a container holding a historic cache of goods or information placed or buried somewhere, with the intention that it will be opened or accessed at a future date. However, when Kryon talks about time capsules, we need to redefine what it means and how they came to be on the planet. Kryon has revealed that time capsules were placed on Earth by the Pleiadians, our spiritual parents, who seeded this planet with Divine DNA, all in appropriateness and love. There are time capsules in Gaia (placed within The Crystalline Grid and the cetaceans) and there are time capsules in your DNA (within your Akash). These time capsules have a different purpose, but they all co-operate together in one plan: The plan to see if humanity can create an ascended planet.

The time capsules within Gaia are about information and ideas. These capsules are about quantum attributes of science and life, waiting to be discovered, to help us move into the new energy. Kryon has said:

the time capsules will seem to be alive by those who can sense them, and they "buzz" with activity to the esoteric "see-er." There is a storehouse of future knowledge and ideas in these time capsules you call Gaia, placed there a long time ago by those who you would call the Pleiadians, and these time capsules will open with new ideas about unity and peace first before they open with inventions.

The time capsules within your DNA are more personal. Kryon has said these time capsules are about

the spiritual inheritance that you came in with that's ready to open up like a lotus. When it does, there will be new awareness. There will be peace in a countenance that is not necessarily peaceful. There will be patience in a countenance that is not necessarily patient. That's when you get to change you, for it releases ideas, emotions and a consciousness that has been within you always, but only now is beginning to show itself in this new energy.

During 2012 and 2013, Kryon gave many channelled messages that focused on the theme of recalibration. This subject is presented in Kryon Book Thirteen, *The Recalibration of Humanity 2013 and Beyond* written by Lee Carroll. It should, therefore, come as no surprise that our relationship with our Akash is also recalibrating, due to a release of information from within the time capsules.

We've told you about some of the time capsules in your DNA. We also spoke of one in particular, which we call instinct. Now, this is a review, but we wanted you to hear it in this room. Animals have instincts and you see it all the time. When certain animals are born in the field, the calf is up and running within hours. The calf knows its enemies, knows what food is poison, and even knows what water is good and not good—all within days of its birth. But the Human Being, working at only 30 percent of DNA efficiency, has none of that. Did you ever wonder about that?

Human babies are born and they are helpless! This lasts for a very long time. There's no automatic anything. Even basic reality is missing. They must to be told that heat will burn them. Walking is something that they know they should do, but it comes with difficulty. Now I want you to turn a page for a moment. I want you to see a Human Being working at 40 percent. Get ready for this. The child is born and pretty soon you start to see them trying to read, because they have read before. Walking starts very early since they are remembering it. They come in, knowing that heat burns them. This is a recalibration of basic instinct. This will be something that is built in to the Human just like the animal on the field, but you've never seen it. You don't believe it! Perhaps you don't even think you've got it? Watch. You're going to see it.

"Now Kryon, isn't that related to the Akash?" Yes. *"Kryon, are there time capsules in the Akash."* Yes. In other words you're seeing a recalibration of your relationship to your own Akashic Record. Now, some of these things cross over to things I have already spoken of, for we've given many channels on the recalibration of DNA. *"Where is your Akashic Record?"* It's in the DNA. *"Are there specific time capsules just for Akashic remembrance?"* Yes. *"What would they be, what's going to happen to the Akash that is different than some of the other things you have been mentioning?"* Let us discuss them slowly.

The Akash of the Human Being is not something you are really aware of day by day. You talk about it in a seminar or you'll read about it in a book, but you don't see it as practical. We use an expression: *you don't really own it*. You're told it's in there, but you don't believe it, necessarily. I sit in front of old souls. It is interesting to me that you don't really know about it. There is part of you that does — the part of your intelligent body called *Innate* knows all about it, and you can use that part with your intuition. If you were to meditate for a moment and ask that part of your body, *"Have I been here before?"* Get prepared for some laughter, and the body will smile and say,

"Oh many times!" Intuitively, this is a feeling. So I want you to *feel* it right now.

Honestly, Human Being, do you really think this is your first time around? Honestly? And the answer will be, of course not. Of course not! The old soul, the wise old soul who is sitting in the chair, has it inbred. He/she knows it! Sometimes you walk around the city and you'll wonder, *"What are they thinking, what are they doing?"* You'll look at groups of adults and you'll say nothing and you're not in judgment, but you can almost remember when you were in their shoes. For they are in drama or working on things that you have accomplished long ago. Why is it that you know you're an old soul, but that's all you know? If I said, *"Do you feel your Akash?"* You would tell me: *"Not really, but I sense I'm an old soul."*

Akashic Awareness

The first time capsule that is going to awaken in the Akash and pour out a new quantum energy is difficult to explain. I'm going to call it Akashic awareness. You're not going to be able to do anything with the Akash if you don't believe it's there, so it's the awareness of it that must be first. The reality of past lives is necessary, and for old souls it's going to be common. There will come a day when very few are going to roll their eyes when you talk about past lives. Just like you know you are alive and breathing right now, you'll know that you did it before, and you're going to do it again. It will be real to you. This is part of a new energy that The Crystalline Grid of the planet is helping with.

Oh, there's more: What else is in your Akash? What do you really think is the main time capsule? We know what it is, and you should have figured it out. It's *awakening to ancestral wisdom*, old soul, because you are your own Akashic ancestors. You know what's in there?

Let's review. What is in the Akashic Record of the Human Being? There are two major things: Experiences and learned knowledge. Some cultures honor their own elders and the older you become in a tribe, the higher elevation you are in their eyes of respect. Why is that? Experience and learned knowledge. Humanity has always looked at this as a positive thing. Can you imagine a time capsule awakening in your Akash that doesn't give you the facts of who you've been, but starts to slowly release what you've done and what you've learned? Can you imagine a baby coming into the planet who starts to explode with wisdom before its 3 or 4 in the same way that you saw the video of the child playing the piano? [A video given earlier in the seminar—a four-year-old playing like a master] What is the child remembering? Experience and learned knowledge. The hands on the keyboard were practiced moves. The knowledge of where to press the keys to make the music was something from the Akash. Can you imagine converting that to knowledge and wisdom, and not just the ability to play the piano? Do you understand what this time capsule could create? What happens with wisdom? Why do we revere those who were wise on the planet? It is because, so often, they were the ones who put things together for us. It's going to happen first with the old souls, and that brings us to the next subject.

The question has been asked, *"Will the Akash start to change, especially those karmic interactions in what you call karmic groups? What happens to that as Humans become more evolved? Will the actual organization of the karmic groups change?"* Let me ask you something: Twenty-three years ago, I spoke to my partner and he wrote down the words, "You can drop your karma." Most of the old souls in this room, have. You know how I know? It's because so many of you have been cast out of your family and friendships. It's uncomfortable to go home, and there are things you don't talk about anymore. You see, I know who's here. You dropped your karma.

Now let me ask you a basic question *"If you've dropped your karma, how can you be in a karmic group?"* The answer is you can't ... at least, not the ones you are used to. So the old established karmic groups are not going to change. Instead, there's going to be a new kind of group, an *old soul group* ... an Akashic group. This is the group that is being formed, and the very purpose of the old soul and the Akashic group is to create wisdom on the planet and shift energy. Let me explain:

We are now discussing how Humans come back into the Earth, and the attributes that might be different. Heretofore, they have returned into karmic groups in order to play out energies of unfinished business. However, now when you have thousands of old souls who have purposely dropped their karma, they cannot be in a karmic group. So what group are they in? They are in the "Non-karmic group" and this might surprise you.

No longer are you coming into groups to fulfill some purpose of an old energy. Instead, old souls are going to come into locations grouped together in places on the planet where they are needed to shift energy. It's not a karmic group, but a new kind of group, an Akashic group of old souls. You know how you're going to be able to tell where they are? Take a look at the young people and what they are doing. There are a lot of them in South America. What does this tell you? There is a shift going on here, dear ones. It's a shift that has a greater energy than almost anywhere else on Earth at the moment. Old souls are being born here in a greater number than almost anywhere on the planet. This is the new group and you can call it whatever you want to, but they're coming in with wisdom and with conceptual minds. They're going to have opportunities to awaken fast and come up with ideas that you've been waiting for, but it's a slow process for you.

I'm going to close with this. I'm going to put out an appeal. I'm going to ask the adults in the room for tolerance of the young. I'm going to ask you to suspend what you think these young people are doing, and instead to back up a moment and pause. They are using terms you have never heard and they're doing things that you believe may be odd or unusual. Some of you look at what they are doing and you're trying to correct it! They've invented something, all by themselves, called social networking. However, if you have been following the Kryon teachings, this is exactly what I told you over ten years ago would happen. I told you: "When everyone can talk to everyone, there can be no secrets."

The last thing that some governments want is to have most of the population communicating with one another freely and instantly. No secrets can be kept, and it exposes things going on that are not in integrity. That is what is happening. Now you have the youth of many countries openly talking to the youth of other countries, and most of them are under thirty. In the Middle East, Israelis are talking to Iranians and Palestinians all the time. They are doing it by the hundreds and thousands. No matter what their leadership is saying, the young people have an entirely different idea of what is going on. This is because they are talking to the actual citizens of the other countries. Some of them are saying, *"When we have the opportunity, we're going to stop this traditional enemy nonsense. We don't want war! We want good hospitals and schools, and what other societies have."* That's what the young are doing.

As for the adults? Many of them don't understand. They see all this technology as some kind of fad or even an irritant, perhaps. They are still tuned into their media boxes, listening to what those in charge wish them to hear and know.

I want you to back up and be tolerant, and understand what these young people are doing. It's a new paradigm on the planet, and it's going to assist with peace on earth. I told you to expect it, even if it looks juvenile or innocent. It is not. This is the old soul at his/her best and you're seeing a lot of it here in South America ... more here than in other places. It may shake some things up before they get better.

Old soul, be aware of your brothers and sisters coming in, who have just as many past lives as you do. Many of these old souls are now under twenty-five years old. Can you do this? This is my plea of the day, for you to start seeing them for who they are. It may even temper how you educate them, and how you perceive them. Our prediction is that when you start respecting who they are, they will turn around and greet you as the old soul that *you are*. The generation gap is about to close a bit, and old soul wisdom and awakening time capsules will help create this. This is the message of the day. I know who's here. I know the puzzles you carry, and the healings you have come for. Leave differently than you came.

And so it is.

Kryon live channelling "The Time Capsules in the Akash"
given in Sao Paulo Brazil — April 20, 2013

Your Akash is rich in experience. As the time capsules release within your Akash, they create new energies of thought in you. Kryon has said that we will begin to think of new things and some of us will consider doing things we have never done before. There is an awakening that begins within you and it's important that you pay attention to your thoughts and feelings because it is coming right out of your past lives and Akashic Record. You may even find you have developed talents that you never had before. That is called mining the Akash. This will help create synchronicities that would not have happened otherwise. Kryon has advised old souls to "pay attention" because there is a greater emphasis in synchronicity for the old souls than ever before.

The Pleiadians, our spiritual parents, came from the previous planet of free choice. Kryon has described what it was like when they crossed the marker of "The Pleiadian Dark Ages." So the placement of the time

168

capsules within Gaia, the cetaceans and us is significant. In fact, it is necessary in the test of whether or not humanity can create an ascended planet, and the reason is explained by Kryon.

As you become more quantum in your consciousness, your Akash is going to start growing in its awareness. It's not going to extend to just its first lifetime on the planet. Instead, many of you will start remembering what happened at the center point. This is the change of consciousness on the Pleiadian planets. By the way, there was more than one. Add that to your puzzle! [Kryon laugh] Right now Humans can't get along with themselves on a single planet. What if you had a planet that was close by? Can you imagine what you'd be doing with them? It gives you an idea of what the Pleiadians were able to do.

The Pleiadians were able to put together something that started in one way, but ended up with a pure aligned consciousness. That's a new term: *Pure aligned consciousness*: Can you imagine an Israeli, a Palestinian, and an Iranian having pure aligned consciousness? Can you picture this? Well, you have it with past enemies right now from your past world wars, so why not in the Middle East?

Old soul, where are these new ideas of pure aligned consciousness going to come from, for you have never had them in abundance on this planet? The answer is that they are going to come from your parents. Not your biological ones, but the ones you call the original source, the Pleiadians. You are aware that you have their DNA, or did you not realize that? They had the DNA of those before them, too. Did you realize that? You have the secrets of peace on the planet, since it's part of your "galactic Akash." You have the secrets and the wisdom that no one has developed here yet. This is why the old soul must return. Did you hear that?

Old soul, you are the future of the planet. You're the only ones who can carry the Pleiadian DNA that is this pure. You're the only ones who can reach down that far and bring up those hidden ideas, because you created and worked them once before, and it was not here. Ideas are not going to be given to you that you've not heard before. You're going to start *remembering* what you did, and skip right to the polished version of how to do it. What happened on the Pleiadian planets can happen here, and you will start with 3D issues and you will solve them first. People will look at some of these ideas and say, *"Why didn't we think of this before?"* You have done this before and we need you now, to do it again. This, dear one, means you're coming back.

Kryon live channelling "The Akash Awakens"
given in Orlando, Florida — January 26, 2013

Here are some final words from Kryon that may feel like a personal message. I believe it relates to awakening our Akash and releasing the wisdom and knowledge held within the time capsules. You may wish to ponder each question that Kryon asks. Feel, sense and observe your first intuitive thoughts. This may give you some insights into some of the answers that you have been looking for.

What is it that you've cast aside? What is it that you've tried and didn't work? What is it that was your passion, but in your mind you have put it aside because you decided it wouldn't work or the time wasn't right? Well, the time is now right!

There's a well of knowledge that is deep in this room, which is the Akashic Record of all who are before me both hearing and reading. It represents the lifetimes that have been lived and the knowledge that has been gained. It is the experience that you've all gone through and it can now surface and become part of this planet's actual Akash [part of the planet's reality].

All of it can now be placed upon that which we would call The Crystalline Grid. That is why you're here, to bring forth that which you know and have brought to manifestation. And I will tell you, old soul; it is why we say that less than one-half of one percent of you have to become Lightworkers in this way in order for the Earth to change.

Kryon live channelling "The Process"
given in Laguna Hills, California — December 4, 2011

Questions for Kryon:

As more humans recalibrate their relationship with their Akash, will it make it easier for others to awaken?

Answer:

Yes it will! Personal recalibration affects what the grids of the planet perceive as what Humans are doing that is benevolent and complete. As you know from the previous book, *The Gaia Effect*, the grids respond to Human consciousness. So in a seeming circle of cause and effect, the grids promote what the Human gives it. That then affects those in the future.

As more and more of humanity awakens to the idea of changing their relationship to the Akash, The Crystalline Grid (in particular) responds. It is the first and fastest grid to change. This is a domino effect, and it then postures the magnetic grid to change. Children are then born on the planet to the new energy of these grids and have the benefit of a faster awakening to mature thinking and the potential of finding the "God inside."

In the past, a lower consciousness of war and survival was the "energy of the day." This has been the energy for all of Human civilization. Fifty years ago, it started to change in anticipation of the 2012 marker. You were already changing it back then. By 1987, it was a "done deal." The potential was strong that you were not going to destroy yourselves this fifth time around and, indeed, you made it.

This is a new energy, a new potential and a new humanity. Everything you individually do is like creating a slightly brighter light to see by, allowing other Humans an opportunity to see what you saw. Without evangelizing anything, or even meeting them, many others will have the benefit of the light you created for the planet.

Can you tell us more about the Pleiadians having more than one planet? Does each new planet of free choice have different attributes in relation to the test of ascension? My intuition tells me that the nature of the test changes slightly for each planet of free choice and it is directly related to what happens in the Universe that is beyond our comprehension.

If you have such complete and correct answers already, then why do you ask them? [Kryon smile]

Let's answer the first one more completely, since you didn't already answer it. The Pleiadian system had multiple planets. One of the nine stars you see as the "Seven Sisters" has many planets that are in the "golden zone" definition. (This is a planet with an orbit that can sustain Human life as you know it.) Early in their science, the Pleiadians settled more than one of them and were able to start other civilizations. Space travel was easier for them. They needed and were given more quantum inventions, something you don't have yet. They didn't use fire and rockets and the force of physics as you do.

Yes, each planet is unique and has its own attributes for invention and illumination and development. The home Pleiadian planet is not a water planet. This is one of the reasons they wanted to also settle on one of their sister planets, very close ones in permanent, non-overlapping orbits that allowed easy travel at certain times during their year.

When the Pleiadians first examined the Earth, they knew it would work. Spirit led them right to it. One of the things they were most excited about was the ocean. It also helps explain why they were so enamored by the cetaceans. They simply didn't have anything like it!

Each planet of free choice was unique as well, and I remind you that you carry the spiritual Akash of these who went before you. At some level, you were on all of these planets, since the "soul group" that is used for all planets of free choice are a shared resource.

Think about it. You are your own ancestors in the sky.

Recent information has been given about the time capsules within Gaia [referring to the twelve polarized pairs, represented by twenty-four nodes and nulls]. As of the writing of this book, there have been two distinct events relating to these time capsules. The first event was the Lemurian Choir in Maui, Hawaii on December 21, 2012, where ALL of the time capsules were stimulated (enabled) for the release of information. The second event was the Kryon channel and ceremony by Kahuna Kalei'iliahi at Lake Titicaca on November 10, 2013, during which the very first time capsule was opened. Can you tell us more about this process and how we can activate Gaia's time capsules?

How can we stimulate our personal time capsules within our Akash?

First, these capsules don't contain anything at all! They are portals to the Pleiadian information that were ready to open with the passage of time (capsules that open to a portal of communication). So opening them simply enables real-time information to be delivered to Earth. A window doesn't contain information. But if there is an instructor standing outside and you open the window, you get the benefit of the information.

These are in pairs, since all balanced physics is also in pairs. Atomic structure is the same, and so is DNA. The structure of all things depends upon a balanced "push pull" energy. You see it as plus and minus, but it's not exactly like that. It's an interaction of the engine of benevolence and life-force. We have also told you that the energy at the center of your galaxy (black hole) is also this way. There are two energies there, not just one. So there is no such thing as a black hole. Someday your science will see this. A "singularity" in your physics is impossible, and that should be a clue. This has been Kryon information for two decades.

Pairs are activated together, and not just a null or a node. So there are only 12 potentials to activate, and you have identified three pairs so far and activated two of them by visiting the nodes. Activation scenarios can happen almost anytime that is correct for the time, but two of them were needed to be activated before 2014. The rest of them should be activated within the final 18 years of the precession of the equinox time frame (by 2030). It is not necessary that I be there with my partner for this. Many will be activated by others who are in touch with this process and close to it. When the time is correct, it will be synchronistic and appropriate to activate a time-capsule pair. You will *know*.

Activation of personal time capsules within the DNA is another complete issue, for these time capsules are very different from the 12 Pleiadian ones on the planet. They are personal capsules, left by you for you within your own Akash. [Kryon smile]

Chapter Seven

The Three Parts of the Human

Kryon often talks about the energy of the three. Three is a catalytic number. The Earth has three main energy grids: Magnetic Grid, Gaia, and The Crystalline Grid. Detailed information about these grids, as given by Kryon, features in my previous book, *The Gaia Effect*. Other aspects of these three grids are also described in Chapter Two: Your Personal Akashic Record.

The energy of three also applies to humans. Kryon has recently identified the nine attributes (energies) of a Human, existing as three sets of three. They are in a circle as a multi-dimensional soup of energy in which they all work together. They do not work separately. One may be stronger or weaker in its potentials, but all nine are in a soup. The three sets of three are represented by the Human Group, the Soul Group and the Gaia Group.

I'm going to explain one set of the three. The other two sets are very esoteric, quite complex and difficult to explain. However, stay tuned because they will be described in my next book (smile). That's right; I'm researching the third book in this trilogy series of Kryon information simultaneously as I write this one!

The easiest set of three to explain are the three energies of the Human Group. They are the Higher-Self, Human Consciousness and Innate.

Higher-Self

Humanity in general sees every Human Being as one individual that represents a singular energy. Most humans that believe in God feel that God is a separate entity. This is part of the Human set-up and our duality. Many believe that you can connect with God, through a series of epiphanies and decisions, and only then can you join this larger energy we call God. This comes from our bias of singularity in 3D. We see ourselves as individual and, therefore, search for a singular source of spiritual power. When we find a spiritual system that suits our culture and our personal ideals, this search is complete. We honor this system, but we often stay the same without changing our lives because the search is over.

The many Masters that walked the planet had a profound connection to God. Often, they were seen as God and worshipped as such even after their death. This is understandable, because humans see themselves as a singular entity. Most of the Masters understood they were not singular. They were showing us what is possible and that we all have the potential to be Masters. The Masters showed us there are many ways to become one with God. This is why the many spiritual systems are seen by Spirit as appropriate for those who use them.

What the Masters were actually demonstrating to us is that the Higher-Self is not separate or apart from the Human Being. Your Higher-Self is your own pipeline to connect with the God in you. It is the hardest thing for us to realize. We prefer to see God as far more magnificent, intelligent and lovable than as something that is a part of us. The Higher-Self, is therefore, part of the system of love that is not singular and is always available in your DNA. It is the portal that opens you to connect with God. This is why learning to love yourself is one of the most important life lessons. When you love yourself, you are indeed loving and honoring God.

When you begin to get in touch with your Higher-Self, things begin to change in your life. You start to realize the divinity within you and others. There is often confusion between the Higher-Self and the soul. The difference between them is this: one describes the whole and the other describes a part.

Your **SOUL** includes all the "selves" that you have. It is your "divine wholeness" and includes the "I AM" presence you have in the Universe. Your soul is 100 percent divine and is the "real" you. It resides in several places at the same time. One piece is within each cell of your body. Another is an energy "stamp" on the magnetics of the planet itself, which indicates that you are here. Your soul knows everything and is far larger than we can ever realize. It is Family. It is LOVE!

Your **HIGHER-SELF** is the part of you directly involved in communication with God. It is a part, or section of you that is "connected" full-time to the family. Your Higher-Self creates solutions for your incarnation on the planet and responds to your enlightenment, your changing path and all new planning sessions. Your Higher-Self is, therefore, the portal, and it is profoundly spiritual.

Why is the portal called the Higher-Self? Why is it higher? Kryon has told us it is the part of us that vibrates higher than any other part of our 3D cellular structure. It is vibrating at the frequency of the Creator. In summary, Kryon has said that the Higher-Self: *is*

177

really a portal to the largest sacred part of you that split off when you came into the planet. It facilitates the very communication with God through prayer and meditation and is the "I AM" layer. It is seen as the pipeline to the other side of the veil, and is often called "The Holy Spirit."

Human Consciousness

In psychology, the term "consciousness" is commonly used to indicate a state of awareness of self and environment. Conscious behavior includes cognitive processes such as thinking, perception and planning. Scientists were once skeptical about the existence of consciousness. Today it is a significant research topic in psychology and neuroscience. In fact, a team of multidisciplinary scientists and physicians have joined forces to create The Human Consciousness Project. Their aim is to research the nature of consciousness and its relationship with the brain. It is recognized that when we are conscious, we are aware. However, awareness is only a part of consciousness. Other aspects of consciousness include free will, reasoning, visual imagery, recalling and making choices.

Human consciousness is what we use every day. It is aligned to your cellular structure. It is what you are using as you read this book. Basic Human consciousness is designed for survival. When you operate in survival mode you are using Human consciousness. When you encounter danger, your survival instincts kick in and you fight or flee. Human consciousness has kept us alive. Kryon has often referred to Human consciousness as the *survival layer*. As long as you are in survival mode you will never get beyond it to experience the multi-dimensional aspects of yourself. Your survival layer depends on you reacting to the outside world. You always have to be alert. You always need to ensure that what you say is the right thing. You look at others and situations and judge what is best for survival. So how do we get out of survival mode? Kryon explains how in a channel called *"The Process."*

You know how to get rid of pure survival? Spirit knows. How many of you have been brought to your knees through sorrow or health? How many of you? I know who's here, and I'm talking to you. You know what I mean, because suddenly, survival goes away and the conscious layer drops before you. Then all you see is the love of God. All you see is gratitude for those around you and a peacefulness of just being alive and well. That, dear ones, is the position you have to be in. But why wait for an emergency? Why not understand it and work on doing that very thing by yourself?

Step one: Get out of survival! *"How do I do that, Kryon?"* Consider this: *"Dear Spirit, I wish to soften my consciousness. When those who would insult me are trying to push my emotional anger buttons, I don't want the buttons to work anymore. I want to disengage them. I don't want to react anymore. I want to sit in peace. That is getting out of survival. I am safe in the arms of God — totally and completely safe. I wish to drop the outer shell that is the Human consciousness layer, the one that instantly and only reacts to 3-D, and walk my life differently."* That would be the first step. That's the first step, dear one. Look in the mirror while you say it.

Do you defend yourself? If somebody criticizes you, are you quick to make it right? How many of you can hear a criticism of yourself, then stop and think, *"Wow, what if they're right?"* It's hard for a Human Being to do this, and you can't do that easily. You've got to practice that one. You know why? Because

179

you're designed for survival. In the old energy, it served you well and now it doesn't.

Basic Human consciousness is designed for survival, and you have passed that marker. It carries an old energy with it that breeds hatred and war, disappointment and depression. It carries self-doubt with it and always makes you feel alone. Do you really wish to wallow anymore in this? It is time to change it from survival to "peaceful existence with wisdom."

I want to take you to the consciousness of the masters of the planet who are all here. If you stood before Christ and said, *"Well, I don't really like what you're wearing,"* what do you think the Master would say? Would he defend? *"Well, it's fine with me. It suits me well, and I got a good deal on it."* (After all, he was Jewish.) [Laughter] But that's not what he would say! You know better. He would look in your eyes and look right through you. He would look into the piece of God that he knows and loves dearly and you would melt before him. That's what would happen. He would love you into a place where you would see the face of God.

Muhammad walked into a cave and met an angel, who told him to unite the tribes of Arabia and give them the God of Israel. That's what happened and he did. He knew the love of God. He walked softly and he was beautiful. He wouldn't give you a defensive answer either, and neither would Buddha. These are masters who long ago gave away the survival layer and worked with an energy of softness from within.

More currently, if you could walk the Earth again with Paramahansa Yogananda right now and look into his eyes and say, *"You know, your robe smells funny,"* what kind of response do you think you would get? In fact, who would ever say that? Believe me, there are some who would. This master would look at you with the love of God and melt you, because you would see in him no judgment, no hurt—only truth. There is no survival agenda with a master. There is no survival consciousness with mastery. Do you see what I'm saying? What happens when you can accomplish that, when you can soften the survival, is that you start getting in touch with *Innate*.

Kryon live channelling "The Process"
given in Laguna Hills, California — December 4, 2011

Kryon also talks about how Human consciousness can change chemistry. This is something we do every day. When we are happy and laugh and experience joy, all of the chemistry in our body is changed. When we are sad or experience fear, all of the chemistry in our body is changed. When we fall in love, all of the chemistry in our body is changed. Human consciousness is, therefore, the part of us that connects with 3D.

Many of us, including scientists and physicians, assume Human consciousness is all there is. However, this is not the case. Human consciousness is limited. How do we know that it is limited? The reason is, that we often have something going on in our body, with which we are not in touch. If Human consciousness is all there is, why doesn't it know what is going on inside us? How come you can have a disease growing in your body and you don't know about it? You have to go to a doctor to find out that you have had a particular disease for a year. Why didn't your body tell you? Why would God design us in such a limited way? It is not our design that is limited. It is Human consciousness that is limited. Remaining in survival mode will prevent you from seeing the other aspects that every Human Being has.

Every Human Being has another form of intelligence that is just as big as Human consciousness. Have you ever heard of the term "muscle testing?" In the natural medicine field, this is known as kinesiology. Kinesiology is the process whereby your body lets you know things that you don't know consciously. Muscle testing is primarily used to identify imbalances in the body. This therapy is best known for its effectiveness in treating food allergies or sensitivities. The essential tool that kinesiology relies on is the muscle feedback system. Our muscle tension is determined from our memories and all the information about our physical, emotional and mental state. A weak muscle test can indicate that stress is having a negative effect somewhere in the system. The body is aware of what it needs to heal. Kinesiology facilitates that information, in order to aid the natural healing process. What is this part of the body that kinesiologists get in touch with? Kryon has often talked about our intelligent body consciousness and has called it Innate.

Innate

Innate is the largest intelligence in your body. Kryon tells us that Innate is something that has understanding with no logic. When we muscle test, we often ask specific questions. For example, you can hold a substance in your hand and ask the question: Does my body need this substance? The muscle test response will indicate either yes or no. Kryon has challenged us to think bigger than this. What about asking the question: Is there something wrong with my body that I don't know about? Yes or no, the body will tell us. We tend not to do this. Most of us, including myself will often need a doctor to run tests to find out what ails us. But if we could have a conversation with Innate we would know exactly what our body needs. Innate is connected to everything, including Human consciousness. Kryon has explained what Innate is and how it works, in many channels. Regardless of your level of understanding, the following Kryon channel is sure to help:

Higher-Self, Human Consciousness, and Innate (some of which are overlapping), are all in the Merkabah. Innate knows everything chemically that's going on in your body. Now I'm going to tell you what else Innate controls: Innate is what sorts out the information in your stem cells. That is Innate's job. I want to ask you some questions: Are you aware that every piece of DNA is identical? Hundreds of billions—trillions of molecules of DNA in you are absolutely identical and unique. They have your chemical and quantum imprint. They have your Akashic Record and your angelic name, and they are all identical. From the tip of your head, to your toe, they are identical. So how is it that they can make cells that are so different? How do they know where they are, or how to coordinate all this?

The answer is because your DNA, these identical pieces, work together in a way that has not been discovered yet. It's critical to health, yet science has not seen it yet. You have to admit that there is an intelligence there that is not what our brain is producing. Your Innate gives information to a very tiny percent of the DNA chemistry, which then makes the genes of the Human body. The stem cells are the templates for these genes. The engine of the race car that propels your body around life is only 3 percent of DNA. Ninety percent is the blueprint that is the template for the race engine. Innate is smart and intelligent. It's what we call "body intelligence." Are you seeing what we are saying? Innate can instruct your body to build a better engine, and the blueprints are there for it... perfect stem cell blueprints in your DNA.

And you might say *"I don't understand any of this. If that's the truth of things, then why don't I know it?"* Here is the answer: It's because Innate, like your DNA, is in a quantum state. It is multi-dimensional and not in 3D. You can't talk to it easily, either. It's not a synapse in your brain. It's in your DNA! Wouldn't it be nice if you could put Human consciousness and your brain, together with Innate? Wouldn't that be something? Right now you are not joined with Innate. You have to muscle test to find out even the most basic things going on in your body...

...How does it work? In a linear world, it looks chaotic, but it's quantum. Let me give you some examples. Let's say you are lying in the hospital. Oh dear Human Beings, this is so powerful, yet the times it happens on the planet so few, yet so beautiful. I want to show you what Innate can do: Innate is in control of your biology, absolute control. It can do anything. It can keep you alive for 900 years if you program for it. You think those biblical reports about those who lived that long had to be flawed? *"They couldn't have lived that long,"* you say. Oh yes they did! Innate made sure of it ... total control of the Human cellular instructions and the engine of the genes.

You're lying in the hospital. You learn of a terminal disease alive in you, and you're going through the processes. It starts to scare you to death. Then somehow, through some magic that you don't understand, you connect to the Innate for just a moment in a state of unaware surrender. Then you have something called *spontaneous remission* and the disease disappears! The immune system comes up to the challenge and wipes it out of your body! The seemingly impossible happens and science looks at you and asks the question, *"How did you do that?"* Maybe if you get scared enough it will happen? No. That's not the answer. But Innate took care of it, and that's how powerful it is. Now, understand that what Innate used was the template for a non-diseased Human that is in your Akash. The blueprint was already there! There was no miracle performed from "beyond." Are you understanding this?

...Innate can do many things you haven't thought about, or even considered on your list. What if you would like to stop aging as much? Innate is very good at that. All you have to do is connect with it. I want to give you a process yet again, which I have told you about before. Are you aware that the Human body reproduces itself and rejuvenates all the organs? It's built to never die, yet it does. It does because that which it rejuvenates is not perfect. But it can be, and it could be, if it only worked a little better.

There is a reason why you age. The reason is the imprint that you have placed upon the energy of the planet. It is why those in the past lived some 600 or 700 years, but you only get 80. Something has happened with the energy of this planet that has actually affected the blueprint of the stem cells. I just said a mouthful. Listen: Every time a cell reproduces to make another one, there is a query within the division process. That is to say, a question is asked. The nucleus of the cell is about to pull apart with cell division. It's about ready to make another one just like itself, but right before it does, there is a question. Innate is the one doing the asking and answering: *"Do I make a copy of this one, or go to the blueprint?"* And the question is answered by this question: *"Is there new information?"* The answer: *"No, so make a copy."*

Can you imagine for a moment, perhaps in that split second of time when the cell is splitting, if the answer was, *"Wait a minute, there's some new information. I want your telomeres to lengthen, go to the original blueprint within the stem cell and enable it."* Then you produce something which is pristine, and better than the old one, and the Human Being alters the aging process, and lives a very long time. Perhaps it improves the immune system? Perhaps it improves many things? But it makes a new one, and not a copy of the old one.

What would that "new information" be? The answer is, that Human Consciousness was starting to change The Crystalline Grid, which is part of the measure of the vibration of the planet. As the planet vibrates higher, more of DNA is enabled. This is the Gaia Effect, and [the information] has been given many times before. It affects Human life.

Your consciousness, Innate, and your Higher-Self are ready to create a body which does not age nearly as much, and where you don't have to worry as much about disease. It's more than just chemistry. It's consciousness over matter. You can start to have peace, and you can demand less drama around you. You become a different Human Being, and your friends will notice — not all of them appreciating it.

Perhaps you are beginning to put this together? These are the things that the masters of the planet told you. This is also no different than what the Ancients knew, talked about, and gave to you. You now sit in a new energy, one where these things are upon you and you are beginning to feel them. What are you going to do with it?

"Well Kryon, you still haven't told us how to do all this." All right, I will: There is a bridge and it's called intuition. Intuition is the multi-dimensional message system for the Human Being. It is not generated from the brain, and it is not perceived in a linear way. It's coming through the portal of the Higher-Self, and it's always correct for you. But you need to learn to decipher it. Spiritual intuition is just a graduate of Human intuition within your own body.

Intuition is the bridge with Innate. Start using that intuitive power which every single Human has. What is the first intuitive answer when you ask a question? Don't discount that information! I know it feels like a fleeting thought, or that you made it up, but don't discount it when it doesn't make sense.

Sometimes, when presented with intuition, you go into a concentrated state of intellectual inquiry. What does it mean? Was it me or something else? Why not instead, speak to your body right now. Innate is YOU, dear one, so you can talk to it: *"Dear Spirit/body/Innate, I choose to meld with you in whatever form you decide. Dear Innate, thank you for being in me, with me, and protecting me. Thank you for the field around me that keeps me safe. Thank you that I'm able to hone the intuition so that I'll know the truth."*

Innate can tell you if somebody is lying to you. Innate is what allows you to know that this channelling is real. Innate knows more than the linear Human consciousness produced by the brain. Innate is a quantum state. It is the quantum part of the Human Being.

In the theory of super strings, scientist say there are eleven dimensions at the center of the atom. Actually, there are more than 27 — they'll find that out. So, what's in the others? It's all known by Innate and you own it. It is information that can be written and rewritten within your DNA, and it can affect your stem cells, and talk directly to your biology. That's not all. For here it comes, full circle.

We have said to you before: Why don't you consider *mining* the Akash? That is to say, why not try picking up those things in past lives that you've lived through, and that you've earned? They are there, lurking in you, just waiting to be used. But because you are 3D, you think they are in the past and they are just something you look at like a history book. You don't understand that in a quantum state there is no time. Use them! Use them all!

"Kryon, How?" And the answer is Innate, through intuition. Innate is ready to pick the ones that you need right now, because it knows and has been waiting for your instructions and permissions in this new energy. Don't pretend you know what you need! Human consciousness is limited to 3D. You know what you *want*, but only Innate knows what you *need* to accomplish what you came for. Isn't that beautiful?

Innate represents the benevolent God in you. It's a system that is bigger than you thought. Many of these things are going to be seen soon. Don't be shocked and surprised if medical science, including that which is called Quantum Biology, starts to prove what I am telling you today. It won't be that long.

How smart is Innate? Let me show you: When a Human Being has his/her spinal cord severed, the result is often paralysis and a wheelchair for life. It's odd, however, that the heart keeps beating. Where are the signals coming from? They used to come from the brain, and regulate the heartbeat. Medical science will tell you it's this or that. But it isn't the brain! The connection is gone. Why do many of those with a severed spinal cord still have reproductive activity? Where is that coming from? What about digestion? That's supposed to be totally brain.

The answer, my dear friends, is Innate. Its' "The Second Brain," because it's connected to the DNA system, and always was. You're starting to get a picture and it's beautiful. That's the message of today.

What are you going to do with this? Why don't you start a process of talking to your cells on a regular basis. Speak to your Higher-Self at the same time, almost as though the two were one. Speak to Innate: *I know you're there!* The beauty of this is that Innate is not set apart from Human consciousness. It's aligned with it. It is the multi-dimensional part of what you already have. Innate is you taking care of you in the best way it can, even if you can't talk to it. Find a way through intuition to *know* more about what is going on within you.

You'll get to a place, dear ones, where talking to Innate is going to be second nature. It's all done through that part of you which is intuitive, and you can do it every moment of every day. That is when you get peace. That is when you start to fall in love with yourself. It's beautiful, possible, and doable. As you walk the planet, the plants will know—the animals will know. They are all hooked into it. Beautiful it is.

That's our message. That's what we want to tell you. It's another exposition of the God in you. I am Kryon, in love with Humanity. Go from this place changed.

And so it is.

Kryon live channelling "The Three Parts"
given in Memphis, Tennessee — February 26, 2011

Hopefully, you now have a clearer idea of what Innate is and, more importantly, how we can become better at communicating with Innate. Kryon told us that the bridge to Innate is our intuition. Most of us experience intuition as a gut feeling. Sometimes, we even act against this gut feeling and the outcome is disappointing. That's when we usually say, "I knew that would happen," and yet we ignored the warning. Using my intuition wasn't something I learned at school. Most of my experience with intuition has been a process of trial and error. The more we *practice* listening to our intuition, the better we become.

Why not have fun experimenting with your intuition. For example, I'll be in the supermarket and ask Innate if there is anything I need. I will get this feeling to buy some cheese. My logical brain will interrupt and remind me that there is already cheese at home in the fridge. I ignore my logic and get some cheese. When I arrive home, I discover the cheese in the fridge has spoiled and can't be eaten. I sure am glad I listened to my intuition. Thanks a million, Innate!

I don't always get it right. Sometimes I ignore my intuition without realizing it. I was getting ready to take my dog for a walk. I always take a plastic bag, in case she leaves something behind (if you know what I mean). My intuition was telling me to take a second plastic bag, just in case. I ignored this very good advice, only to be found in the park staring at my dog in horror as she was leaving behind her second deposit of the day on our walk! That was a bad time to have ignored Innate (sigh). Never mind. The truth is, I'll have many more opportunities to practice. How about you?

In the meantime, I'd like to introduce another channel Kryon gave about Innate. Some of the information is repeated from the previous channel, but there are new ideas that will enhance our knowledge and understanding of this marvelous aspect of ourselves called Innate.

Innate

The word *Innate* is part of Human consciousness. All of you have this at the corporeal level and we are going to discuss that today in a way we've never discussed before. We will be telling you only a little bit about it, but hopefully enough to tweak your interest and make you understand that there is more to you than you think — much more.

Innate has been described in the past as the *smart part of your cells*. Now, that might indicate that there's also a *non-smart* part, but let us say that it's a more ignorant part, and believe it or not, that ignorant part is your brain. Now the brain perceives many things and it's a most excellent calculator. It's the best memory and relational computational instrument on the Earth today. Everything that you have experienced is in your brain. It tempers how you behave, what you do, how you act, what you believe, and how you perceive things. But let me tell you where it falls short. It doesn't know anything about what's going on within your cells or your emotional body. It may send signals to operate your body, but it is blind to what happens after that. It is also easily confused.

Your Brain is Not "In The Loop"

You can intellectualize this for a very long time, yet you will never find out from your brain how your cells are doing. Do you have an allergy to something that your body has not experienced yet? Perhaps it is a food you have never tasted or a chemical you have not seen. How would you know? As you begin to eat the food, or ingest the chemical, shouldn't the brain yell, *"Don't do that! You are allergic to it! You will pay the price!"* But it does not. It is not connected to cellular structure. But the Innate is.

The Innate is the smart corporeal body. It knows everything about your overall system. It actually is as smart as your brain, but in a different way. So, what can a Human Being do to find out if he/she is allergic to something? Let's say that is you, so you can ask your brain, but it has no idea. So instead, you place the food or chemistry in your hand and *muscle-test* it. That is called kinesiology, a big word for something very simple. Muscle-testing is using the body's *Innate* to give you a "yes or no" signal about something it knows about, but that your brain does not.

So in the process of kinesiology, do you understand that you have acknowledged that there is a part of your body system that knows more than your brain? Indeed, this is a process that has been used for centuries, and it's very accurate.

This Innate knows a lot more than what you are allergic to, my friend. It is also tuned in completely to the quantum parts of your DNA that know everything about your spiritual and cellular evolvement. Innate handshakes with your Higher-Self at all the *three Human group levels*, and that is difficult to describe. If you put this information in a circle chart, you can draw the lines between the groups and you'd see what I mean. It's your smart body, and it's connected to everything.

Let me ask you a question, dear one: Don't you find it odd that there are certain kinds of diseases that can lurk within your cells, that can attack you, yet you only know it through your discomfort or through your death! What kind of brain do you have that would not tell you about this? You never have the signal through your brain about any of it except discomfort and pain! But Innate knows about it the moment it happens. Innate knows when it entered your body. As your white blood cells go to the places they need to fight, your entire immune system goes into alert! Yet you have no idea about it, since your brain is just doing what it always does — it computes and remembers. But, in this case, it does a very poor job helping you survive.

About Innate

What is Innate? Where is it? This is difficult to explain. We told you, dear Human Being, that the elusive Akash information is not in your brain, either. You cannot go to your brain to find out who you used to be in a past life. The Innate is the same. It's not in your brain, but instead it's in every cell of your body and every molecule of your DNA. The difference between Innate and the Akash is that Innate is *on top (a linear concept for you)*, and it is always broadcasting, always there. If you know how to listen to it and where it is, you can tune in. Muscle-testing is one way of knowing, a very basic way. Some of you also know that Innate responds to acupuncture. Did you know that? Your brain does not.

The Merkabah—Innate's Quantum Field

Innate is aware of all things at the cellular level and is broadcasting all the time. It broadcasts so well that it flows into that which you call the Merkabah of the body. Now, the Merkabah is a quantum field around your body that pulses very strongly with esoteric information, including corporeal health. Many have the ability to see and read this field.

A medical intuitive can stand before you in various degrees of success and *read* the messages from your Innate. This intuitive person does not have to muscle-test to know you've got something going on within your cells. They can *see it* or *sense* it within the field around your body. Now, you may have thought that a medical intuitive is looking at your liver or your heart, doing some kind of analysis. That's very linear thinking and is not what is happening. That's your box of belief working overtime. Instead, the medical intuitives are sensing the quantum energy within your field that your Innate is broad-casting about your health, of what's going on in the chemistry, and of what might be developing inside you. It's different than you thought, isn't it? That's the Innate and that's only one of the things that Innate does.

Mining the Akash — The Role of Innate

What I'm going to tell next, we have given you before. However, I wish to explain it better in this communication. Your Innate is also a governor of what you personally need. Let me explain: Turn a page with me. We have talked in the past about *mining the Akash*. So let us open that door for a moment. Is it possible, dear one, that you could go into the vast storehouse of the attributes of your past lives and pick out something that you need today? The answer is yes. It's called mining the Akash, and it is a staple of the Kryon teaching. However, the way it's accomplished by the individual Human is really difficult to describe. It's a personal intuitive process. However, one attribute of it that is often misunderstood is that *permission from the Innate is needed*. This is because the Innate *smart body* knows what you need. It is then the governor, or the filter, giving you permission regarding what can be pulled out of your Akash and used. It will say *no* to frivolous things and *yes* to the things that will allow you to cure yourself of disease, live longer, and increase the efficiency of your DNA. It's a smart body regulator.

Innate doesn't care how you look. It cares about your health. If you want to go into your Akash and pull out something that you need for survival, it's right there with you. If you want to make clearer skin, it won't respond. Do you see what I mean? It's the governor for *mining the Akash*. By the way, the Akash is very ready to be used for this. [Kryon wink]

You have earned what you've lived, dear ones, and it's very available. It lies in a *quantum soup of lifetime information* that is ready to be used. If you have a disease in your body right now, and perhaps you want to mine the Akash in a way that will create healing, you can. Like all nonlinear things, it requires a new, mature consciousness and practice to work. But the body is ready for you to "go get" the cellular structure of a past life that had no disease. The blueprint for this resides within you since you earned it and lived it. The Innate is responsible for *spontaneous remission!* Science has no idea how a Human does this. The Innate can help you "go get" the things within your *earned Akash* and place them into your cellular structure. That's how smart it is! Imagine clearing disease so completely that there is no sign it was ever there? It happens all the time. Imagine being able to drop a chemical dependency overnight? It's exactly the same principle.

Did you ever sit in a meeting and something is said or a feeling can happen, and you get chills? What are they? You might say, *"They are chills of validation."* Guess where they came from? The Innate! The Innate has the ability to *signal you the truth*. The brain does not. In fact, your brain will often get in the way. It's the brain that contains your *box of belief*. It's the brain that contains the perception of who you are based on experience and memory. It's your 3D survival instrument. But the brain can't give *truth*. It can only give you what it perceives as the truth, based on logical, processed, computed, synaptic reasoning and only based on your past experience.

Your brain can tell you not to touch the stove because of what happened once before. But it can't give you chills of validation from information it does not have. The intellect wants you to believe that your brain is supreme. However, the brain is only one part of the body system and not a very intuitive part. It is the Innate that knows the truth. The Innate is connected to the quantum parts of your DNA and, therefore, also knows of your spirituality and the truth of God inside.

The Next Step

One of the attributes of the future Human Being is to build a bridge between your Human consciousness and your Innate. This is one of the three things in the cellular parts of the nine attributes lesson, the Human energies part. This needs to be a bridge of new tools so you no longer have to muscle-test. In fact, you can become your own medical intuitive. Doesn't this make sense? So, when a virus or bacteria invades your body—something your brain can't warn you about—you will *know it* anyway! This bridge will begin to complete the Human Being's evolution and is a logical next step for longer life. I know this makes sense to you. You should be able to sense these things when they occur rather than going to a doctor for tests. Going to a doctor for tests is not a bad thing, but it should validate what you know is happening and not be the discovery of it.

The Second Brain

Innate does so many things for you! Some of you are starting to get a bigger picture of where I'm going with this discussion. Here is a concept that we've not really broached before. We're going to give it a name, but please do not misunderstand it. You only have one word for your intelligent control center, and the word is called *brain*. So we are going to give you a concept that the Innate is your *second brain*. It doesn't function like your first one at all, but it is smart and it is intelligent and it knows what you need. Sometimes it can even replace a function that your logical brain normally does.

Let me show you what I mean. Here is a puzzle, a conundrum of medicine: When an accident happens that severs your spinal cord completely, it leaves you with no feeling or muscle function from the [neck] down. This is because the signals from the brain to your muscles are no longer able to be sent. The pathway for those signals is severed. You then spend the rest of your life in a chair, perhaps even being fed by others. But the puzzle is that there are some things within you that continue to function anyway. One of them is your heart. Another is digestion. Many of these things continue to work, even though you are told that your brain, the central nervous system, the organ that sends all the signals to make things work, had its signals severed. The conduit where the signals are sent within the spine is broken. So what keeps all these organs below the neck going?

Your heart depends upon signals from the brain to function. It needs the electrical pulses sent from specific parts of the brain, creating a synchronized rhythm, in order for the heart to beat. Yet the brain is disconnected and the heart keeps its rhythm. How can that work? Now I'll tell you: The Innate takes over and continues the signal. It's always there, for the Merkabah is body-wide, not centralized in one place as your brain is. The organs will continue to function, but the pathway to the muscles is gone. Even reproduction can still happen! The heart keeps going and digestion continues, and all without connection to the brain.

Innate is smart! It's a second brain. Medical science is often puzzled over this, and I just gave you the answer. So Innate is the intelligence in your body that is smarter about cellular things than your brain. Now I want to wrap this all up.

What are you supposed to do with all this information? I want you to get in touch with Innate. It's the *heart connection*, dear ones. The Higher-Self, Innate and Human consciousness are the three Human energies that need to meld—Human consciousness, Higher-Self and Innate.

When DNA starts to work at a higher efficiency, there are bridges that start to be built between these things. You'll start to feel them when you recognize and sense truth. When you start to have discernment and cognize things for what they are, you stop looking around for answers. You are far more self-contained, and your answers are often the same as those around you who have the same discernment engine. All this now comes from within, instead of an outside source.

Many will tell you this is all nonsense. They tell you about God and ask you to believe them. They tell you that you were born dirty, or that there are societies trying to control you, or that everywhere you look there's a conspiracy against you. They generate fear, and the result is Human fear, confusion, separation and even war.

What if you could start understanding the truth from the Innate within? You would understand that you are a piece of God on this planet, and you can discern what is and what is not happening around you. The Human Being becomes smarter when the two brains come together and you're able then to see your own health situation, to catch things before they get out of hand, and even to sense the truth of God within the beautiful system of your Akash.

We told you this in the Akash discussion earlier. Every single one of you has a different diet based upon what works for you. There is no such thing as an enlightened diet, except the one given by your own discernment. The Innate is smart. It works with your Akash and it knows all about your soul aspects. It is connected to your Higher-Self. It knows what diet will work for you, based on your immediate past lives. This is in your Akash, and your Innate is in touch with it.

Now, as you start to build a bridge to Innate, everything starts to change. The questions that you ask in this room (and they're always the same) will not have to be asked: *"Dear Kryon, how can (your name goes here) mine my Akash? I (your name goes here) want to go here, I want to know this, I want to know that. How can I (your name goes here) create this and that in our lives?"*

Dear one, the day is coming when you will never have to ask these things, any more than you would ask a person on the street how to walk. Someday, when it comes to esoteric things, you won't feel you're in the dark or that there are missing pieces. When Innate starts to be present in your consciousness, concepts will start to meld and the missing pieces will start to fill in. You're going to be a lot smarter about who you are, and one of the things that's going to occur is you'll know you're not from here! You will sense it! You're from the great central sun. You're from where I am from, and you'll know that you're eternal! You'll know that you've had more than one life, and it will be something that you *know* just like Innate *knows* it and not something you intellectualize with the computer in your head.

It's the heart connection, dear ones. Innate is what creates emotion. Let me tell you, dear ones, that Innate helps you fall in love. Innate gives you energies that you can't explain. Innate makes you just a little nuts (nobody can explain the "in love" feeling), but Innate knows all about it. Innate can change every cell of your body, and it will *ring true* with information and help for you personally. This will create more discernment and a wise Human. There's nothing like it, and the most important thing is that "truth is truth," and more and more Humans will see what you see. Can you see how Innate would serve humanity and how it shakes hands with your Higher-Self and knows about God?

This has been our story for this day—about something in you that is amazing and ready to work for you. Perhaps you may have not known the extent of it or what it was? Perhaps you didn't know how it worked or how important it is? Now you know a little more. Finally, the beautiful part: It's not an entity inside you, dear ones. It's you—the bridge from the corporeal body to the Higher-Self, the smart part of your cells. And so it is.

Kryon live channelling "The Mysterious Innate" given in Gaithersburg, Maryland—August 31, 2013

Innate is designed to give us what we need. Innate will help us mine the Akash. The more we practice and communicate with Innate, the better we get. This involves listening to your intuition. When you give pure intent to change your life, to change your habits, you will always receive full support from Innate. It's a partnership that is available to you, if you choose. Humans who communicate with Innate are the pioneers of humanity. I believe that eventually, modern medicine will acknowledge and communicate with Innate throughout every step of medical treatment. It wasn't that long ago, that mainstream medicine didn't believe in germs, because they were invisible. Today, germs are visible under the microscope. When the planet has a quantum invention that shows a human's quantum field (Merkabah) I think it will forever change our approach to health and healing. In the meantime, we are very blessed to have Kryon giving us this advance information that we can utilize now.

If you are interested in additional information on Innate, please visit the "Extra's" tab on my website: www.monikamuranyi.com

Questions for Kryon:

In the new energy many things are recalibrating. There is a recalibration of Gaia, the Universe, The Crystalline Grid, humanity, wisdom, knowledge, awareness, perception and love. Can you tell us about the recalibration of the relationship that humans have with their Higher-Self?

Answer:

This is astute of you to ask, and indirectly it has been answered within the "recalibration channellings." But specifically, the relationship with your Higher-Self can be measured esoterically by *how strong the portal is with your own pineal*. It's about the communication to source that changes this relationship and more.

In the past few years, you have started using sounds to enhance the communications and it's working well. This is just an example of some very new ways to start strengthening your pineal's quantum attributes. This will serve several purposes all at once: (A) The pineal's portal expansion will start to create a much closer relationship with your Higher-Self; (B) You will feel this happening through increased intuitive communications; and (C) Your Innate will start creating a better bridge to your 3D consciousness.

So, work harder on recognizing intuitive communications. This is one of the biggest keys, since intuition is the only way Spirit can communicate directly. It can't do it through your 3D brain synapse, so this involves your Higher-Self and your Innate. See how it all fits together? It's a recalibration of how you perceive your own thinking process.

So the strength of your connection to the Higher-Self is measured by how well you recognize intuitive thought. How are you doing?

What advice do you have for Lightworkers who are in places where many humans are in "survival mode" and there is a very low vibration of Human consciousness?

Holding your light is not dependent on who is around you. A light bulb gets its light from the power of the socket it is plugged into. It doesn't depend on how many other light bulbs are around it.

As you find yourself in places where there is simply no one of like mind, you are still plugged into source and you still have the full energy of your light being to draw from. But since it's "darker" where you are, you must try a little harder to shine alone so that others see you clearer. This just means you must be more balanced.

Low vibration consciousness is not your enemy. It's just a place that needs light more than another place. Your balance in these situations shows others what you have, which many of them may desire, but they have no idea what to do. Your balance, therefore, is your light, and it will show! When you are presented with confrontation or drama, hold your balance! Don't react with anger or allow your emotional buttons to be pushed. This is work! Don't be afraid to go into areas that are dark. This is why you exist!

So this is the answer and always will be the answer. It defines "being a light in the darkness of the normal world." When people ask: *"What do you have that allows such a balance? I notice that you don't react as others do. How do you do it?"* That's when you can tell them about the God inside and how you have recalibrated your life.

Many of us are able to communicate with Innate via muscle testing. Will we eventually be able to communicate with Innate through other means such as telepathy?

No. The progression of your spiritual evolution regarding Innate will be this: Eventually you will simply "know" what the Innate knows. It will happen in stages, but your intuition is again the key, for it's your intuition that will give the messages about what is happening in your body.

For some, this is not good news, for intuitive thought is very elusive and hard to pin down. It's elusive because it doesn't come from your normal 3D synapse (brain), where most of your thinking is accomplished. Intuition is a multi-dimensional communication and so it's difficult to recognize. That's the work we are telling you about, since it requires practice to receive it and understand it.

We have told you that when you have a better grasp of intuitive communication as delivered to your consciousness, you can then start to have all manner of things begin to happen for you. One of them will be a far better idea of what is happening within your own body.

Innate is ready for this! It wants you to *hear* it! Eventually you will become your own medical intuitive.

Chapter Eight

DNA—It's More Than You Think

What do you know about DNA? Perhaps you know a lot. Most of us, including myself, only have a basic knowledge. Our DNA (deoxyribonucleic acid) is the core blueprint of a Human Being.

There are four different kinds of chemical nucleotide base pairs that are the building blocks of DNA. The sequence of the DNA bases is what makes up the genetic code. The Human genetic code contains around three billion base pairs and occurs a hundred trillion times in our body. The double helix structure of DNA was discovered in the 1950s. In the mid-1970s, scientists developed methods to start determining the order or sequence of the chemical "letters" in DNA. In 1990, the Human Genome Project (HGP) was launched, to provide a better understanding of the roles genes play in the Human body. The project's main goal was to map (sequence and understand) the three billion letters of Human DNA, called the Human genome. There was a great level of hope and expectation that the mysteries of life would be revealed. The HGP was an international effort that included scientists from many countries. It was funded by the US government, with a budget reported to have cost around three billion dollars over a thirteen year period.

Scientists learned that there were far fewer genes than originally thought. At the last count, the Human genetic code contains around 23,000 Human genes. The HGP revealed the basic chemistry of DNA. Lee Carroll has described it as finding the "letters" within a giant book. The problem is that no one has been able to discover what the language is that can give us clues about what the words are within the giant book! Furthermore, within all the letters and the chemistry of the Human genome, only three percent has a recognizable code. Only the protein encoded DNA chemistry carries a clear code for making genes.

This means that more than 97 percent of the Human genome in the DNA does not encode protein sequences. Scientists called this "non-coding DNA," because its function is unknown and appears to do nothing at all. Since its discovery "non-coding DNA" has more commonly been referred to as "junk" DNA. Don't you find it incredible that nature would actually create a living organism that has 97 percent of DNA that is junk and doesn't appear to do anything?

If you have read Kryon Book Twelve, *The Twelve Layers of DNA*, you will already know what the "junk" DNA is and what it does. The reason scientists have not been able to identify "junk" DNA is that it is quantum. Science has yet to understand multi-dimensional energy, but they are making progress. What this quantum portion of our DNA does is provide instructions to the three percent of DNA that makes up our biology. *The Twelve Layers of DNA* gives a full revelation of what's in those instructions. Your Akashic Record is a portion of your quantum DNA.

In September 2012, a group of scientists claimed to have cracked the "junk" DNA code. Their findings have been hailed as the biggest breakthrough in genomics in a decade. In the project named "Encode," scientists found that 80 percent of the "junk" region helps dictate how and where proteins are produced. They discovered that swathes of DNA, once thought to have no purpose, actually form a complex "control panel" for our genes. They have concluded that this DNA is not junk at all, but absolutely vital for the functioning of our cells. One-fifth of this category of DNA is made up of "switches" that turn some genes on and others off. It is now believed that, in order to understand genetic illnesses, such as hereditary heart disease, some forms of diabetes and Crohn's Disease, we need to understand these regulatory elements as much as the genes themselves.

Source: http://www.telegraph.co.uk/science/science-news/9524165/Worldwide-army-of-scientists-cracks-the-junk-DNA-code.html

http://www.telegraph.co.uk/science/9534185/Junk-DNA-and-the-mystery-of-mankinds-missing-genes.html

Let's review the information given by Kryon:

To you and science, the very premise of DNA is bio-chemical. That is, what you have in your body, what you believe is responsible for the blueprint of life, is totally explainable by science through the chemistry and biological processes. But there are attributes within DNA that I wish to again discuss. There are multi-dimensional spiritual attributes within DNA that are quantum. The actual majority of the chemistry that you can see in the Human Genome is in a quantum state. Although your science cannot measure a quantum state at this time, nor the field around it, there is evidence of it within the puzzle of the Human Genome.

We have told you that the DNA in your body carries with it a tremendous amount of unseen information and energy. We speak of DNA as an entity, not as a chemical double helix. That is to say, 100 trillion loops of DNA all work together as one energy to be called "your DNA." This group is unique. It has to be, for it is absolutely, 100 percent you. Because of the quantumness of DNA, it can contain a huge part of your spirituality. [This has been defined in Kryon Book Twelve, *The Twelve Layers of DNA*]. Not only does DNA contain the record of all that you have been on the planet, but your relationship to Gaia as well. It contains all that you have ever done and the spirituality of what you've learned in every lifetime. This information is literally imprinted within it.

Now listen to me: Over eons, no Human ever loses any spiritual revelations they have ever had. Do you understand? With intent, any Human can awaken to the point at which their DNA holds what they've learned over all lifetimes. You awaken the DNA itself with your intent and epiphany of God inside. All of the spiritual things that you have learned will come flying back and be yours again. How could they not? You opened the door originally and you own them. This has to be good news to the individual who wonders what it's going to be like if he comes back. Will he have to start over? Will he have to go through the things again that he's gone through this lifetime? The answer is no. It remains free choice, and many lifetimes might go by without any kind of spiritual quest, but in this shift, many are beginning to "remember" who they are and what they know.

Some of you have actually said that you do not choose to come back again, for it has been difficult this time. There is an intrinsic, innate feeling to some of you that this is your last time. Yet I will tell you, dear ones, that this is what you said the last time! Here is what happens: The first thing that masters and old souls want to do when they arrive on the other side of the veil is come back... and that's you! Most of you will, and when you do, you will pick up where you left off, not restart. That's in the DNA. It's beautiful. The wisdom of the ages is imprinted within the DNA. It's quantum, and therefore huge. The crystal in the Cave of Creation stores this for you and activates your DNA when you return within a different Human body.

Isn't it interesting that now that humanity has seen the Human Genome, they see how unique it is? Isn't it interesting? DNA is totally unique. Not one Human Being has DNA like the other, not even identical twins. Only a fraction of it is identical in twins (less than 5 percent). But not the non-protein-encoded quantum parts. They are absolutely unique to each Human.

There is more. Within the DNA are attributes of the *piece of God* that you are. The imprint of the Higher-Self is there. The angelic name that I call you is there. That name is not a name in linearity or one spoken in the air with vibration. Instead, it is a name that we sing in light. And when it is spoken, it vibrates with majesty. That's the truth! Feel it! The imprint of who you really are is in there. You carry with you pieces and parts of the lineage from another planet and other areas of the Universe. The energy of those who helped seed you with humanity's spiritual portion is there as well [Pleiadian]. Appropriate, it is. Beautiful, it is. Loving, it is. All of that is there within your DNA, and in order for it to be there, it has to be a quantum energy.

Now, let us again speak of the 3D biology. When the Human Genome Project was finished, all the chemicals in the double helix had been identified. In that very, very small double helix, three billion chemical parts were then known and identified. It is so small that this DNA molecule must be seen via an electron microscope. So complex it is that it has three billion in chemical parts. Then the task began of identifying what the parts did, and science began to study the enormity of what was there. They were looking, indeed, for that which created more than 23,000 Human genes. So they looked for the coding, the linear protein coding, so that they could understand how these things worked.

Science had waited a long time to see "the blueprint in action," and they did. But the shock came when less than five percent of the DNA created genes. Indeed, they saw linearity and they saw the coding in the protein-encoded portion of DNA. This small portion created the genes, but the rest of it seemed to be random, even chaotic. More than 90 percent of DNA seemed to be scrambled and useless.

My partner talked about that today [in lecture], where a quantum state appears to be chaotic. It appears to be random, for there is no linearity to be discovered in a true quantum reality, none at all. One of the things that keeps you from seeing a quantum state is the linearity bias that you have in your 3D reality. So you, indeed, stare at that which is quantum, but to you the concept of what it might be is invisible. This DNA attribute of randomness could not be taken lightly, for science was looking at something that was unexplainable. Imagine, 90 percent of DNA seemed to do nothing at all! The biologists knew better, but there simply was no explanation at hand.

On to New Information

So we start from that point in order to reveal a few things that you need to know, many of which will be eventually confirmed. When it is, you'll remember where you heard it. [Kryon smile]

DNA is far larger than you think, and even today, science is starting to acknowledge that the 90 percent of DNA that is seemingly random may not be a language or code at all. Instead, it may be what they would call "influential chemistry" that somehow modifies or configures the five percent that is the engine of the genetic blueprint. The irony here is that this is exactly what's happening, but not in the way science is looking at it.

The 90 percent of DNA is a reflection of your spirituality. The Akashic Record, the Higher-Self, that which you seek that you call "a portal to the other side," is there. In a quantum state, these things are not actually in the chemicals at all. Think of all of those chemicals together as a bridge, somehow a pipeline, a portal or quantum pointer to everything. Instead of thinking in a linear way that there is a compartment or a box where your Higher-Self is, think of a doorway. If you could go there and see the quantum state of it, you would enter a pipeline that takes you to everything that is. So understand that this 3D/quantum chemical bridge is a sacred influencer of the genome, and it's very large, containing most of the information in the Human blueprint of life.

DNA is More Than You Think

Now, let us speak of DNA as you've never heard us speak before. It is time you knew the rest of the story.

Science considers your brain to be the center of consciousness, but it is not. The brain, the highest ordered neurological group they can see, is filled with a complex synapse. Therefore, it must be responsible for what is called Human consciousness. It is not. The brain is only the 3D engine that responds to the 90 percent quantumness of DNA. It is the engine of the synapse and it's vastly complicated. But the brain is only the receiver of information to create electrical signals that do as they are instructed, as influenced by the DNA.

One hundred trillion parts of DNA working together communicate as one. Did you realize that? Science doesn't know how this happens, and the communication link from your head to your toe somehow has one purpose. Is that your brain? No. It's the DNA all together, creating the Human Being. DNA "knows." It all works together. This isn't something you are going to find in the medical books, but it completes a large missing link that science gives no credibility towards. DNA communicates with itself! It has one "mind" and it "knows" what is happening in every part of your body.

The new information is that DNA provides a "field" around you that is multi-dimensional. That field is your consciousness, not your brain. That which your brain does is in tandem with the DNA. Your brain dreams ... or does it? The synapse is there to show it, and in your deepest REM sleep, out comes so many complex things. Those things are all in your DNA, supplied to your brain. So the DNA even supplies instructions and influence to your brain's dream activity for you. These things are difficult to explain, since we are not speaking about linear things, but that which is quantum.

All of you dream in a quantum state. That is why there's no linearity, and things don't always make sense. Those who have passed away and those who have not are all together in your dreams, yet they are looking at one another. Dreams don't make sense because they're not in the reality you are used to. That's your DNA talking ... the Akashic Record coming forward and playing "the tapes" to your brain. Science does not acknowledge this, for it cannot see the field, but the DNA is Human consciousness and the brain simply is the 3D engine of the synapse that supplies the bridge for your reality.

"Kryon, is there evidence of this?" Oh, yes. Very much so. When a Human Being has an accident and the spinal cord is completely severed, it leaves the body inert. This is the paraplegic who can no longer move anything—not a finger, not a toe. And yet the heart keeps beating, does it not? Digestion continues, does it not? The kidneys and other organs function, do they not? Even reproductive activity is possible! Everything keeps going, yet you learned in school that the brain sends electrical signals through the spinal cord and keeps your heart beating, doesn't it? Well, if the spinal cord is severed, what

keeps your heart beating? I will tell you — it's the blueprint of DNA!

When the engine of the synapse is broken, the DNA finds other pathways and instructs the body to continue the life force. That is why the organs continue even though control of the muscles does not. Interesting, is it not? There is proof there if you look. Science finds it curious, don't they? Therefore, you might say that your DNA is actually an esoteric, ethereal brain, containing things that your regular brain does not contain. You'd be right. There are all manner of very spectacular attributes in your DNA that are here to look at, which current science has yet to even see.

DNA "Knows"

The biggest attribute that we wish to discuss is this — this multi-dimensional DNA field is *knowing*. That is to say, it is built to extend life. It knows who you are. It contains the blueprint of your sacredness, and is one of the largest tools you have for health, for joy, for opening the door. It is in the DNA field, not the brain. That's where it is. And in that truth, there is celebration. For it releases you from having to create what you think you need.

Let me give it to you this way. If you're going to use that field as a tool, now that you know what it does, you're going to work with your cellular structure to manifest things. The normal Human experience is to gather knowledge on *how.* *"How do I communicate? What is the best thing to ask for? How do I specify it so the DNA will know what I'm asking? Do I have to be a certain way or be in a certain place? Do I follow many steps that will open the door?"*

None of the above! If you could visit your cellular structure, your Akash, your sacred life lesson, don't you think it would know what was happening? It does, perhaps even more than you do! All you have to do is speak to that which is the

211

quantum part of you and it knows what you need. So we are asking you to relax the linearity of the lists that you give to God. For suddenly, we're telling you there is a quantum energy that is the *sacred you* who knows what you need.

Therefore, your meditations and prayers could be shifted to become wiser as you speak to your own cellular structure, to your own Higher-Self. You might say, *"Dear Spirit, dear DNA, examine the life that I have and give me those things which will enhance it."* Perhaps that's the healing you came for, dear one? Don't you think I know who's here? Perhaps that's a miracle that will give you joy in the face of the sorrow that you're in right now? Don't you think I know who is here, what you've gone through in these last days? I counted the tears when they fell, and so did the DNA field! You feel so alone, not understanding there's an entourage around you the whole time, and they would love to touch that field that is your DNA! They'd love to touch it. But not unless you say it's OK to do so.

Understand this: DNA is more than chemistry! It is a field and a portal. These things are *the mechanics of Spirit*. We're starting to give you advanced information and there have been those who have known how this works and assigned sacred geometry to all of it. They're accurate and it's correct. But it's a field.

A Master's Ascension

Let me review something with you that's ancient, wise, and tells a profound story. In your own scriptures in the western world, there is a story of a master named Elijah. This was the only Human Being in history to select his time of ascension without death and have it recorded by the one who would take his place. Therefore, you could see it within the writings of the one who witnessed it. I want to review it, for even all the way back then, there is proof of the field.

212

They say Elijah stepped into an opening, asking Elisha to record what was going to happen. Now Elijah was a master with great wisdom and knowledge and he is today what you would call an *ascended master*, and Elisha loved him. In the linearity of humanism, there is an entire group of people who expect his return. I have some news for them. Get out of your linearity, for he's been back a long time! For the energy of the masters is part of the energy of the great shift that is upon you. They intermingle with the vibration of this planet. They're all back, and it's what you're feeling. In a quantum state, they're in your DNA. Don't you sense this? There is so much expectation around 3D things that were never meant to be 3D. So much information is given in metaphoric terms, so you might understand that perhaps prophesy itself could mean things outside of your linear reality.

Elijah walked into the open with Elisha watching, but he did not *die*. Instead, he claimed his sacredness. Indeed he left, but not without some *fireworks*. For Elisha indicated that he turned into a chariot of fire, accompanied by three entities. In the best that he could see and describe in his linearity, Elisha described what it looked like and what it felt like. Now, take a look at this, for you will find that it was not necessarily angels from above who came and got Elijah. Instead, something happened *on the ground* and Elijah turned into light and he left.

Let me tell you what that was. That was Elijah energizing his field of DNA! This field has a name, the name given at that moment Elijah was riding a chariot of light. The name was given in Hebrew: Merkabah. And I will now reveal to you, as I have before two times, that your DNA field is indeed your Merkabah. It has sacred geometry connected to it, for this multi-dimensional field has structure. If you could see it, you'd see the structure of the double tetrahedron, and it's beautiful. It's not just a ball of light. The name Merkabah would indicate that something rides within it, and it is the chariot of your divinity. Each Human Being has this, recorded by Elisha watching the master ascend. In addition, the chariot contained three parts, which was the reunion that I have spoken about in the past of the three parts that split from you when you arrive on the Earth, and recombine when you leave. I will give more about this in the next channelling. That's what we want to share in these moments, for that's what each one of you has — exactly what Elijah had.

Biology and Intent

Let's talk more about biology, because now it gets a little more complex. There is an intermingling of the 3D and the quantum that we wish to describe to you now. It's something that is new, for the vibration of this planet and of humanity, especially of those who are working with the light, is creating a new tool set. You're going to start to see it and it's going to be visible through examination of the 3D chemistry of DNA, even at the 3D level.

Science is now looking at what they call *markers* in the protein-encoded DNA, which creates the Human genes. These markers, as they are described by science, are those that are the pieces and parts that would indicate predispositions — attributes that might weaken certain cells so that later in life they would allow disease, such as cancer. They're starting to see these markers, perhaps in certain families where mothers and daughters and their daughters and their daughters all had the same kind of disease. They're starting to see the genetic markers that create predisposed weakness.

Let's talk about the markers, for this is the first time we have disclosed this. First the premise: For years we have told you that your intent to talk to your cellular structure has power. This intent is your communication to the DNA field to alter something within the 3D cellular structure. You might say, it's your own multi-dimensional "voice" giving instructions to the quantum part of your DNA, which then results in the actual chemical changes that are occurring in the codes within your 3D genome. But now the results are going to be seen, and you can begin by removing the markers, and when you do, they stay removed. This means that something quantum you do today can change the chemistry of your gene-producing DNA so greatly that it will NOT be passed to your children. You can break the chain.

Blessed are the Human Beings who realize that as they purify their lives with the light of the Creator, it will affect the biology of the protein-encoded parts. You can erase the markers. It's one of the first times that the 3D has intermingled with the quantum so that science can someday look at the same Human Being over time, knowing that DNA never changes... yet it did! It's yours and it's unique and you changed it. There will be no answer for them, but the 3D facts will show it, that you eliminated the marker.

The joy of this, and the beauty of this, is that the lineage of the young women who do this will be shown, for their daughters will not have the disease, nor will the daughters of their daughters. It's a new gift and reflects the power of the times. Can you really change those who are your children-to-be? Indeed!

I know what you are thinking. The crowd who sits here says, *"Well, it's a little late, Kryon. I've had my children. So why do you sit here and tell me these things?"* Are you not understanding where this message is going? Are you not understanding the profundity of what happens when old souls allow us to give this information to Earth? Do you not understand your energy has generated the allotment of allowance for us to come in today and give you this, so that young women and young men who are Lightworkers each will hear it and know what it means to them? Do you understand you're your own ancestors? Has this occurred to you? I see you as actual history, sitting in the chair, from all over the world! That's what I wanted to tell you today.

You don't each have one name to me. I don't even see the gender that you are. I see you in a quantum state and that's why it's so profound that you would let us come in and visit you in this fashion. The woman sits in the chair in front of me. She has no idea the warrior she's been, or how big she was when she was a man. Yet she carries around with her the feeling of the warrior and she knows she's strong. I look at the big, burly man and I see the mother toiling with all those children and the man knows it. He can feel it. He's sensitive and can actually feel the love of a mother. Who is it he used to be? And how has it affected him today?

Old soul, it's affected you today because every single lifetime gives you layer upon layer of wisdom. It has brought you to the chair today or reading this today. For this is the lifetime where you have awakened and realized there is more, a lot more. It brings you as a seeker to a place where you can say, *"What can I do for myself and the Earth?"*

I'll tell you what you can do. You can become compassionate on this planet. You can walk around and show your light on this planet. You can change the markers in your own DNA! Think of who's listening to this message and what it might mean to their children and their children's children. These are the tools we spoke of so long ago, and the proof will come down the line of the reality of this message.

All of this that I have told you today is correct and real, and will be seen naturally in its own way. But I wanted you to know the sacredness that is here within a structure you thought was only chemical based. DNA is far larger and more sacred than anyone has ever imagined.

So what are you going to do with this information? Why don't you walk out of this place different than you came in, feeling a little more enabled? Perhaps you will feel a little better about the possibilities before you? Perhaps you might even know that what happened today is real.

Kryon live channelling "DNA Revealed"
given in Melbourne, Australia — March 13, 2010

Earlier I mentioned that Lee Carroll refers to our genes as "letters" in a book. In order to understand the letters or codes we need to understand the language. As you read the letters and words within this book, what helps you to understand what I've written? The answer is learning the language and understanding when to use spaces and punctuation marks. If we don't use spaces and punctuation, we have difficulty reading the words. For example, the following sentence has no spaces or punctuation:

awomanwithouthermanisnothing

Did you understand the sentence? Did you create your own spaces and punctuation? Let's look at how punctuation can change the meaning.

A woman without her man is nothing.
A woman: without her, man is nothing!

Can you see the importance of spaces and punctuation? Back to DNA. Some exciting discoveries are being made. One article in particular stands out. The name of the article was *Scientist Proves DNA Can Be Reprogrammed by Words and Frequencies*, written by Grazyna Fosar and Franz Bludorf. Here is an excerpt from the article:

Russian scientific research directly or indirectly explains phenomena such as clairvoyance, intuition, spontaneous and remote acts of healing, self-healing, affirmation techniques, unusual light/auras around people (namely spiritual masters), mind's influence on weather patterns and much more. In addition, there is evidence for a whole new type of medicine in which DNA can be influenced and reprogrammed by words and frequencies WITHOUT cutting out and replacing single genes.

Only 10% of our DNA is being used for building proteins. It is this subset of DNA that is of interest to western researchers and is being examined and categorized. The other 90% are considered "junk DNA." The Russian researchers, however, convinced that nature was not dumb, joined linguists and geneticists in a venture to explore those 90% of "junk DNA." Their results, findings and conclusions are simply revolutionary! According to them, our DNA is not only responsible for the construction of our body, but also serves as data storage and in communication. The Russian linguists found that the genetic code, especially in the apparently useless 90%, follows the same rules as all our Human languages. To this end, they compared the rules of syntax (the way in which words are put together to form phrases and sentences), semantics (the study of meaning in language forms) and the basic rules of grammar. They found that the alkalines of our DNA follow a regular grammar and do have set rules, just like our languages. So Human languages did not appear coincidentally but are a reflection of our inherent DNA...

... **Esoteric and spiritual teachers have known for ages that our body is programmable by language, words and thought...**

... Of course, the frequency has to be correct. And this is why not everybody is equally successful or can do it with always the same strength. The individual person must work on the inner processes and maturity in order to establish a conscious communication with the DNA. The Russian researchers work on a method that is not dependent on these factors but will ALWAYS work, provided one uses the correct frequency...

Source: http://www.collective-evolution.com/2011/09/02/
scientist-prove-dna-can-be-reprogrammed-by-words-and-frequencies

Science is beginning to measure and investigate the multi-dimensional parts of our DNA. Many medical doctors are discovering that the cells of the body are receptive to the environment and outside stimulus. Dr. Bruce Lipton is a stem cell biologist and internationally recognized speaker, who bridges science and Spirit. He is the bestselling author of three books: *The Biology of Belief*, *Spontaneous Evolution* and *The Honeymoon Effect*. The research done by Dr. Lipton has radically changed our understanding of the process by which cells receive information. This research shows that our genes and DNA do not control our biology. Instead, DNA is controlled by signals, from outside the cell.

Dr. Lipton likes to emphasize that you are not a single entity. You are made up of 50 trillion cells. This makes you a community of cells and each cell is a mini-version of you. In essence, what drives you is being driven by your cells. Cells respond to a signal from their environment. Dr. Lipton says there are two signals that cause a cell to respond. One signal is a physical chemical. This includes hormones, growth factors, neuropeptides and drugs. The other signal is a vibrational energy field. The most recent biophysics research shows that cells prefer and respond better to vibrational energy. Allopathic medicine focuses attention on the physical chemical signals while physicists endorse the role of energy fields being more important to controlling life.

When Dr. Lipton did some experiments with cells in a petri dish, he made a remarkable discovery. Cells that were exposed to a bad environment became diseased. Normally, the cure for disease is to inject the cells with a "treatment" chemical. Instead of doing this, he simply placed the cells back into a healthy environment. The cells then healed without chemical intervention. You are, therefore, a complement of the environment you provide to your cells.

What environment are you providing for your cells? Is the environment conducive to your cells being healthy and filled with a vital life force? The environment can be both physical and mental. The physical environment includes things like what you eat, drink, chemicals around you, pollution around you, level of exercise, etc. The mental environment includes things like your level of stress and emotional state. How many of these things can you control? Your answer will depend on how you view yourself. A victim will think they can't control any of them. An enlightened co-creator will think they can control all of them. Okay, most of us are somewhere in the middle of these answers. Don't let your response distract from the purpose of the question. The question is only raised so that you can make the connection about how our cellular structure works. What we think and believe directly affects our biology.

Dr. Lipton has discovered there are only two fundamental components that provide for life. They are our *cells* and the *signals* they receive. There are also only two possibilities that create disease. Something is either already wrong with the cell or something is wrong with the signal. Statistics reveal that less than five percent of the population has a disease as a consequence of a birth defect. That tends to suggest that our fundamental beliefs are wreaking havoc! So if we wish to change our DNA, it makes sense that we change our beliefs.

To conclude, each one of us is unique. We all have an individual chemical inheritance and Akashic Inheritance. Remember what Kryon said about our Akashic Inheritance? It means that one individual can thrive on being a vegetarian, while another is enhanced from eating meat. The significance of this is that you cannot use the same template for every Human Being. You will, therefore, respond differently to different modalities of healing. Learning to communicate with your own Innate wisdom will greatly help you to discern what is best for you. How do we do this? Kryon has encouraged us to listen to our intuition. Kryon's advice is to practice, practice, practice, so that we can reach a point where it is automatic. I wish you continual love, joy and success on your journey of self-discovery and renewed acquaintance with Innate.

Questions for Kryon:

How can we increase the efficiency of our DNA?

Answer:
1) Change your perception! Own the full awareness that your DNA has the potential for operating better than it does. Most of the planet has no concept that would match this. You must recalibrate the things you have been told and that you have learned. You are able to change your own DNA!
2) Understand that "how DNA works" is a process created by the "data" within DNA that is located in the 90 percent of the quantum chemistry in every DNA molecule. You can change that data, since it's

responsive to Human consciousness. Your cellular structure "listens" to your thoughts and alters the data within the DNA.

3) Pay attention to what your personal Akash might contain to help you. It's possible that other lives you have lived and worked through have DNA that worked better than what you currently have. We teach that you can "mine" the data in your DNA and bring it forward to your current life. This is a fast track for health and a longer life.

What level of DNA efficiency is required before humans will be able to grow back limbs?

There is no quantitative answer in the form of a percentage, for the percentage of DNA that is working is relative to the catalyst of Human consciousness and the reality of what is happening on the planet.

A sleek jet plane sits on the runway. It's perfect. It's a personal jet, outfitted with the latest engines and navigational aids. It has the name of the pilot engraved on it and is beautiful in its design. But it can't go anywhere because the runway is too short.

The length of the runway will be determined by the workers who can extend it. But there has to be a consciousness that wants to extend it, and an agreement with others to extend it. So Human consciousness is the runway that enables you to soar to new heights in your cellular progress, no matter how enabled your DNA becomes.

Growing back a limb is already in the template. Other creatures on the planet can already do it, so there is a precedent already available for you to look at. It's coming!

Chapter Nine

Past Life Healing

The search for God or the Creator inside is intuitive from birth and is responsible for over 85 percent of humans believing in the after-life. However, only a fraction of humans believe in having a past life. Slowly, this is changing. The increase of past life regression therapy has greatly increased people's awareness of past lives and belief in reincarnation. Thousands of lives have been changed or healed as a result of experiencing a session.

Today there are many past life regression therapists around the world. One of the pioneers for this work is Dr. Brian Weiss. Dr. Weiss is a graduate of Columbia University and Yale Medical School, and is the former Chairman of Psychiatry at the Mt. Sinai Medical Center in Miami. Like most traditional psychotherapists, Dr. Brian Weiss was grounded in empirical science that is provable. Imagine his astonishment, when one of his patients began recalling past life traumas. Over the course of several sessions with this patient, his skepticism was eroded. Using past life therapy, Dr. Weiss was able to cure his patient and embark on a new journey of healing.

The details of this remarkable episode were given in the best-selling book, *Many Lives, Many Masters*.

In this book, Dr. Weiss recounts his experience in treating a patient in 1980, who was seeking help for her anxiety, panic attacks and phobias. She was emotionally paralyzed, terrified and depressed. For eighteen months, Dr. Weiss used conventional methods of therapy to assist his patient to overcome her symptoms. Finally, in desperation, he tried hypnosis. In a series of trance states, his patient recalled "past life" memories, as well as information from spiritual entities. In a few short months her symptoms disappeared and she was able to resume a happy life that was filled with peace. While Dr. Weiss did not have a scientific explanation for what happened, he could not deny what he had witnessed and experienced.

Since then, Dr. Weiss has written several other books on the subject and conducts national and international seminars and experiential workshops and training programs. He has also appeared on *The Oprah Show*, an extremely popular TV show that was watched by millions of viewers.

Many individuals have been able to confirm their past life experiences with physical evidence. A great example was given in Dr. Weiss' book, *Miracles Happen*. During a past life regression, a British woman, Jenny Cockell, remembered a previous incarnation as Mary Sutton, who lived in Ireland in the early twentieth century. She remembered the children she had borne as Mary, and in the 1990s, she discovered that five of these children were still alive. In an emotional reunion, Jenny reconnected with her children—as their reincarnated mother! Jenny recalled her past life memories of the childhood events that had occurred more than seventy years prior. All of the children confirmed the accuracy of what Jenny recounted.

The on-going research and careful documentation of past life sessions have greatly helped to validate and legitimize claims of reincarnation being accepted on the basis of clinical data and not just belief. There is now an extensive collection of carefully collected knowledge and wisdom that provides scientific proof of reincarnation.

Another pioneer of past life regression therapy is Dr. Michael Newton, founder of The Newton Institute for Life Between Lives Hypnotherapy. Dr. Newton has written many best-selling books, including *Journey of Souls: Case Studies of Life Between Lives*, *Destiny of Souls: New Case Studies of Life Between Lives*, *Life Between Lives Hypnotherapy* and is editor of *Memories of the Afterlife: Life-Between-Lives Stories of Personal Transformation*. He has also appeared on numerous radio and television shows.

One of the key attributes of Dr. Newton's work is the attention given to the "Life Between Lives," as he calls it. The accumulated information, as described by patients, has resulted in an attempt to understand what happens to our souls when we take our last breath on the planet. I believe that the detailed description of what happens to our souls, as described by patients experiencing a past life regression, is somewhat limited by our Human bias of singularity. Kryon tells us that, after we die, there is a period of three days of remembrance of who we were through our Human filter and not with the mind of God.

Kryon has said that, during this time, we connect with our guides and members of our soul group from both sides of the veil. Kryon mentions that we are only seeing a part of it. Despite these limitations, the results that people have experienced from receiving a "Life

Between Lives" hypnotherapy session are profound. I greatly honor those who give these sessions. It has allowed thousands of people to experience their eternal "soul" and gain insight in their current life challenges.

In Dr. Newton's book, *Memories of the Afterlife: Life-Between-Lives Stories of Personal Transformation* thirty-two individual stories are presented about ordinary people seeking spiritual regression. One of these cases involved an energy worker called Samantha. Her story demonstrates some of the attributes that Kryon talks about regarding our life lessons and soul experiences that we choose from the other side of the veil.

The condensed version of Samantha's story is as follows:

Samantha booked an appointment with Trish Casimira, a hypnotherapist who trained with Dr. Michael Newton and specializes in regression therapy. Trish was Samantha's last hope. Samantha's life was in ruins and she had given up on life. She wanted answers to help find out what happened. Three years ago she had been happy and content and had a thriving practice as an energy worker. Her relationship with Spirit was strong and deep and helped her to create powerful healing work.

All of this changed when she decided to date again. She met a man and instantly her guides told her to be with this man. Samantha's reaction to this suggestion was the opposite. He was not her type, and furthermore, he had no concept of Samantha's spiritual path. As Samantha prepared to leave, with her rejection speech already formulated, Spirit again said that she was to be with this man. She had always trusted Spirit, so she ended up giving this man her number and agreed to dinner.

Samantha had many objections that she raised with Spirit, but she always received the same answer. She gave up arguing with Spirit and dated this man for one month before she fell deeply in love. Within six months they were discussing marriage. He was fascinated and enthralled with Samantha's spiritual nature and began to open up to her teachings. Nine months later they were house hunting together and making future plans. Then suddenly he announced that he no longer loved her and left.

Samantha was devastated. She spent months in prayer trying to understand. She was so certain that Spirit wanted them together, that she couldn't understand why they weren't. As Samantha's depression became more severe, she began to lose her clients. She was angry with Spirit. Her anger turned into apathy and she gave up caring. She closed her practice, moved to a new city and tried to start over. Despite the passage of three years, she still cried herself to sleep every night and felt completely betrayed by her guides.

During her "Life Between Lives" session, Samantha began to discover the beautifully orchestrated lesson that she had helped plan and create. Some of the things she experienced, as related in Dr. Newton's book, included the following:

- She met her ex-husband and wept as she recalled their agreement to come together to have children, but there was no agreement about love. She forgave him and herself for all the years she tried to make the marriage work.
- She met a former lover and understood their contract was to raise each other's consciousness. She met several other people who had been instrumental in her life and recalled their agreements.

- She looked for the man who had broken her heart, but could not find him. As she looked around, she finally saw him in the distance. When they met, she asked him what had happened. He replied by reminding her about their agreement. He was from a group of very young souls. No one from his group was ready to awaken spiritually, but he wanted to try. She agreed to help him, as she was going to be a Lightworker and it would serve her purpose to assist.

  She asked him what had happened regarding their relationship as she thought they were in love and would grow old together. He gently responded by saying that was not part of the agreement. The agreement was for him to try to awaken and there was a possibility that he wouldn't follow through. She had agreed to help him understand his divine self.

  She remembered the agreement, but stated that her life was in chaos; she no longer trusted her guides or herself, because they told her to be with him. She had listened to her guides, but she felt they had failed her. She was so sure they were supposed to be in a relationship. She had allowed herself to fall in love, thinking it was part of a greater plan. Her life was devastated when he left, as she had changed her whole life to be with him. She didn't understand how he could cut off his emotions in the way he did and just leave.

- He asked her to think back to exactly what her guides said when she met him. She realized they had simply said "Be with him." They didn't say for how long. As she fully integrated that they had never agreed to fall in love, her pain dissolved and she was able to forgive him.

During this session, Samantha's heart opened and she realized that the energy of forgiveness was a major life lesson. She saw that her latest experience was perhaps the hardest. In allowing her heart to be broken, she learned more about forgiveness than in any other way. She was also told that she had a choice. She could choose to judge and hold on to a lower vibration, or she could forgive this man for jilting her, forgive Spirit for what she thought was misleading messages and she could forgive herself for not seeing the higher path from the very start. When Samantha could see the lesson from her soul, she immediately realized how brilliant the plan was and even more pain melted from her. Her session was complete and she had finally received the answers and peace that she had sought.

A year later, Samantha's practice was thriving again and her work was better than ever. Her sense of judgment, blame and forgiveness now is very different and she is able to help others with this new perspective. Her heart remains open and she is able to start dating again. Samantha is living her life in the "now" and realizes happiness is a choice.

How did you feel about Samantha's story? Did it bring you a new perspective? Was there a message for you? Samantha's story aligns with the phrase: *Things are not always as they seem. Trust, all is well!*

Previously, I mentioned that our Human bias may limit our understanding of our spiritual overlay. This is one the most difficult things for us to comprehend. Even when people have a near death experience or a past life regression there is still a Human bias toward what is being seen, felt and experienced. In 2013, Kryon gave a channel to further clarify our external existence. This channel has been published in Kryon Book Thirteen, *The Recalibration of Humanity 2013 and Beyond.* It revealed lots of information about our Akash and our soul experience, making it an essential channel to include within this book on the Human Akash. Often we find things (that appeared hidden) when we review it a second or third time.

The Human Soul

First of all, the Human Being and the Human Being's soul are seen as one item to us. It is never split up in our reality and is in many places at once. But for your understanding and for this lesson, we have the soul in only four places at once. The three winds are three of the four, and the other place your soul resides is *home*. That's where I am, dear ones, and we don't call it a *wind* because there is no wind when you're at home. There is no action for or against, and there is nothing pushing or pulling. It is so difficult, if not impossible, to describe something to you that is so close to you, yet so hidden. *Home* is not one of the winds, for it is where you always are.

A piece of God is in you, yet what it is like to be on my side of the veil will remain hidden as long as you are a Human. It has to, for the test of energy that you are working on as a Human must remain in a certain kind of reality and consciousness for you to exist on the planet and work the puzzle. But there's no *wind* when you're home. Home is the place you are when you are not in one of the winds. Home is your natural "God state."

How Humans "See" God

You're a piece of the *soup of God,* which is measured in innumerable parts, yet all is one. The very essence of *entanglement* [a physics term describing a quantum attribute where things are locked into one reality regardless of distance] are the attributes of God. When you are in touch with your Higher-Self, you are in touch with all the parts of you. Sometimes humans think that they're getting messages from angels, and these angels are given messages from other angels, and so on and so forth. Humans see a hierarchy of authority in everything, since it exists in their own reality. But with God, there's no such thing, for the wisdom of God is a singular wisdom, which is always the same wisdom and is fully present all the time, everywhere. The truth is the truth, and because you have a piece of God in you, you become aware of an absolute truth as you awaken spiritually. This is why you can take an awakened Human Being from another part of the world that is foreign to you, speaking another language that is not yours, and find the same truth. The God inside you is the same as the one inside them.

So as we give this lesson, honor your intuition, that part of your mind that discerns using spiritual logic. Some of you may actually have a revelation of what we are speaking of as we discuss the Three Winds.

The Three Winds

Human Being, there is nothing more honored within the Human life scenario than the Three Winds. They represent one of the three states that humans are always in. Two of them are brief and one of them is long. There is the Wind of Birth, the Wind of Existence, and the Wind of Transition. In your words, you would say birth, life, and death. We don't use those words since they are biased to a 3D reality, which often is your only view of the truth.

The Wind of Birth

The Wind of Birth is different from the actual physical event that you call *birth*. For us, the Wind of Birth is you right before you enter (taking your first breath). In each "wind," we're going to start by dismissing the fallacies and giving you the truth. So let us discuss as much as we are able and start with the energy at the Wind of Birth.

Imagine yourself as a piece of the whole, a part of the love element of the Universe, and a part of the wisdom of God. You're ready to go back to your planet, but you do not have the mind of a Human. What is involved? What energies spin around it that get you to this place? Who is able to be in the Wind of Birth and is there a system?

These things are difficult to describe, for they are not linear. Understand that you are aware of only linear things, since it is your reality. Your 3D reality as you sit there reading is only aware of one solitary life on Earth. But in this quantum Wind of Birth, we are *seeing* you standing at the precipice of another reality, returning to the planet after many lifetimes [speaking to old souls now]. So as you stand there, you are about to reconnect as a Human Being into the planet's energy in a certain way. The "wind" of the 3D reality you are about to step into blows against you with great force. You seem to "lean into it" as we make our final love words to you. You are about to disconnect from the reality of Spirit, willingly give away your memory of all that is, and return to Earth yet again. What a beautiful time!

The Power of the Akash

The Akashic Record holds within it the ability and potential for enormous energy, depending upon what the Human has done in past lives. If the Human has awakened to spiritual potential before, then there is more energy than if they had not. Therefore, the potential creation of an enlightened old soul is literally available at the Wind of Birth, for it's about prior knowledge and experience and what you've done before on the planet. It's about who you were, what you have accomplished, and if you ever awakened to the workings of the *light puzzle* before or not, if you are returning or if it's the first time.

So the Akashic Record is not just a record of how many times you've been here, but rather, how much spiritual knowledge and life experience you have awakened to through all your planetary experience. The Akash is a sacred library that you pick up and hold through each lifetime and then into the next. You add to it every time you come and go on the planet, and it helps to develop and alter what your next life may be about. Remember the axiom we have given in the past: *You will never have to return to a less-aware state.* Once you open the metaphor of the "spiritual Akashic jar," all spiritual learning is available from all lifetimes, all accomplished learning.

The Human Spiritual System

The puzzle during your life is about how much of this truth of being part of the Creator you can accept. How far can you open the quantum door to see this truth when you are alive? This single attribute determines how enlightened you become during life. Listen: It's not how much knowledge and experience in is your Akash, but how much you allow yourself to believe it. There are many old souls on this planet who have an amazing amount of spiritual learning, yet they don't want to touch that "spiritual jar" within them at this point in their lives. This is the free choice of the Human Being we speak about.

There is immense planning that puts you at the Wind of Birth. What did you accomplish during the last lives, if anything? Who were you and what did you do? What energies did you start that were not complete that you wish to continue? What soul group were you in? Who were your parents? Are you in certain soul agreements to become their grandchildren? That is more common than you think! There are so many things that go into the planning of the "entry energy" of your life, and each life potential is different and unique. The planning is done by you when you have "the mind of God" on my side of the veil.

Humans don't like the fact that there is no generic spiritual instruction manual that states, "*Here is what happens and here is what to do.*" Listen, dear ones, humanity is honored way above that! Are all your children the same? Do books on how to raise children always work for your child? The answer is no, because each soul is totally unique. But humans still wish to have a list of things to do and not to do, as though each soul somehow came out of a spiritual machine that made them all the same. No. Instead, Spirit honors each soul with unique choice and a tremendous variety of energy selections.

The Great Artists

There are certain attributes that humans receive on the planet, and we'll call them creative attributes. These are almost quantum attributes that may take several lifetimes to complete. What often happens to these *creatives* is that they go through a series of lifetimes *as though it were one* in order to have completion of their creative cycle. Famous artists will come back, and the first thing they want to do is pick up a brush and continue what they did before. Famous composers, famous poets and sculptors will come back and simply keep going! It's so obvious, yet you deny this in your scientific way.

So the creatives are different from the others, and their puzzle is to bring the planet the greatest treasures of art through a unified series of lives, yet personally they try to sort out the puzzle of "what they carry inside is valuable, but nobody knows it." If you've noticed, most of the great artists who have ever lived and are here today carry a burden that is easily identified as "lack of self-worth." Do you see the set-up? It's ripe for personal discovery, isn't it? So can you see the Human standing in the Wind of Birth, ready to continue what they only began last time? With the "mind of God," there is a smile on their face as they *hear* the music that they will compose, for it's with them when they arrive.

As you stand at the Wind of Birth, you are completely and totally a unique creature with incomplete energies. It takes more than one short Earthly life to create Human attributes that grow into maturity. Even non-creatives (most of you) have a lineage of starting something that never got fully completed. Sometimes it's within relationships. Sometimes it's learning or teachings. Old souls are good at this coming and going and often pick up where they leave off as they slowly change the planet by their very presence upon it. The old soul is, "*Sowing the seeds of light on the carpet of linear time, not even knowing that he will also be harvesting those exact mature plants of wisdom as he returns in a subsequent life.*"

Therefore, dear one, you don't *arrive* with a blank slate, but you have to know that, don't you? The old soul feels it. The only ones who arrive with a completely blank slate are the newbies [first timers] and we'll talk about that in the next *wind*. But this is a room of old souls who are hearing and reading right now. Each of you is here with a spiritual jar that is filled with the experience of living on Earth, and sometimes even the attribute of "awakening to your own mastery."

You are standing at the Wind of Birth and you're about to come back to the planet. Laid upon you are all the potentials and possibilities based on your past experience, and the imprint of "who you are." You're coming back as part of the spiritual family of Earth, which is what your soul group does. Where will you be? What gender? The most difficult thing for me to describe to you is that the planning is not linear and it is not something that you would see on a logical financial spreadsheet. It's energy based and very often influenced by others. It's, therefore, also family based.

If you have awakened to spiritual truth in a past life, there is strong potential it will greatly change the next life. So an old soul will go to another place that perhaps a young soul would not go. All of this is in the planning before the Wind of Birth, and you're ready for it. You really are. Listen: No Human soul comes to the planet unwillingly or as punishment. Perhaps you should memorize that statement!

The Wind of Existence

We arrive now at the Wind of Existence. This is what you call *life*. Let us give you the attributes. First, no matter what you have been told by spiritual *authority*, you are not here as punishment. You're not here to be tested. Sometimes we call your life a *test*, but it's a test of *energy*, not of you! Gaia then measures the energy of the planet and passes the results to the very fabric of time and existence — to the Great Central Sun. It's the measurement of the vibration of the Earth via The Crystalline Grid, which plays a part in a much larger scenario that we have not discussed much.

Therefore, the *test* is whether humans can change that Earth measurement by their consciousness. That's the test. Again, humans are not here to be tested, but rather you're here as family. The bridge between the Wind of Birth and the Wind of Existence is not subtle. It's where you remove everything you know about the truth and come in with it blocked out. When you step into that Wind of Birth, you're no longer aware that you are a piece of the Universe. There is no longer the connection to the consciousness of God itself. You don't *remember* where you came from or what you've been through.

The newer energy now has you awaken to intuitive *potentials of remembering* these truths. They are in your Akash, but available only through intent. As we have indicated, some old souls don't necessarily awaken at all! Sometimes an old soul who has had a very difficult and profound previous lifetime will soar through this current life as a *vacation* from spiritual things and never claim they are interested. But, dear ones, you know who they are when you meet them and you can see it in their eyes. Some of you have even married them! They may not be here at a meeting like this either, but it's the energy of this very thing that attracted you originally.

The Old Soul's Purpose

Dear ones, you have to understand the uniqueness of life. It's why we say there are no rules that state that you some-how must awaken to help the planet or that you have to send light while you are here. There simply are no *have to's,* because the system is complex with variety. This time around, some are simply here to hold the energy of who they are and where they are. The next time around they will do the work, but for now they just hold a place. Some of you have had these very attributes and it's necessary and needed on the planet. Like a spiritual relay race, some carry the baton swiftly and some sit and watch, but *all* are part of the event.

Some old souls are simply holding the energy, unaware of any metaphysical journey at all. So this would be like *old soul re-calibration or rejuvenation.* However, some of you might say, *"I'm not certain I like that. It seems like a waste of an old soul's life — of 80 years or more!"* Dear ones, is it a waste of three weeks when you go on vacation? No. You often come back rested and ready to work! It's complex and you look at things in the light of "a lifetime." But for us, it's simply a passing day. It's all about timing. So don't make up your mind what is working and what is not based on your "lifetime clock."

Old souls will have the greatest impact on the planet in the new energy. The ones who have been here the most often will know better what to do than ever before about the conditions they find when they arrive.

The Wind of Existence Categories: New and Learning

NEW: The newbies are always arriving. They have to, because the planet has a geometric expansion [population growth] rate. So logically, do you understand that there are new souls arriving all the time? It's obvious. But you can recognize a newbie in a minute when you start talking to them. You say A and they hear B. You'll ask them to go left and they'll walk right. They'll have no idea about anything, how anything works between humans. They don't really understand if a thing is good or bad. Appropriateness of behavior is a mystery—and it often shows.

They don't know how life works in general. You will slap your head in amazement because you can't believe anybody could be that way! They're new. They don't know about Human nature. They're the ones who can be easily tricked by another Human Being who wants to trick them. Again, you will slap your head and think, *"Did they just arrive?"* Yes, they did.

They are naïve to the max in all directions and you've seen them. Each of them will have to come back a number of times before they start understanding the whole process of how life works, so there's always quite a number of them. They are not about to be in a meeting like this and are better off being in a meeting that teaches "how humans work." Many of them wind up on the psychologist's couch to discover more about themselves and, oddly enough, many even end up being psychologists themselves! This is because Human nature is such a vast mystery to be solved by them that they are fully aware how much they need help, so they become the helpers of other newbies.

LEARNING: Within a few lifetimes, many arrive at a certain state where there is an intuitive awareness of how things work on the planet. There is a better emotional balance and then that Human is a *learner*. Spiritual knowledge can start to be collected.

Learners are an obvious category. These are the ones who are the potential awakeners, for these are the ones who have the potential to come to a place like this, hear the truth, recognize it or not, and leave. If they don't feel it's something they relate to, it just means the timing isn't right. Again, remember the axiom about returning to a less-aware state? You can't. So even if you don't agree with something or act on something today, it doesn't mean you forget it. Today's foolishness can become tomorrow's wisdom. It just depends on your perception.

Timing is everything. My partner has asked many times, *"Kryon, why did I have to awaken to the truth in the middle of my 40s? It would have been so much more efficient if it had been in my 30s!"* The answer I have given is all about timing. It's about placing him at the age he needs to be in order to do what he does now, and also what he's going to do next. I'll get to that.

And so, dear ones, those who sit in the chairs in front of me and who are reading are all in the *learning* category. These are often the older souls and the ones who have awakened to spiritual questions. They sense what is happening on the planet and want to know more. They have a new awareness that the energy is changing and that the Earth needs them. They also know that each path is different, so they are sitting in this room now or reading this transcription with that in mind.

This is the way it works, old soul. Some of you have awakened to the spiritual truth of the "Creator inside" many times. Your library is thick with spiritual purpose. Some of you have just awakened in this lifetime and realized you're an old soul. So since you are all here listening and reading, I give you a diversion. It's a complexity you didn't expect and one for the new energy.

Karma

How does karma play into all this? The learner, who is the one who gets past the state of just "arriving on Earth," now has something called karma, and it's a big energy to work with. So let's explain what it is.

Karma is "unfinished family group energy" that continues from one lifetime to another. It pushes and pulls you around life, and it has nothing to do with predestination. Instead, it has everything to do with *predisposition*. If you have a lot of karmic energy around you, then you are predisposed to move left or right when certain conditions happen. This is based upon the energies of the past and mostly from Human interaction.

We gave you information back in 1993 when Kryon Book One, *The End Times,* was published. We told you that old souls now have permission to drop the energy of karma and steer their own way through life, co-creating the energy of what they want instead of having to battle the past. We continue to tell you that karma is an old system of learning and that you are now beyond it.

Karmic energy is still needed for the learners who are not ready to drop it and need to walk through lessons based upon it. Karma is not available to the newbie [first-timer], since the new soul coming in has no past energy to pull from. By the way, that's why they are clueless! But by the second or third time around, they start creating their own karma from the energy of ordinary life that then pushes them to do things in the next.

Once the old soul has dropped karma, it means that he has severed it completely and the next time around, it won't be there either. Again, here is a quantum attribute that states that, "what you create within the patterning of your spiritual DNA today stays forever. It does not have to be done again in the next life." Again, this is not predestination, but know that what you do in this life shapes the next, and in this new energy it is profound, old soul!

Contracts

I want to talk to you about *contracts*. The very word is misunderstood. Do you feel you have a spiritual contract to *do something* on Earth? Some of you will arrive on the planet and will think, *"I am here doing what I'm supposed to be doing in this city because it is my contract."* So while you are seemingly fulfilling your contract, what do you do when another person comes along with a better offer but you have to move to another city? It might be a spiritual offer, placing you in a far better place to help people. Oh no! Here is a big puzzle. What happens with your spiritual contract?

Part of you pulls in the direction of, *"I must stay here and do what I came for."* The other part of you is torn with indecision. Finally, you bolster yourself and say, *"My contract is that I must stay here and do my work. No matter what, I will fulfill my contract with God."*

Let me give you a word to remember—nonsense! Your contract is in invisible ink! Listen, old soul: Every single day of your life has a rewritable spiritual path. Did you know that? This is the essence of co-creation. The only contract you have is to *be here*, and it is being fulfilled as you read this. So pick up the spiritual pen and write what you need every day. If synchronicity comes along and sweeps you into another area, view it for what it is—it's what you asked for! Feel the truth of it as it occurs. Go with your intuitive feeling and write a new contract for the day, which can disappear tomorrow as you rewrite it into something even better.

Old soul, you've never had an opportunity like this before. In this new energy, you can change the Wind of Existence to match what you need. In these next few years, you'll decide a number of things collectively on this planet. Through very slow attrition of the old energy dying out, you will gain the upper hand.

The Wind of Existence is you, working the puzzle, old soul, and you're not in karma and you're not in a contract. Instead, you're in *manifestation mode*. It may not seem like it, but give it a chance. We've said this before: When you start getting out of survival mode and stop worrying about every single thing, you eventually arrive into manifestation mode. The *worry mode* is what your parents were taught. You inherited it, but it's not what enlightened beings do. Instead, they manifest what they need and they don't worry about what they don't have, for it comes to them when they need it through the process of synchronicity—an enlightened concept that gives credibility to divine wisdom inside.

The Wind of Transition

The last wind is the Wind of Transition. You call it death. What can I tell you about this that you don't already know? Well, I think I can tell you a lot. First of all, the rules: You don't know what you don't know. You don't know when it's going to happen. Did you know that we need to keep some of you here for a very long time? It's because you are not done with what you started. For others of you, we need you to transition sooner than later in order to follow your own plan. We need you at a new place on the planet soon, when you're young. We need your Akashic knowledge to awaken early and keep developing what you're developing now, because you'll have the energy of youth.

We need you to be a certain age so you can run for office, just as you planned it. We need to have you young for other reasons that should be very obvious to you as you think about it from our standpoint. So, you don't know when you are leaving. Cast away the fear of this transition, so you understand the reasons that are profound and the ones you helped create when you were on my side. The very awakening process helps to decide when you're going to transfer the energy and move through transition yet again.

I want to give you an attribute you probably haven't thought of: Death is fearful. In the corporeal sense, you have an incredible will to survive. The last thing anyone wants, even bacteria, is to die. Survival then pushes you to live and nobody simply walks into death without fear. This will remain, and it's the way it should be. But there is a gift for you that we give you, and you don't even know about it.

At the moment of transition, when your heart stops and you take your last breath, we are there. All the angels from the Great Central Sun are there, too, and they kindle a light that puts you at peace. It's a peace so great that fear cannot exist. In a fraction of a second, you know it's OK. You might call it a *spiritual anesthetic*, but we call it the gift from the Creator.

So the Wind of Transition from our standpoint, a quantum standpoint, is beautiful. It represents that instant when you realize you're finished with this life. It's only for a second, and then it's gone. Then you move into the process of a three-day remembrance of who you are. Part of you is still on the planet and part of you is with us. All of it is beautiful.

Some humans have gone through a near-death experience and explained it the best they could, but they all say they came back different. Oh, Human Being, they saw a piece of it; they saw a piece of the Creator and when they came back, they exclaimed to you, *"You won't believe it! I was dead for a moment and I heard singing and saw light."* Just ask them and they'll tell you. So this is the gift of transition that we have never talked about before. There is no sting in death, Human Being. The only sting is for the ones who remain and don't know where you are. They feel you are gone forever, but you are not. Neither are the souls of those you have lost over the years, dear listener and reader. Did you know that the parents you may have lost will be with you till your last breath? They are holding your

243

hand the whole time. This is complex, but it's part of a beautiful, multi-dimensional system of soul grouping. Some of you know I'm right, since you have sensed them.

Human Beings, you have to know that your soul group can be in several places at the same time. We've given you that information before. Souls can be reincarnated somewhere else on the planet as a corporeal Human, and also be with you at the same time as what you perceive as a guide. Don't ask the question about "how," because it won't make any sense in your reality. It's a beautiful system. Death has no sting!

If you lose somebody you love, I want you to remember this: They may appear still and cold and gone forever, but that's just in 3D and it's not the truth. They are alive and well and looking at you, pleading with you to see the energy of love that they represent. They are not gone.

Those are the Three Winds for today. I love to talk about these things, for they are near to me all the time. I work with all three, and I'm working with them right now. The energy that is Kryon is a group. It's just like all of you are, since you have these attributes also. I'm part of a group right now who are working with those at the Wind of Birth. I am also welcoming those going through the transition — right now. This is the role of Spirit through the Higher-Self that is yours. Discover God inside. When you do, you will also see that the plan is beautiful, dear ones.

Kryon live channelling "The Three Winds"
given in Saskatoon and Calgary, Canada — February 23-24, 2013

As I conclude this chapter I would like to share two more cases from Dr. Newton's book, *Memories of the Afterlife: Life-Between-Lives Stories of Personal Transformation.* I believe they help us to gain a different perspective on events that are sad and tragic.

Case One: A woman, who was in continual torment and distress following the loss of two close family members, decided to experience a "Life Between Lives" regression. The deaths she was grieving for were due to suicide. Nothing this woman tried helped. Nothing, that is, until she experienced a series of past life regression sessions.

The results were spectacular. Her soul remembered how the two awful suicides were carefully planned in order to challenge and bolster her courage and inner strength. Understanding was also gained when she recognized that her current life is only one in a whole series of lives planned to help gain strength and courage. These sessions allowed the distressed woman to see the powerful events of her life from a different perspective. The insights she experienced were the perfect catalyst to move from being a victim to a consciously empowered and enabled Human Being.

Case Two: A "Life Between Lives" session greatly helped a woman gain new understanding and insight to a tragic event in her current life. Her son was a taxi driver who was brutally murdered at the age of twenty-six by a stranger. During her session she received two insights. The first was that in a past life she had been raped and murdered. Despite this brutal death, she did not feel the sting of the horrific events in those final moments before dying. This gave her peace around the nature of her son's death. The second powerful insight that she gained was that her son had taken someone else's place that was meant to die that day. Her son had saved the lives of five people. The murderer was originally on his way to murder a storekeeper and his wife and three children over an earlier altercation. She discovered that her son sensed the passengers' intent to commit murder and subsequently stalled driving which resulted in him being stabbed, not the family of five.

These past life healing experiences perfectly demonstrate the tremendous amount of love that is behind a tragic event. It also demonstrates how our potentials are constantly changing based on what we do in the "now." Can you see how the energy around past events changes when we change our perceptions and emotions? What about past events in your own life? Have you changed how you feel about them based on what you know now? Kryon has explained what happens when we rewrite the emotions and energies around events with an enlightened mind:

The father that abused you is now the "partner in karma," and [is] an entity who did a good job of stirring your life up. The brother who committed suicide and shamed the family is now the one who gave you a gift ... a kick in the pants to find out more about spiritual things. This is a powerful new attribute that shows a new enablement for humans, and is primal to the teachings of Kryon and the other channellers of the New Age. As you rewrite the emotions, you change your very time line in this place called Earth.

Question for Kryon:

As the body of evidence increases, that humans reincarnate, how will this change the organizations that have a belief system in which their doctrine says we only have one expression of life on the planet?

Answer:

There will never be 3D "evidence" that Humans reincarnate, just like there will never be evidence that God is real. But it will some day become so self-evident that there will be no question that it is the *way of things*.

If these things were able to be proven, then there would be less fairness in the free choice of humanity to "find" the truth of God inside. Instead, these things must be an "a-ha" of belief from the Human Being. Each Human has to internally "know" what the truth is for him/herself.

As elusive as this sounds, this happens with some things even now. How do you "prove" that you love your mother? Love is an emotion, but it's also a concept. "Loving another" is a *conceptual reality* and not a process. A conceptual reality can't be proven, but a Human can still have absolute assurance of the love they feel for another! How? This is intuitive power at its best! In fact, it's so different from brain synapse that it actually upsets the brain.

"Being in love" often upsets the brain's logic and makes a Human temporarily dysfunctional! So what kind of energy can do that to a highly structured brain? The answer is a dynamic, multi-dimensional energy that defines truth better than anything else within you.

Falling in love with God provides the template of truth to be presented in this same way. The "way things work" starts to be self-evident to those who wish to create the bridge to their own soul, or Higher-Self.

Doctrines change slowly as Humans awaken to common-sense solutions instead of the mythology of the past. But they do change. Sometimes when they do not, then the organizations slowly slip away due to lack of interest. Overwhelming truth has a way of changing almost everything: For example, a doctrine that states that Humans are the only species in the Universe and that a certain prophet is here to work with only them is a very common one on your planet. But imagine one day when others in your galaxy land and greet you and look like you and it's broadcast everywhere. It's a "game changer", isn't it? Everything has to be rewritten in your religious traditions about what you thought was true. If you do it right, God becomes far grander, and the plan of the Universe starts to include far more Humans than you ever thought were there. Does God love them the same? What place does the "one prophet" now have? Can the organization expand, or will it deny the truth in front of them and try to exist within the mythology of the past?

Humanity won't be interested in worshiping a God who does not reflect the reality of life.

Chapter Ten

Akashic Communication

The previous chapter discussed how thousands of people accessed their Akashic remembrance during a past life regression session. But is it possible to remember past life details without being regressed? The answer is yes, however, the majority of cases where this occurs are in children. Perhaps your own child may have told you about their other family? Perhaps as a child, you tried to explain these memories to your parents, only to have them ignored.

The late Dr. Ian Stevenson, who served as chairman of the Department of Psychiatry at the University of Virginia, School of Medicine, devoted forty years of his life to scientifically documenting the past life memories of children from around the world. He interviewed around 2,500 children from the United States, England, Thailand, Burma, Turkey, Lebanon, Canada, India and other places. These children claimed they could remember a number of incidents from a past life. He checked documents, letters, autopsy records, birth and death certificates, hospital records, photographs and newspaper reports. In at least 1,200 cases, there was factual evidence that proved the accuracy of the children's past life memories.

Dr. Stevenson found the following statements to be true for most of the childhood cases he investigated:

- *As soon as the child could communicate they would start to describe a previous lifetime.* Often the child would say their name was different to the one given to them by their current parents. The child remembered various family members, physical features of the house and the village or town they had lived in previously.
- *The child remembered details of their death in the prior lifetime.* Dr. Stevenson also found that individuals who died of traumatic wounds, such as bullet or knife wounds, were often born with birthmarks or scars that mirrored the wounds.
- *The child's previous family was eventually identified.* In the cases where the child was able to meet with the family from the prior incarnation, the child was able to identify family members and discuss family secrets known only by members of that family.
- *Personality traits, personal preferences, and habits often persisted from one incarnation to another.*
- *Their gender usually stayed the same.* Dr. Stevenson found that only 10 percent of cases had a situation where the gender was reversed from one lifetime to another. (This figure is the same one Kryon gives regarding gender changes).
- *Physical appearance was similar from one lifetime to another.*
- *Relationships were renewed through reincarnation.* This was validated through a study that involved

31 sets of twins. (Kryon has explained that we often incarnate with the same karmic group).

- *Almost always the past life memory began to fade between the ages of five and eight.*

Source: http://www.iisis.net/index.
php?page=semkiw-ian-stevenson-reincarnation-past-lives-research

Is it possible that adults remember past life memories without being regressed? The answer is yes, but it doesn't happen very often. I would like to share an incredible, true love story. To protect their identities, the hero of this romance has been renamed Lance and the heroine Liberty. Lance's most recent life was as a notable celebrity. He was featured in TV shows, films and he performed numerous times in Las Vegas. He had a very active career in entertainment from the 1950s until his reported death in the late 1980s. Chances are, you have probably seen this celebrity (smile). Lance was very aware of the many lifetimes he had lived. He even created a specially designed jacket that had specific images and symbols that marked each incarnation he felt he had lived!

Instead of your typical boy meets girl romance, these two individuals found each other (again—remember we incarnate in karmic soul groups) in the late 1950s. Despite an age difference of 21 years, there was an immediate attraction between Lance and Liberty. They were drawn to each other like a moth to a flame. The threads of their previous lifetimes of love continued to be woven together. Due to Lance's popularity, the couple had arranged to be secretly married. Sadly, the relationship was cut short when Liberty tragically died in a car accident just a few days before the wedding. Liberty's next incarnation provided another opportunity to meet, but ironically this time there was a 42-year difference between their ages.

The next time they met, Liberty was five, while Lance was 47. Again, despite the age difference, the Akashic remembrance was present and felt deeply by both of them. Lance instinctively knew who she was. Despite her young age, Liberty immediately felt something special about Lance. As Liberty grew up, she followed his career and would mysteriously receive an anonymous birthday gift each year, which she intuitively knew came from Lance. When Liberty was 24, she once again encountered Lance (who was 66) and they renewed their relationship. Their continued love affair was enhanced by their joint recollection of the many lifetimes they had shared. Imagine the impact this would have on your relationship! It gives new perspective and explains the continuation of unfinished business that began thousands of lifetimes ago.

The fact that they could both remember their past life connections with each other in adulthood is quite extraordinary and amazing. However, that's not all! During a deep meditation, Lance revisited that fateful day when Liberty had died in the car accident just days before their wedding, and saw a different potential. He described some of it to Liberty and dared her to see the potential for herself. As Liberty began to meditate, she saw several potentials around her previous death. One of the potentials was that the car accident did not occur as Lance was driving. In that scenario they got married, had four children and Lance's career went from famous entertainer to recording engineer as he settled down to family life. In that same scenario, despite Liberty escaping death in the car accident, she still ended up dying young from cancer. Incredibly this was the exact same potential Lance had seen. This is a great example of how Kryon says our potentials are constantly changing, based upon what we do in the NOW.

Kryon has mentioned how sometimes we fail to recognize each other. Many times we encounter people with whom we have shared a past life and yet we don't even recognize them! This is part of the duality we have. So why is it, that for most of humanity, we can't remember our past life experiences like our own current life memories? The answer was provided by Kryon during a channel about our elusive Akash. This channel has been published in Kryon Book Thirteen, *The Recalibration of Humanity 2013 and Beyond*, and finally reveals why we can't remember our past lives. It's because our past life remembrance is not a brain function. The Akash is in your DNA, not your brain, so Akashic communication is very different.

The Akash of the Human Being is a history of everything the Human Being has experienced on planet Earth. Now, there are more Akashic attributes inside you that go beyond humanism, but they are very well hidden and not the subject of tonight. So you might say that most of what you have, as we define the Human Akash, is your direct experience on Earth. This Akash is also well hidden and it is elusive, but it shows itself all the time in ways that you don't recognize. So we start here by describing how it can actually be inside you, yet you would not be aware of it at all.

The Akashic Puzzle

Most Human Beings have no concept that they deal with the Akash every day. Most humans are *driven* by it, yet they never know it. So I want to set the stage by telling you right now that the Akash is not something that communicates with you in a traditional way. It's not what you would expect. Let's back up a moment and look at the overview. The Akash is a system, dear ones, and it is beautiful. I sit in front of you, knowing who is in the room and knowing about your lives, all of them. I know the puzzles you carry around today. I sit here as an advisor who has never been Human, watching you work a Human puzzle, which is amazing to me.

You are what you might call *a soul group* who are all specialists in *biological being expression* [Kryon's description of a group who specialize in walking through multiple Human lifetimes]. The creative source, which is God, who has made the Universe, the galaxies and all that is, has an elite grouping of specialists, and it's you! You are part of *the soup that is God* who specializes in doing what you're doing. It's a difficult role, so only a few trillion are selected to do it. If you want to know what's at the core of your soul as a specialist, it's love and compassion. That's the core. It's not always seen that way, but it's there, and when you come into the Earth, your mission is to give it away—to share it with the very energy of the planet. The Akash is a system that helps to drive humans into situations of learning and solution.

The attribute of the *piece of God* that you are, stays on my side of the veil. You come into the planet as a biological being, and hidden from you is who you really are, as you try to make your way through a dark Earth. Hidden from you is how you are trying to find the light that's inside of your own cellular structure. You've got the hard work. All the masters who walked this Earth tried to show you this Human God part and told you it was there. But it must be discovered.

Kryon has been here a long time. I've been here with you when we watched the grids being set when the Earth was being formed. It was just like before, when we watched other planets in other places being formed, knowing that someday you'd be doing what you're doing now, over and over and over. Certain groups of you come in first, and then others of you come later. That's the system. In this system, there is a real attribute of structure that honors consciousness, free choice and the concepts that we're going to talk about right now. All this is to say, that the Akash is not a mistake or a mystery or a system of chance. It's a design, and it's designed to help you.

The Akash is intrinsic. It's there at the beginning and it came with you in your biology during your "awareness creation." It is a part of you that can never go away, can never be erased, and you live with it every day. It is part of the system you're born with, but it can be enhanced, understood, and changed to create your evolutionary process.

The Elusive Akash

Now, here is what makes this Akash elusive, dear ones. This system, this beautiful system, wants to be in your pocket as a help through your life all the time. But it responds almost completely to the *Human free will* attribute on the planet. If humans decide that the planet should go backwards into darkness, the Akash behaves differently. If humans decide that humanity will increase in Human consciousness, the light will begin to take over, and the Akash responds differently. So now you see that it's dynamic, and not "set at birth." It changes as you change. So the first thing is that it's always moving.

It is so elusive! If I ask any of you, *"Tell me about your past lives,"* the chances are, that even the most enlightened of you would say, *"I'm not really sure. I may or may not have been here or there. I cannot seem to pick a separate lifetime out of the soup that is my consciousness. I have some strange memories, but I'm not positive that I might or might not have been this or that."* You'd be correct! So, why is the Akash so elusive?

The reason is this — listen carefully, for this is new information. The Akash is not a brain function. It is not where the synapse of memory occurs, so when you are trying to answer the Akashic question above, you are searching for these things in a structure of consciousness that works with common memory and synaptic attributes of the Human brain. The Akash is not in your brain, so you won't get the memories you are looking for. Instead, the Akash is in your DNA. So, suddenly, we have a situation where Akashic communication is very different. It's not linear, and it's not able to be remembered like your brain remembers anything. It won't give you facts. It's elusive! So how does it *get* to you?

DNA communicates to you and your consciousness in a different way than your brain does. We have described this in the past, and it is complex. But I'll say it anyway: Information carried in your DNA has to get to your brain eventually in order for you to cognize it [become aware and believe it]. It then arrives in your consciousness and works a certain way, which we will describe next. It does so with what we call *overlapping multi-dimensional fields*. This is not a mystery of science, for in your electronics, you have this type of communication all the time. DNA doesn't *talk* to you in memory, synapse, structure or linearity. It talks to you in *emotional concepts*. The process of overlapping multi-dimensional fields has a name in electronics, and it's called inductance. It's also the way that the sun transmits information and even astrological attributes through the sun's heliosphere, into the magnetic grid of the planet through overlapping multi-dimensional fields. So this is natural, it's happening all the time, and it's fractal [has many repeating parts]. But it all happens at the basic DNA level. You have a field around your DNA that interacts with your consciousness through something we have called the "smart body" or *Innate*. So don't over complicate this. Just know that the Akash is elusive because it does not allow you to remember as you normally remember things. It's not traditional. It's part of DNA communication.

How Does the Akashic System Affect a Human?

Let us speak of how it works, what the energy of it is today, and where it is headed. The Akash has what we would call *drivers*. Drivers are what communicate certain feelings about the Akash into your brain, and it allows you to sense something. It does not come as memory, as we said, and the Akashic system does not necessarily feature the communication of an individual past life. [That may come later with DNA awakening and processing]. Normal Akashic drivers do not broadcast to the brain who you were, where you were, or when you were. There are no names and no genders, even though you think you may know. What it does, instead, is to give you *experiential, emotional concepts*.

The Akashic drivers for humanity, at the moment, are the same ones that have existed for eons. The things that you will sense first from your Akash, that drive themselves into your consciousness, are survival instincts. They are about past experiences that created *fear, drama and unfinished business*. You know I'm right. What is it you sense, old soul? It's what you're afraid of. The Akash will deliver this to your consciousness, not as a remembrance of what happened, but as a *survival emotion* of what happened. These Akashic attributes are called drivers because they drive you into action, or in many cases, non-action. You feel something, and you won't *go there* or do something because of what you feel. Is it intuition or Akashic remembrance? The concepts you receive are at the DNA level and they radiate to your brain and drive you through this exposure to the emotional part of your thinking. Why are these things such low energy? Why fear and drama? Why unfinished business and, yes, let's call it what it is — guilt. Why? You are an old soul! Don't you deserve something better than this? We have given you the information before. The energy of what you have created on the planet drives Gaia's consciousness and the efficiency of your DNA and the future of humanity. It represents your free will up to this point, and that's changing.

The Recalibration of Personal Akash

Imagine an Akash that is realigning its drivers. What if, instead of fear, drama and unfinished business, the Akash started to present something else to you? It will, dear ones, for this comes with new energy and the recalibration that is going on right now. It represents a change in Akash communication, because you are increasing your vibration. All of the cells in your body know what is going on in this new era. You might ask right now, *"Well, Kryon, does that mean that everyone's Akash knows?"* The answer is yes! The difference is whether the brain will allow it to be felt or not. Now, here is where the pineal comes in.

The brain also has its drivers, and some are spiritual drivers. You call them *filters*. Others call them *filters* The brain allows things to be cognized [believed] or not, based upon past experience and commitment of "the way things work." You are creating a new consciousness, and part of that is the allowance of the Akash to talk to it. Those in this room who are listening to this message and others who are listening and reading later may start to understand that, as they increase the light of their awareness, they let in truth. It starts to change the communication of the Akash. The pineal works better, the filters are clearer, and the Akashic drivers start to change.

Much of humanity has filters that will not allow new spiritual thought. They are committed to their own box of belief and, therefore, the DNA may broadcast new information, but they are not "tuned to the station." But humanity is enabled for the shift, even though they may not receive it yet. This is the beauty of the system of the old soul, for you have created a worldwide enablement that can be "seen" by each and every Human if they wish. Free choice is like that.

Now, in a moment, we'll talk about one of the most power-ful and common drivers and how it works. But first I want to tell you there are always exceptions to the rules, because these things I am telling you are not absolute for every single Human Being. There are always those who are different. The reason is because your life's path, what you came for and what you are doing on the planet in service to humanity is unique to you. It's not generic to every soul. So as I give this information, it's an overview, and that's all I give you. So let's talk about one of the profound exceptions to the common Akashic drivers, and this is where you're going to start realizing what I'm saying is accurate, since you can actually see it.

The child prodigy is not driven by fear, drama or unfinished business. The child prodigy who plays the piano like a master when he is four is driven solely and completely by his . The painter who paints like a master when she is eight is being driven by her and that's all! The prodigy could care less about survival as long as they have their craft. It's all consuming, very linear, and all they can think about. This creates a puz-zle in psychology where you will have a Human Being without the possibility of having any remembrance of a complex talent they never could have experienced in this life, yet it's there. The puzzle for psychologists is: How could this be, where it is not part of the brain's remembrance? DNA is it to the brain as fast as the brain will receive it. It's the craft of many lives. These are special cases, dear ones, but you see it often enough for you to know that it doesn't fit with synapse and memory. That is the Akash at a multi-dimensional level, pushing something to the child that's conceptual — art, music, poetry and sculpture. It takes lifetimes to make a master artist, and they will be born over and over, continuing with the craft that they had before. All they want to do is keep going with it. That's very different from your process, and the possibilities of all the things that I've talked about are reduced to for them, the one focus for them, and you get to see it in a child prodigy. By the way, this is why so many artists are dysfunctional, for this continues and they are oblivious to survival reality, others around them, and are only interested in themselves and their craft.

Karma

The thing that drives most of humanity is one of the drivers you have labeled . Now, karma is much more than unfinished business. Karma is not punishment for past deeds, dear ones. That's an attribute of judgment, which is not of God. Karma is sensing past experience and having an emotional response so that you will either do it again or stay away from it. Karma is powerful and most humans feel it, but have no idea they are receiving a specific driver from the DNA's Akash. Karma doesn't often even feature completion! Sometimes it's a policeman becoming a policeman, or military men becoming military men again, or mothers becoming mothers. It's a driver of remembrance of things both positive and negative. Sometimes it's just emotion. Sometimes it drives someone into a classic mindset that is problematic.

You want to know that classic? It's a classic issue that psychologists really have a hard time with. It's hard to describe, but you know it exists when I describe it. Sometimes things that you sense from the DNA are not pleasant, but you them as — and you can't live without them. That's karma. There are Human Beings who come into life and who are convinced they don't deserve to be here. If that is their consciousness, the DNA tries to cooperate with it. You knew that, right? Cellular structure takes cues from Human thought. Lack of self-worth will manifest itself with problems that create, you guessed it, more lack of self-worth. It also creates drama, and some people just can't seem to get away from it.

The Human who is abused early in life has many choices. They probably created the puzzle to see if they can break the pattern (karma at its best). Sometimes, however, it just validates what they feel, that they shouldn't be here. So that Human will often get out of one abusive relationship and move into another and another! Friends will look around and say, At the Akashic level, they are responding to the same instructions over and over. It's a victim comfort zone. Do you see this?

This is what the Akash does. It presents to you concepts of existence. It will make you afraid if you've been afraid before. If I told you, dear ones, that you had been killed because of your belief, you'd probably believe me. Old souls have been — most of them. If I asked you how many times it happened or where it happened, you'd be guessing. See what I'm saying? The Akash deals in concepts, not factual memories. It also gives you concepts that are invitations to change.

Past Lives in the Akash

Some interesting concepts are transmitted through the Akash. Let's talk about past lives. Past lives carry the concepts into the Akash that are inherited [Akashic Inheritance]. So, if you were a warrior and were killed in the battlefield, you may not like the smell of gun smoke. These things are passed to you in unusual ways. Some of you can stand in a battlefield and smell it! Some of you like it, since it's the smell of victory and release — more concepts. But you know there's something there and, dear ones, that's a concept. It goes into your central sensory perception. That's the Akash at its best. You're not as much as you are something that exists to this day inside you.

The past life reader has to sort all this out. They have to linearize something that is not linear. It's elusive, you see. Past life readers can sense the quantum field around you created by the DNA [The Merkabah]. This is where a good reader can help pull out individual lives in that "soup of concepts" that you would never be able to do. This explains how a good reader can help you with blocks and past experiences that you can't seem to get yourself.

Now, the old soul has an added Akashic attribute. The old soul, the one who has been here by definition for thousands of years and lifetime after lifetime, has experienced just about everything there is to experience. So what do you think is in your Akash, old soul? I will tell you: It's the same as everyone else's — drama, fear and unfinished business, until now. The old soul has a storehouse of awakening lifetimes and that's the difference. In the new energy, that is what the old soul is going to start remembering. So being an old soul up to this point didn't hold near as much in the Akashic way as it does now.

Things are recalibrating. This is a recalibration of the Akash as well. It's how you feel, what you do with it, and how it drives you to do things. The most interesting attribute within the old soul is that old souls feel they have things all figured out. Been there, done that. There's nothing new and in that they have cognized and committed to a way of life, or what they think is a way of life, on planet Earth. It's so interesting, and often totally wrong.

The New Akashic Drivers

Turn the page with me for a minute. I now want to tell you about the new drivers of the Akash. They are , and . These are going to be the ones that are going to be broadcast from the old soul DNA to old soul brains. This will start a process of helping them think out of the box of traditional thought. Old souls will start to see that they are not victims of life. They belong here! Self-worth will increase, for it will know that humans deserve to be here. It's time!

This process will allow the Akash to speak to the brain and the Innate body in higher concepts, those of compassion. Ask a surgeon about how Human Beings often keep themselves alive in a hospital for months just to see a grandchild graduate. Ask a doctor if he's ever seen mind over matter. A doctor who works closely with death and dying will have amazing stories about how Human Beings can get up from their death beds, when some of them decide they are worthy of being here. What do you think of spontaneous remission? This is the Human changing course.

The Results of New Consciousness and a Changing Akash

The Akash speaks to you through concepts. The new energy carries different survival drivers for the old soul. Into your brain will be delivered concepts where there is no more karma. It has been voided, as we told you more than 20 years ago [Kryon Book One]. We told you to drop karma, for it is not needed anymore. Go forward with Akashic energy that you create yourself for your future instead of a concept from the past.

Some of you are mystified and feel odd, because without the driver of karma you seem empty. Well, let me tell you, it's time to understand what that feeling is. It means that you control your life! It means you're not a victim of the circumstances that push and pull you around. You've dropped the old energy driver of karma and so now it's time to create! That's conceptual, and Human Beings who don't get that message think there's something wrong. Some liked the other feeling and equated it to "being normal." It's a recalibration. No more karma.

Past lives will not have the influence that they used to and the things that you used to remember about the past are starting to recalibrate. Now you will begin to remember success, love, compassion and results that come through high thinking. You are going to want these things again. Do you see where this is going? Imagine a Human Being who is driven only by positive things. Imagine a Human Being who is driven so completely by positive things that he/she will develop books and television shows and movies about positive things. Imagine how that might change what others see and feel. Imagine how the few can show something to the many, which might change the planet! Imagine the funding for these things being easy, because old souls with money see it, too!

Dear ones, you are going to start remembering, not old mythology, but the of God. You are part of the puzzle, and you now carry the solution. You deserve to be here and the more you awaken, the longer you are going to live. Conscious awareness of a compassionate mind will extend life. You will never see an angry God in your compassionate mindset. You will never see the mythology of a Creator who has judgment. That never existed! It's a Human thought placed upon God. Gaia will become your partner on Earth, not a frightening force you have to give offerings to, any more than you would a Human partner. You will fall in love with Gaia. Do you see the differences? This is the elusive Akash, which is recalibrating itself to become a lot less elusive. This pushes Human Beings into a whole other Then you start realizing that the masters of the planet all had it.

In closing, we ask you yet again: Who is your favorite master? Who? Put yourself with him or her right now. How do you feel? Your answer will be, So I ask you again, what did they have that would allow you to feel this way? The answer is what you are learning to have for yourself; it's peace where there is no 3D reason to have peace, calmness where there is no 3D reason for calmness, an awareness of beautiful, esoteric things that are out of the sight of those who only trust what their eyes can see. It's the love of God that becomes prominent in your life and completely voids the lies of victimization and fear. You are relaxed and treat others differently. The Akashic concepts of mastery are manifested in your daily life, and things that used to be a problem simply become parts of the challenge of Human living and not a survival issue felt at the core level or pushing your "buttons" of fear.

The brain is the great central station of the transit of consciousness energy. You are in control of what you will, and will not, allow into it. It's time to allow a new Akash to speak to you of the glory and the majesty of the system that you helped create.

Questions for Kryon:

Many children have vivid recollections of a previous incarnation. Often these memories completely fade between the ages of five and eight. Can you explain more about this?

Answer:
Human development creates this. When children get to a certain age, many things change within the growth of consciousness. The things you speak of are not forgotten, but replaced with what we will call "survival synapse." Slowly, children become more aware of what is around them, including their peers and child-survival issues. This is when self-image starts to appear, and children start to expand their lives to include more complex personal issues around them. Their brains are still developing and chemistry is also involved.

As long as life is fresh and simple and uncomplicated, the memories of the past are free to flow in. But the survival instinct and chemical changes that begin at about 7 years old will take over and overwrite most of these things to the degree that the child will someday not even remember they said them.

Pay attention to the infants, for they have messages of innocence and simplicity that will teach you a great deal about who they are, and who you are.

Why is it that some individuals have been able to remember specific details from previous incarnations (without assistance from a therapist) but most of us do not?

The Akashic system that you are studying in this book is complex. Some of humanity is far closer to it than others. This has nothing to do with how enlightened a person is or if they are an old soul. If a Human comes in with a very strong past life that affects them daily, that person is one of those who you are speaking of in your question. There may be a residual Akashic energy of "lack of self-worth" or "fear of others" or "don't go near the water." These could all be energies from immediate past life experiences, some of them so powerful that they consume the person and he/she must go to a doctor for help.

So, who is to say how the Akash is "remembered" or not? The answer is that there is a system that you all are aware of when you are on the other side of the veil. You actively choose to have a "sensitive Akash" or not. My partner, for instance, has a very strong residual of being a Navy officer who was then killed in a very famous World War II battle. It changed his life direction and affected his decisions. But other than that, he has no other past memories.

Some Humans remember multiple past lives, since it later helps them if they choose to look at these memories as tools of self-help. Others, however, may suffer from these residual energies all their lives and never realize that these things were given to them within their own plan to see if they would "work the puzzle" of life.

So the answer is that each Human designs his own system and then works that system if they choose to. It's a beautiful thing, is it not, to know how involved you are in your own incarnation? You are not a victim of life, but rather the designer of it.

In closing

Ihope that your heart has been opened and that you remember your magnificence. There is a circle of life that is part of a beautiful and elegant system. Every divine Human Being that walks the planet is loved beyond measure. You are far grander than you can ever realize. The multi-dimensional pieces and parts of you are known throughout the universe. Your epiphanies and self-realizations will forever change the planet. Deep within your Akash is an infinite pool of wisdom and experience. The invitation is there for you to go and claim it!

As you practice mastery, you may find yourself at peace, regardless of the circumstances around you. As you drop your karma, pay attention to any synchronicities that come your way. As you mine your Akash, don't be surprised at the new thoughts and talents that emerge. Be prepared to release any old fears and phobias that no longer serve you. These can be challenging to release, as they are like an old friend that has been with you forever and there is a sense of loss, even when you willingly wish to let them go. Be gentle, kind and patient with yourself.

I would like to leave you with some profound words from Kryon about the Human Akash:

So here you are with this information. Interesting, isn't it? There are three places where your Human energy exists at the same time. (1) The Cave of Creation — it keeps a record of who you are as you come and go, and imbues your lifetime of experience to the vibration of the planet even after you have gone. It is the multi-dimensional system that captures the Human experience for Gaia and it stays with Gaia. (2) The DNA in the Human body helps you while you are alive in each lifetime, for all that you ever were is information and energy that is stored in the double helix. All thousand lifetimes are there, if you've lived a thousand of them. They are all accessible. You never have to relearn anything spiritually, since it's cumulative — that is, it stays with you from lifetime to lifetime. All you have to do is open that spiritual jar of intent to remember, and out will come the wisdom of the Ancients. This ought to tell you something. All of you are your own ancestors. Did you think of that? (3) The Crystalline Grid — a spiritual grid that lays over the planet's surface that remembers everything that humans do and where they do it. This grid is also being reactivated as you approach 2012, for it is becoming more quantum, in that what you do in real time is being transferred to Gaia through this grid in real time. This means that the energy of humanity is affecting the vibrational level of the planet in actual time instead of waiting to receive the energy after you pass to the Cave of Creation. This also creates a feeling of time going faster for you...

...Lastly, there is a backup system for all of it, a redundancy that isn't the kind of "backup" that you think of — for your backup is something that is linear, in case you lose the first one. This "backup" system is one that assists the others all the time. The information of those three combined Akashic systems is stored in a living mammal on this planet. It has to be this way, for it is the final layer and it connects you not only with Gaia, but it connects you with the rest of the life on Earth in a most profound way. The system is stored in the whales and dolphins of Earth...

...They hold the records. It is the cycle. The whales are in Gaia; they're under the water. They're mammals like you. They contain the information. The Akashic cycle is complete. The very water of the Earth also glows with everything you've done, who you are and who you might be...

...Gaia exists for the sacred Human Beings who are on this planet in lesson. I give you this in love today. I want you to think about something. Everywhere you walk, you're known by the Earth. What a system! Why do I give this to you today? It's so that you continue to feel loved and cared for. It's so you know there's a hand-holding going on between Spirit and you and Gaia, if you want it. There are so many things here for you if you want them. Old soul, you sit here for a purpose. Maybe you needed to hear this today. Important you are, precious you are, and a master you are. Now go claim it. Live a long time. Be joyful in the process. Don't make up your mind what's supposed to happen. The worst thing you can do is predispose what God has for you, based upon what you think is happening now. Instead, relax, be joyful in all things, and fall in love with yourself.

Leave this place differently than you came.

I am Kryon, lover of humanity — for a good reason.

And so it is.

About the Author

Monika Muranyi has always had a deep affinity and connection with our planet Earth. She has a Bachelor of Applied Science degree with Honors obtained at Southern Cross University, New South Wales, Australia. Monika has worked in various national parks within Australia and New Zealand for over fifteen years. She is an accredited Electro Magnetic Field (EMF) Balancing Technique™ Practitioner (Phases I to XIII). Her passion also includes photography. Many of her photograph's can be seen on Lee Carroll's website, as well as her own:

www.kryon.com and www.monikamuranyi.com

Monika has carefully researched the information within this book, and travelled to many places during the process of discovering and understanding her own Akash. Some of the places where she has travelled include Australia, New Zealand, United States, Chile, Argentina, Brazil, Uruguay, Bolivia, Peru, Ecuador, Colombia, Venezuela, Mexico, Russia, Ukraine, Poland, Bulgaria, Hungary, Switzerland, Spain, Italy and Portugal.

The inspiration to write and produce this book is a result of Monika's desire to share the wisdom and teachings of Kryon, so that others can mine their Akash and create their highest potential.

We hope you enjoyed this book.
If you'd like to receive our online catalogue featuring
additional information on Ariane Books and products,
or if you'd like to find out more about the Ariane
Editions,
please contact:

Ariane Éditions Inc.
1217, avenue Bernard O., office 101,
Outremont, Quebec, Canada H2V 1V7
Tel.: (1) 514-276-2949,
Fax.: (1) 514-276-4121
info@editions-ariane.com
www.facebook.com/EditionsAriane
www.ariane-books.com

The Great Human Potential:
Walking in One's Own Light
Authors: Wendy Kennedy, Tom Kenyon
Edited by Martine Vallée
(ISBN: 978-2-89626-133-8)

The information that is shared in this book is what we consider the most appropriate vibrational match for where you are right now. When we give information, we always look at the vibrational level of the majority of whom we think will be reading this. We do this to give you a version of the truth that will best serve you in accessing your highest potential.

We are truly excited for you as you embark on this journey. This window in time is rife with amazing potential that is only limited by your imagination. The greatest challenge for you will be to release the constraints of your past beliefs and judgments and know that all things are possible. *That is what ascension is all about.*

Despite negative aspects, games or manipulation, when you recognize that you are a creator being, you can change your version of reality. And when enough of you decide that you want a different version of reality, then a brand new timeline is created, followed by a change in current events, all leading to a brand new world.

So, there is only one thing left to do: dream your most beautiful dream!

Ariane Online Store

www.ariane-books.com